Filming on a Microbudget

D1331471

Filming on a Microbudget

Paul Hardy

www.pocketessentials.com

This edition published in 2008 by Pocket Essentials
P.O.Box 394, Harpenden, Herts, AL5 1XJ
www.pocketessentials.com

A CIP catalogue record for this book is available from the British Library.

ISBN: 978-1-84243-301-0

2 4 6 8 10 9 7 5 3 1

Typeset by Avocet Typeset, Chilton, Aylesbury, Bucks
Printed and bound in Great Britain by CPI Cox & Wyman, Reading

Acknowledgements

Thanks to everyone involved in Blood Actually: Amelia Tyler, Al Convy, Natalie Gardner, Chris Pinches, Paul Ullah, Charlie Falagan, JJ Bates, Charlie Morton, James Lawton, Sophie Hancock, Harry Webb, Simran Panesar, Huw Bowen, Tim Robottom, Bo Davies, Abigail Tarttelin, Damian Hayes, Nino Marsala. Also thanks to Warwick District Council, Heartbreak Productions, everyone at Spencer Yard, and The White Horse Pub in Leamington Spa.

Contents

Introduction

This book will tell you almost everything you need to know to make a short film on as little money as possible. A 'microbudget' for short films is a cash spend of around £500 ($1,000) or less, but that shouldn't put chains on the quality you can aspire to; a fundamental trait of every microbudget filmmaker I've ever met is that they exploited whatever resources they had as ruthlessly as possible and never acknowledged the word 'impossible' if they could come up with an original way of doing something. With the right mix of ingenuity, contacts and tenacity, it's possible to make a film that looks like tens of thousands of pounds, on a budget within the reach of even the most modest wage. And technology is on your side. First the Mini-DV format and now the emerging HD formats have brought reasonable picture quality within easy reach, video editing is now possible with quite ordinary PCs, and better equipment can be found at subsidised rates from media centres and workshops across the country.

But there's one thing that can't be improved by technology: you, the filmmaker. To begin with, you need the ability to imagine a series of images that tell a story. After that, the only thing that can improve you is experience.

9

INTRODUCTION

You should watch as many films and as much television as possible (especially the ads, since they're effectively short films), and with a critical eye. And you must make films, even if you're just going out and grabbing some footage to use for an editing exercise. You're the one that's got to make the films, and you'll still make mistakes, but hopefully the way will be a little smoother.

Having made many of these mistakes myself, I wouldn't want you to repeat them without being warned…

This edition has been updated to reflect the changes in technology that have come about since the last version, mainly the advent of High Definition video into the microbudget arena. There's also a new case study film, *Blood Actually*, which I shot and edited during the writing of this book and which you'll be able to watch online at www.pocketessentials.co.uk/bloodactually.

NOTES FOR INTERNATIONAL (NON-UK) READERS

The basic procedures for making a film are pretty much the same throughout the world, which means that the vast majority of this book will be relevant to you. But nevertheless, it was written with a British audience in mind, and there are some points where you will need to exercise your own judgment:

– **Currency** The prices quoted in this book are all in pounds sterling, a currency that only applies to the UK. You should check exchange rates in your part of the world to get a rough translation. For example, the US

Dollar is trading at a rate of £1=$2 at the time of writing. This will doubtless change as time goes by – I've seen it dip to nearly £1=$1 in my lifetime and while that's unlikely, it's far from impossible.

– **Prices** The prices given in this book are rough estimates of UK prices for certain goods and services. However, translating these numbers to your currency may well prove inaccurate, as things will likely cost more or less in your country. For example, the suggested UK mileage rate of 40p/mile will not translate to US prices as gasoline has always been much cheaper in the US than the UK.

– **Sales Taxes** In the UK, we have 'Value Added Tax', currently at 17.5% and applied to most (but not all) goods and services. This of course does not apply outside the UK, but other sales taxes at different rates and with different rules may well be of relevance.

– **Video Formats** Standard Definition video formats come in three flavours: NTSC, PAL and SECAM, and which one you use depends on where in the world you live. This book mainly covers PAL, and if you're filming in NTSC, you'll need to look up the relevant differences. It gets more difficult when you have to send a film to a foreign festival and have to translate between the two, which may require a visit to a specialist video company. High Definition formats don't differ so much, but NTSC countries will generally film at 30fps and PAL/SECAM countries will generally film at 25fps.

– **Power** Electricity is delivered in different voltages in different countries. In the UK and the rest of the EU it comes at 230V; in the US it's 120V. Most of the time this is just annoying if you go abroad, but for film-makers plugging in lots of lights onto a domestic ring main, it alters the amperage that the lights draw; an 800W light in the UK will draw 3.48 amps, while in the US it will draw 6.66 amps – pushing you much closer to the point at which the circuit breaker cuts in (or if you're less lucky, the point at which the house burns down).

– **Units of Measurement** The UK is unusual in that it has two parallel systems of measurement – both the Metric and the Imperial Systems. The Metric system (e.g. metres and centimetres) is familiar to most people in the world (unless they're Americans), while the Imperial system (e.g. feet and inches) will sound very familiar to Americans. They should, however, be careful as some Imperial units (mostly to do with weight and volume) are different in the UK, even if they have the same names. This is because the US didn't reform their system of weights and measures in the nineteenth century as the UK did. The systems used in this book reflect the most likely measurements to be used in any given situation, and are therefore a bit of a mixture. Consult the internet for translations.

– **Emergency Services** If you get in trouble while filming in the UK, you may need to dial 999 for Police, Fire, Ambulance, Coastguard or Mountain Rescue. In the US you call 911. In the EU you call 112 (which also works in the UK, and on GSM mobile phones almost everywhere). Consult your local phone directory if you live elsewhere.

– **Local Laws**... will vary from country to country,

state to state, city to city, town to town. Some cities will require you to pay for a permit to do any filming outdoors. Some won't care in the slightest as long as you don't block the road. Health and Safety regulations will vary. Requirements for insurance will be different. Contractual laws will be different. There's no way to really summarise all the possible differences, so consult your local screen commission or other local sources to get accurate information.

– **Copyright** is treated differently in different countries. In the UK, copyright is inherent in any completed work, such as a script, film, or piece of music; elsewhere you may need to register the work in order to get copyright protection. Differences in copyright law may also mean that a piece of music which it is legal to use in one jurisdiction may be illegal in another, possibly because the composer's rights last for longer after their death.

Development

THE IDEA

Getting an idea for a film is tough. It helps to read widely, as many newspapers as possible, watch a broad range of television and see as many films as you can; the more knowledge you have of the world, the more resources you have to draw upon. Extrapolating further events from something that really happened to you is often a good source, but many stories are stranger flights of fantasy that come from something in your unconscious; they might start from a grain of reality but something else must be added. In my (highly subjective) experience, the key has always been daydreaming; the willingness to let your mind wander without restraint. Taking long walks always helps this to happen, and I personally find public transport to be enormously helpful. But try not to be anxious about getting an idea, as that gets in the way – just relax your mind and it'll often wander off down some interesting paths. If you're not working alone, brainstorming is also a very good technique; get together with friends and a whiteboard/flipchart/whatever and knock out some ideas. Let ideas pile up without judgement and then see what among them sparks your interest.

Another way to get ideas is to work backwards. Make a list of all the things, people or places that you could use to make a film, and see if that sparks your imagination to come up with an idea. Robert Rodriguez (*El Mariachi*, *Desperado*, *The Faculty*) made a short film called *Bedhead* with his brothers and sisters as performers, the family house as a location, and only what was already available in the house for props. It went on to win multiple awards.

Once you've got an idea, you need to subject it to a few very tough questions before you turn it into a film:

– **Is this actually a story?** Not every idea will be useful. It's necessary to learn about story structure and what actually makes stories work before you allow your idea to progress beyond idle imagination. Skip forward to the Script & Structure section on page 18 for more information but it's a good idea to read some books on screenwriting as well.

– **What's my audience?** Not every idea will be of interest to anyone besides yourself. It's important to be aware of the needs of the audience right from the very start, whether that audience is very small (your immediate family) or massive (the world), or anything inbetween (women, men, OAPs, under-fives, religious groups, national groups, people who watch BBC4 rather than BBC3 etc.). What does a given audience expect? What can they cope with? Will they even understand? Even if you only have a vague notion of who your audience are, you must remember that they're the people you're doing this for (unless you only ever intend to screen the film to yourself).

– **Is it the right length?** Short films can be anything from a few seconds to 40 minutes or so. The longer the film, the more difficult it's going to be to make; if your story is running long, it may be worth considering using it to build an idea for a feature film. Longer fictional shorts are very difficult to find distribution for, and ten minutes is often considered an appropriate length in the UK. Many short film schemes require this, and cinema distributors of short films tend to stipulate this as the maximum. Ten minutes will allow you to go into some depth with an idea, and is a good benchmark to set yourself. There is also something to be said for making a very short film of 60–90 seconds; while this may not seem like much, bear in mind that television commercials are often shorter and yet capable of telling a perfectly good story. It's an excellent way to learn a very efficient approach to storytelling which will pay off when you make longer films.

– **Do I have the resources to do this?** If your idea concerns space aliens battling Roman soldiers upon the bloody fields of the Somme, then the answer is probably no. If it involves the titanic struggles of your child to throw a ball through a hoop, then the answer is probably yes. Take a look at the idea and work out if you can do it – what props does it need? What equipment? Are there large travel expenses? How many people are in the crew? Are there large crowd scenes that will be difficult? Time is also a resource –

are you completely free? Do you have holiday time coming up? Can you only shoot on weekends? There are lots of things that are surprisingly difficult, and you often won't appreciate these until you've made a few films, so it's best to keep your first project small, and build from there.

SCRIPT & STRUCTURE

Story Structure

Writers sometimes like to give the impression that ideas strike in a burst of genius, needing only to be typed out and delivered to set; films collude in this, often showing the process of screenwriting as a matter of banging away at the keyboard until all the pages are filled.

This is a lie, but an understandable one. The actual process of writing isn't very photogenic, as it involves a lot of hard work, dead ends, rewriting, and staring at a blank screen wondering where to go next. Even if you do have a burst of genius, it won't be enough, because you need to find a way of structuring your idea into a story.

Story structure is nothing to be frightened of; it hides beneath the surface of every story you've ever heard or seen and normally goes unnoticed, unless you know what you're looking for. There are two main story structures you'll be familiar with:

- **Two Part Structure** has, as the name implies, two parts: Setup and Resolution. Example: A woman goes through a theft detection gate in a shop, which beeps. She protests to staff that she's stolen nothing (Setup). Which is when a charity collector next to the gate reveals the remote control that's causing the beeps. She reluctantly pays up (Resolution). This basic system of reversals of expectation is at the heart of all storytelling, but is most often seen only in short films or within scenes of longer films, because it's a little inflexible by itself.

- **Three Part Structure** is necessary to tell longer stories, and does so by adding another section: we now have Setup, Conflict, and then a Resolution. An example is: A man and a woman spot each other across a crowded room, make eye contact and like what they see (Setup). But they are each joined by another woman, and it looks like these new women are their girlfriends, dashing their hopes (Conflict). But the two new women turn out to be merely friends of the original couple; and the new women suddenly see each other across the crowded room, make eye contact and like what they see (Resolution).

Satisfy the Audience in an Unexpected Way

The trick is to give the audience what they want, but not in the way they were expecting. In the Three Part Structure example above, we expect to see a pattern of Boy Meets Girl (Setup), Boy Loses Girl (Conflict), Boy Gets Girl Back (Resolution). But instead, what we get for the third part of the structure is Completely Different Girl Gets Girl. It fulfils our expectations because someone's got someone – just not the people we were originally expecting.

The audience will have expectations of a story – expectations that you have given them and which you cannot ignore. If they see a romantic story happening, then you need to give them the resolution to the romantic story – but you'll only be doing it well if you do it in a way they didn't expect.

Subtext

Another way to keep things interesting is by using subtext. Subtext is a layer of meaning hidden beneath the obvious meaning you'll find in the script – but hidden in a way that makes it possible for the audience to figure it out, thus creating that little spark of involuntary participation that draws them into the experience.

You can find examples in almost every seduction scene in cinema history. In *The Thomas Crown Affair*, the mastermind of a robbery (played by Steve McQueen) is being chased by an insurance investigator (Faye Dunaway), but she's only acting on a hunch. They play chess, but the game is only what's happening on the surface (the text); the way they play the game, with lots of little looks and nibbling the end of pawns (the subtext), reveals that she's pursuing him in a romantic as well as an investigative sense. In this instance, subtext is revealed through performance in a fairly blatant way, but it's still more interesting to watch than if the seduction had been put into straightforward dialogue. Showing how people feel is always more interesting than having them explain it.

Subtext in dialogue scenes can turn them from dull exposition to electrifying turning points in the story. A classic example is the line 'round up the usual suspects' delivered by Captain Renault (Claude Rains) at the end of *Casablanca*. In this one line, he simultaneously orders his men to conduct a routine series of arrests following the murder of Major Strasser, protects the man who actually shot Major Strasser, and reveals an abrupt and complete change of loyalty from the Nazis to the French Resistance. If all of this had been put into dialogue, it would have taken half a page and bored the hell out of the audience. Instead, it's a single line that's gone down in cinematic history.

Show, Don't Tell

The best principle for storytelling is: show, don't tell. We usually speak of 'telling a story,' which makes sense when your story is written in text or spoken out loud, but in film, what you should really be doing is 'showing a story.' The basic process of filmmaking is to string together a sequence of images that tells a story – NOT a sequence of speeches. Changes and revelations should be, as far as possible, transmitted to the audience in a visual manner. Consider the examples I gave above: is it necessary for the man and the woman locking eyes across a crowded room to have to explain to someone else that they really fancy each other? No. If an audience see something for themselves, they become more involved than if they had simply been told the same information. Of course, it's not always possible to make a film without having people speak to each other, but if the dialogue has subtext, the principle still works; if two people are talking about something innocuous but there's a deeper meaning, then the audience has to make that little bit of deduction which gets them more interested in what's happening.

Keep it Simple, Stupid

One common mistake is to overestimate the audience's ability to make connections. Filmmakers tend to do this because they're very familiar with the story and the characters and already know what things mean – so surely it should be obvious to everyone else, right? Unfortunately, this is not always the case. Try to look back over the story and see it from the eye of a first-time audience: what do they know about the scene and the characters? Small details that might seem to speak volumes might not even be noticed. Knowing how much they can be expected to understand while not boring them with too much information and detail is a fine art but one you're going to have to learn. If in doubt, the venerable KISS principle applies – Keep it Simple, Stupid.

Start Late, Get Out Early

When's the best place for your story to start? As late as possible. When's the best place for it to finish? As soon as possible. If you can start in the middle of something already happening (a chase, for example), that's a wonderful way to grab the attention of the audience – their minds will be racing to construct the events that happened before the film started. Don't have anyone stop to explain what happened before, though – go for the visual explanation over the spoken one every time. Then at the end of the film, make sure you know when it's finished. The moment after the epilogue is not the end of the story; the end of the story is the moment when whatever was at stake has been resolved (boy and girl get back together, hero kills the villain etc.). As soon as this final event has happened, try and finish the film as soon as humanly possible, at that very moment if logic allows. The same principle applies to individual scenes. Why show someone turning up at a doorstep when the moment it gets interesting is the conversation they have inside? Why show them leaving when the next interesting thing is what happens when they get home? Every single thing you show should have some relevance to the story; it may be permissible to show someone turning up on a doorstep if their appearance is a massive shock; it may be fine to show them leaving if the person they were visiting is staring daggers at their back. But if there's no story reason to show something happening, don't show it.

The Writing Process

When you start writing, the last thing you should be doing is jumping right into the script itself. First of all, you need to figure out what it is you're going to write. Here's a rough idea of how the process works…

– An **Outline** is a step-by-step, scene-by-scene layout of the story. Each scene gets a single line, a quick summary of *what* happens, rather than going into details about *how* it happens. The purpose of an outline like this is to help you figure out the story, the character arcs and the structure. It's common to put each individual scene on an index card so they can be shuffled about while you're designing the story; using individual entries in a spreadsheet program is another good way to do this.

– **Tell the story to someone else**, just to get an idea of whether or not it works. You'll see it in their eyes if it does. If not, you'll see a slight frown as they try and think of something polite to say. If you get the latter response, it's probably time to do some more work on the outline.

– A **Treatment** is the next step – a detailed description of what happens in each scene that could easily be longer than the script itself, but is purely a working document you use to figure out the details of exactly what happens in each scene. Confusingly, a 'treatment' is also used to refer to a much shorter description of the main points of the story – one sheet of A4 for a short film – to be used as a selling document to interest producers and funders in getting the film made.

– **Write the script**. This should go pretty quickly if you have a detailed treatment, as you've already done all the hard work. The first draft is a document you will love and cherish and believe to be the greatest thing ever. Unfortunately, you're wrong. Put it away for a week, and then look at it again. You'll soon see flaws. So the next step is...

- **Rewrite the script**. If it's really bad, you may have to go back to an even earlier stage, but this is all good, because at least you're improving it and not rushing to production with a script that's rubbish. A good technique here is to read it out loud, especially when working on the dialogue, as you'll soon hear whether or not it's actually possible to say this stuff. You'll probably have to rewrite it more than once; you may well find that you don't really figure out what the story's about until you stumble over something while doing the fourth draft, which means you have to rewrite everything from scratch – but as long as the script keeps getting better, it's worth it. Three to five drafts of a script are quite common.
- **Get people to read it** and let you know if they think it works. You'll almost certainly still find problems, but as before, at least you get the chance to solve them.

Script Format

Do you need to write a properly formatted screenplay for your short film? No. What you need is a blueprint for your film which will enable you to get your ideas across to other people. A script is the default way to do this since most films will require a mixture of visual action and dialogue.

Properly formatted scripts (which are different to plays or TV) also have a very useful feature which will assist you in making the film: on average, a single page of formatted script equals one minute of screen time. Working out the length of your film is a matter of counting the pages, then allowing for a couple of minutes' variation. It's also a minimum standard of professionalism – if you send someone in the industry an unformatted script, they may file it in the bin because writers who can't be bothered to learn script format usually haven't bothered to learn anything else. Screenwriting programs are commonly available these days, but if you have no access to these and need to set up your word processor from scratch, these are the basic settings:

- **Slugline/Scene Heading (e.g. INT. EVIL LAIR – NIGHT)** All capitals. 1½″ from the left edge of paper.
- **Screen Description** 1½″ from the left edge of paper.
- **Character Name** All capitals. 3½″ from left edge of paper.
- **Dialogue** 2½″ from left edge of paper.
- **Personal Direction/Parenthetical** 3″ from left edge of paper.
- **Effects (e.g. Fade in)** Right aligned. 1½″ from right edge of paper.
- **Top and bottom margin** 1″ .
- **Font for everything** 12pt Courier.

Some films can and should have a different blueprint. A film that is entirely visual and has no actors (particularly animations) is best designed with a storyboard. A film that is to be improvised by actors may require a list of scenes and information on the characters, rather than specific instructions on what to do and say. A film with no dialogue and no actors may simply require a shotlist. It's up to you to decide what your production needs. There's an example of script format here – a 'Spec Script' such as you would write for submission to a production company. There's a 'Shooting Script' on page 210 as part of the Case Study.

FADE IN:

EXT. BUSY STREET — DAY

A NAKED MAN walks from a side street and plants a banner in a council flowerbed- "SCRIPT FORMAT TUITION"

INT. WALK-IN REFRIGERATOR — NIGHT

The location has changed but the Naked Man is here still. He shivers and clings on to the banner.

> NAKED MAN
> That location thing is a slugline, okay?
> INT means Interior, EXT means Exterior,
> then you say where it is, then you say
> what time of day it is. Very important
> for lighting!

He points at a window, which shows the moon.

> NAKED MAN (CONT'D)
> (whispering)
> I'm whispering to show you that personal
> direction, in the brackets there. Don't
> overuse it! Actors don't like being told
> how to do their job. Can we go somewhere
> warm now?

EXT. ACTIVE VOLCANO - RIM — DAY

CRANE SHOT up from LAVA TRACKING IN on Naked Man as he DANCES on the blistering surface. FOCUS PULL onto banner as it falls and BLAZES into charcoal.

> NAKED MAN
> Who do you think you are? The DIRECTOR?
> No camera directions!

The Naked Man bursts into flames.

> NAKED MAN (CONT'D)
> Keep paragraphs four lines or less!
> Readers get frightened if they see a big
> block of text.

He falls into the pit.

FADE OUT

Figure 1 Script Format Example

What Goes into the Script?

Not everything needs to be said in the script. If the script has such things as 'The lead character closes her eyes. Camera TRACKS BACK to reveal a WIDE SHOT of everyone standing in a line, gaping in awe. ZOOM IN on main character as she opens her eyes and STARES down the lens…' then the reader will not see the story in their mind's eye, but be distracted by the camerawork – something that won't be happening when they actually watch the film.

Remember that the script is not a *technical* blueprint for the finished film – you'll be doing that with story-boards and shotlists later on. Scripts have many uses, and all of them are about communication; a funder is looking for an interesting story; an actor is looking for an inter-esting character; most people just want the script to make them feel enthusiastic about getting involved in the film. The purpose of a script is to give as close as possible an impression of the experience of watching the final film so that people know what it is they're working towards. And since you can't make a film on your own, being able to communicate this to your colleagues is vital.

One thing you don't need to worry about while writing is scene numbers, as these only get in the way while you're writing. Most screenwriting programmes will allow you to easily add them, so leave this stage until you start storyboarding – at which point you will need the numbers as a way to link the storyboards back to the script.

Storyboarding & Shotlisting

Storyboards: Starting to Direct

A storyboard is another, more detailed way of creating a blueprint for your movie, usually done once the script is completed. A storyboard looks like a comic, and that's almost precisely what it is: the film in still images. You don't need to draw a frame for every single moment, only for each of the shots you intend to shoot. And by doing so, you're creating a rough edit of your film before you've even shot it. This is the stage in filmmaking when you make the fundamental decisions about what exactly you're going to shoot – the stage where you start directing.

And since this is when you start directing, it's time to consider the three main ways of constructing a scene:

- **Single Shot** – The simplest way is to cover the entire scene in one shot. This sounds like a nice easy way to do things, but means that if you make a mistake (and you probably will if you're on your first film), you won't be able to conceal it in the edit.
- **Shot by Shot** – the most obvious way to construct a scene is to think of each shot in turn, in the order that they'll appear in the edit. This tends to work very well for sequences that contain actions of some sort, when we may never have to return to the same shot on a character or object in a scene.
- **Coverage** – However, many scenes are largely

SINGLE SHOT

Covering the scene in one shot. Has to be done for very good reasons as it profoundly affects the scene and is difficult to adjust in editing.

1

Wide (critics MLS), pushing in. Critics discuss film theory while Anti-Critic fumes

1 cont'd

Still pushing in. Anti-Critic now seen to be fiddling with a device

1 cont'd

MS on filmmaker at end of push in as he stands and zaps a Critic with the device

SHOT-BY-SHOT

Each shot intended to be edited into the scene in the order shown. Very good for scenes involving visual events, can be spectacular, but not so flexible.

1

MLS Critic One jabbering away about film theory

2

MCU shot on Anti-Critic raising sonic nausea inducer

3

MCU Critic One getting zapped by nausea inducer and throwing up

COVERAGE

Each shot covers a large part of the scene; exact order of shots to be decided in the edit. Usually best for dialogue scenes, which need flexibility.

1

MCU on Critic One, covering her side of the debate, until she gets zapped and vomits

2

MCU on Critic Two, covering his side of the debate, including reaction to zapping

3

MS Anti-Critic, fiddling with device and then zapping Critic Two. Acts as a cutaway from the dialogue, and ends the scene.

Figure 2 Storyboard Strategies

composed of people talking to each other, and these scenes are best shot with coverage. In this system, we film the entire scene from a variety of angles, creating a number of shots which can be cut into the scene at any point we wish, allowing us to decide the structure of the film in the edit – which we'll need to be able to do since the cutting of dialogue scenes often depends on actors' performances, which aren't always very predictable.

The shots commonly used in Coverage are:

– A **Master** shot of the entire scene from beginning to end. You'll normally only see this at the beginning of a scene, to establish the space in which the scene happens.
– **Singles** on each character, covering all their actions. Possibly several of these at different shot sizes.
– **Cutaways** Details on any physical action, like the pouring of a drink, fingers tapping etc. Sometimes you need these to tell the story; sometimes you need them to cover up problems in the edit.

Shooting coverage just by itself is, in the long run, quite a dull way to shoot a film, but it will get you started. In practice, you'll often find yourself combining the Shot by Shot and Coverage styles within a scene, as there's often action which needs to be filmed in a specific way even while characters are talking and requiring coverage on them. As you gain more experience, you'll quickly see that you can mix in plenty of cool shots, as long as you always have enough coverage as well.

There's an example of a full storyboard on page 215 as part of the Case Study.

SHOT SIZES

A few rough conventions for shot sizes. Not everyone agrees on these, so be ready to explain what you mean when speaking to a new acquaintance.

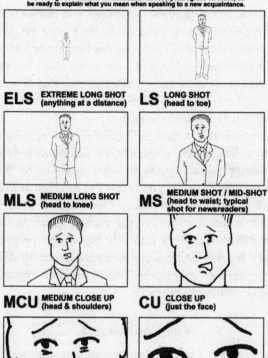

ELS EXTREME LONG SHOT (anything at a distance)

LS LONG SHOT (head to toe)

MLS MEDIUM LONG SHOT (head to knee)

MS MEDIUM SHOT / MID-SHOT (head to waist; typical shot for newsreaders)

MCU MEDIUM CLOSE UP (head & shoulders)

CU CLOSE UP (just the face)

BCU BIG CLOSE UP (facial details face too close for CU)

ECU EXTREME CLOSE UP (any very tight shot)

ALSO:
2-SHOT - Any shot with two people in frame, usually between MLS and CU.
WIDE SHOT (WS) - The Wide Shot makes no reference to the human figure; it could cover a whole room or a landscape. Often used as an establishing shot.

Figure 3 Shot Sizes

Shotlisting

Once you have a finished storyboard, you can work out how many shots you need to do. And once you have that information, you can work out how many lighting setups you need to do, and how many shots for each one. And once you know that, you can have a rough guess at how long it will take to shoot – and a full schedule is just round the corner.

The shotlist is a tool for planning, and planning is key to getting a film made. On set, you'll probably use the shotlist as your guide to what needs to be done since the storyboard is a bit bulky. Put in as much information as you think necessary. Once you've made the list, put it into two orders: the editing order, and the likely shooting order. I find that spreadsheet programs are best for shotlisting, since they allow easier shuffling and sorting for this purpose. There's a sample shotlist in the Case Study on page 219.

Video Storyboard

Now you have a rough idea of what you want to film, why not grab a camera, some friends and shoot a test version? You don't need the real props although shooting in the real location can be a big help. Edit it together on whatever system is available and see what it looks like. These 'video storyboards' are a great way to discover problems with pacing, storytelling, whether or not you've put in enough coverage, shots that you ought to do that you didn't think of before, and practical problems that might come up during the shoot.

Preproduction

Scheduling

Filmmaking is a problem-solving exercise, and the key to problem solving is planning. You cannot create a story with unrealistic requirements and then expect everything to end up exactly as you envisaged. There's so much that can go wrong when you're making a film that you need to be as certain as you possibly can of what's supposed to happen. So you need to make a schedule. There are two aspects to scheduling: the overall production, from preproduction through to distribution; and the shoot itself.

The Overall Production

The first question is: When do you shoot? You set a date several weeks in the future, and how far in the future depends on how many things you already have available. The key thing is usually auditions, as they take a while to organise, and also locations, if you need to wait to get permission from a large organisation.

For the purposes of the following example, we'll assume that you've picked dates six weeks ahead. Bear in mind that this isn't a hard and fast schedule, and every film is different; it's possible to throw something together in a few days if you already have most of what you need, but you may find this a useful framework to build on.

- **Preproduction Week One** is mostly about finding people. This is when you advertise for actors and make enquiries about your key crew. You may also want to be looking out for locations. You don't want to be thinking about equipment or props unless there's something unusual or difficult that you need to find.
- **Preproduction Week Two** is about selecting people – you'll be selecting the actors you want to audition, and hopefully nailing down your key crewmembers. You may also want to be looking out for locations as well.
- **Preproduction Week Three** is the week of the audition, when you'll make your decisions on the cast and book them for the shoot; you should also be finding most of the rest of your crew by now, although this process often goes on longer. You should have a pretty good idea of what locations you want to shoot in by now. This is also a good time to look for equipment.
- **Preproduction Week Four** is all about getting your locations sorted out. You should know where your locations are, and now you'll be booking them. You'll also be booking equipment for the shoot by now, and looking for props and costumes.
- **Preproduction Week Five** is mostly about sorting out props and costumes (and if you need to have

costumes fitted, now's a good time), but also about the Recce – you may have visited locations before but now you need to take your key crew around so they know what they'll be dealing with. On the casting front, you might well be looking for extras if you need them.

- **Preproduction Week Six** doesn't have much specific stuff planned – just kit pick-ups and rehearsals, maybe make-up tests if necessary. The reason to keep this free is that some of the stuff you should have done earlier will inevitably take longer, and the final week is when you'll be taking care of all these details.

A ten minute drama will generally take between three and five days to shoot. It's best to have these in a row, and running over a weekend; shooting on consecutive weekends is fine, but bear in mind that it might incur things like extra travel costs.

The postproduction schedule can be more flexible, but it's a good idea to move as quickly as possible – all too many people let postproduction slide on for months without getting the film made, when you could finish postproduction in four weeks. Again, these timings are only a guide and it's possible to do things a lot faster.

- **Postproduction Week One** is mainly about taking equipment back, and capturing footage. You shouldn't jump straight into the edit – give yourself this week to clear your head.

- **Postproduction Week Two** is when you do the first edit, known as the 'Offline' edit. This can take a good five days for a ten minute film. Once this is done, you lock the picture and stop making edits that change the length of the film.
- **Postproduction Week Three** is when you get to grips with visual effects (if you have any, and it's probably not a good idea to do too much in your first film), and sound issues. You'll be adding music at this stage (unless you're working with a composer, in which case it'll take longer to get the music ready), and looking for sound effects.
- **Postproduction Week Four** is when you complete the 'Online' edit – adding all elements and grading the picture quality. You'll also mix the sound, and master the film to your chosen formats. You may also author a DVD for the film.

The Shoot

You should by now have numbered the scenes in your script, which you'll need now in order to keep track of them. Make a list of all the locations named in the sluglines (or setups if there's only one location), and arrange them in the most convenient order (see 'Out of Sequence Shooting', below), noting which scene numbers need to be completed for each one.

A shooting day is usually between ten and twelve hours; you'll normally expect to complete roughly ten setups a day, but if you have to move to another location, that'll usually take at least an hour, and remember that it takes time in the morning to get set up – usually about an hour but quite possibly much more if things are disorganised. You'll find an example of a day's schedule, along with an explanation of how it was arrived at on page 224 as part of the Case Study.

Catering

Food can have a serious effect on the morale of a crew; if you feed people badly, you may find them grumbling behind your back and not giving their all. If you're only using your friends, you might be able to get them to bring packed lunches or pay for their own meals, but if you're using anyone with professional experience, you're expected to provide a free breakfast and lunch. If you don't have much money, the cast and crew might forgive you for some shortcomings; a trip to a high street baker to get sandwiches will probably be enough, or handmade rolls (even cheaper). You should have tea and coffee available at all times, or cold drinks and water if you're expecting hot weather, along with a good supply of biscuits, chocolate and snacks. Ask everyone involved if they have any particular dietary requirements – there's always a few vegetarians on any shoot, and more people than you'd think have special diets for health reasons. Lunch should be given an hour in the schedule. In the event of absolute disaster, people are sometimes willing to work through lunch and eat food 'in the hand,' but make sure everyone agrees to this before you spring it on them.

Call Times

Although everything depends upon when you can get into your locations, 08:00 (8am) is a basic starting point for a first crew call, with the cast called separately depending upon when they're needed – those needed for the first scene will come in with everyone else and go straight into make-up if necessary. Others will have later call times, but always allow enough time to get them through costume and make-up; the schedule for this is a separate challenge all by itself.

Out of Sequence Shooting

Films are shot out of sequence to make your life bearable. Imagine you have a dialogue scene in a dark, moodily lit recording studio in which you want to cut back and forth between two people as they talk. But the lighting setup for each angle takes half an hour or more; do you really want to do that every time you need to make a cut? No. You shoot everything needed from one angle (also called a 'setup' – see below) first, and then from another angle, and so on until you've got everything on your shotlist. Shoot the widest angle first, then work your way in to the closer shots. A few repetitions of the action while it's wide will act as rehearsal for the close-ups (when the actors absolutely have to get it right). Otherwise, scenes are shot in the order that it's convenient to shoot them – many considerations will come into play, such as the availability of performers, locations, daylight, local requirements and so on. Get ready to juggle.

Lighting Setups

Lighting setups are the thing that will determine how long you need to stay in any one location; every time you put the camera in a substantially different place, you create a new setup and need to adjust the lighting. Only experience will give you a rough idea of how much, but you should go through your shotlist and decide which shots are to be done from which angle/setup, and then total up the number of angles/setups; indoor lighting setups will take longer (up to an hour or more sometimes), while daytime exterior setups may only require the placing of a reflector to bounce a little light onto someone's face to even out the effect of the sun – the work of a few minutes.

Camera Movement

What sort of camera movement you use also makes a difference. Exterior handheld work is the fastest, since the camera doesn't need to be 'set up' as such, just loaded onto the shoulder. The longest setups usually involve a track, when the camera is moving on wheels; these movements have to be rehearsed over and over to make sure that lighting is correct throughout (and it's even worse when you throw in a jib as well). The same can apply if a handheld camera has to move about a lot in a scene; the hardest thing to do is create lighting that works in any direction no matter where the camera chooses to look.

Performers

People make mistakes, especially when it involves long, complicated dialogue scenes. If you have a shot where someone has to make a simple physical action, it will usually go a lot faster than a shot with dialogue. This is nothing to do with the professionalism of actors, but simply a measure of how much more difficult a dialogue scene is; you'll want to get it right, so give them a little more time.

Using the Weekends

Bear in mind that Saturday, Sunday and public holidays present a variety of problems and opportunities separate from other days. Sunday is a good day to do a crowd scene if you're relying on friends and family. Saturday on the sea front may be a difficult shoot because of the people; but Saturday in an office is great. Plan your shoots around weekends to get the most out of the peace and quiet while it's there.

Night Shoots

Sometimes you need to shoot at night, but bear in mind what time of year it is and exactly how many hours of night you'll have. Scheduling a ten-hour night shoot of exteriors in July is difficult; doing it in January is fine, but get prepared for the weather. Lunch breaks should be scheduled as normal, but it may be wise to provide (or pay for) a hot meal instead of just sandwiches. It's best to put night shoots at the end of the schedule, since getting back to a daytime schedule requires a couple of days off. Or better still, shoot Day for Night if you can – see page 138 for more details.

Weather Cover

Weather in the UK seems designed to defeat film-makers. Luckily, light rain doesn't show up on camera, and you can keep filming with the assistance of plastic bags on equipment and lots of umbrellas, but waiting for the heavens to clear is a familiar experience to most of us. On such short shoots, it's difficult to have something else available to shoot, but if the rain sets in to stay you'd better have something else to do or you might lose the entire production. Arranging for 'Weather Cover' can range from having a location you can run to and keep shooting in if it rains, to sound recording you can be getting on with, or to carrying a whole set around with you to shoot in. Whatever it is, make sure there's something you can be getting on with if the heavens open.

LOCATIONS

The best locations are the ones you get for free, and when you have no money, you're always looking for the best location. The easiest way to accomplish this is to write a story set in whatever locations you already have access to – your home, your workplace, public spaces, and so on. Most streets, roads and highways in the

United Kingdom require no permission to film unless you have to block pavements or otherwise cause a nuisance.

Some areas are obviously more difficult – airports and anything next to a military base, for example – but city centres are also becoming more troublesome, as local authorities now take a dim view of unannounced filming, partly because of the nuisance value but also for security reasons. Not to mention that large parts of city centres are actually in private hands, where security will simply move you on if you have no permission to be there. That's not to say that it's impossible to film in such places – but it may take some persuasion, so make sure you have a back-up plan.

Things to Look For in a Location

- **Relevance** Is it right for the film? Bear in mind that many locations can double for somewhere else or be made to look different with minimal set dressing.
- **Availability** Is it going to be open at the time you need? Is it going to be open long enough? Can you persuade someone to open it for you?
- **Accessibility** Is it within range of everyone who needs to get there? Are the doors/entrance big enough to get equipment and props through? Is there disabled access?
- **Location-Specific Rules** For example, hospitals may require mobiles to be switched off, certain areas in a building may be off-limits, farmers like to have gates left closed.

- **Parking** Is there parking nearby? Is there enough? How much does it cost?
- **Power** Is there electricity on site? Is it adequate to your needs? At the very least, you'll need a socket to plug a kettle into. If you're out in the middle of nowhere, take a small camping gas cooker.
- **Light** If the sun is your main light source, does it have adequate access to your location? Where will it be shining at various times during the day (take a compass with you to check)?
- **Noise** If you're recording location sound, is there a source of noise pollution nearby, such as a major road, factory, nightclub, field of excitable sheep etc? Is it noisy all day or are there quiet times? Can you live with the noise? The most annoying things are air conditioning systems and fridges – make sure you ask if they can be turned off.
- **Safety** Is the location safe? What are the fire regulations? Do they require all your equipment to be PAT tested? Is there a danger of casual theft? What's the area like for personal safety?
- **Insurance** Does the location require you to have public liability insurance? Large bureaucratic organisations are keen on this.
- **Water** Will always be required for drinking and cleaning. If you're out in the country, it's better to take water with you than rely on a standpipe.
- **Facilities** Are there sufficient toilets nearby? What are they like? If you're out in the middle of nowhere, will people mind going behind the bushes, or is it wiser to shoot near a country pub? If you're using

facilities not associated with the location itself, make sure you've arranged it beforehand.

- **Changing** If your actors need to change costumes, is there somewhere private they can do this?
- **Backstage Stuff** Your make-up artist will need somewhere to work, equipment will have to be put somewhere when it's not in use, actors like to have somewhere to hang around between takes (often called a 'green room'). Remember to take some fold-away chairs with you.
- **Communications** Is there mobile coverage? Is there a working phone box nearby? In the event of an emergency, you need to be able to dial 999.
- **Events** Check that there's nothing going on during the shoot. A location may be quiet on recce, but could be the site of anything from a carnival to a funeral during the shoot.
- **Sensitivity** If your production contains material which people in the vicinity might find offensive – e.g. lots of swearing next to an old people's home, demonic rites next to a little country church, racist characters spouting off next to a mosque – you should consider things very carefully. Some things can be worked out – the racist character might be part of a film that is anti-racist, and the mosque may well approve if they're approached in the right way – but some things can't. The only rule is: be considerate.
- **Weather Refuge** Is there somewhere people can run to if it really starts pouring down? Somewhere tea and coffee can be made?
- **Proximity** How near is the location to other poten-

tial locations? It will save an enormous amount of time if you can keep your locations within a small area. For example, if you have an office scene and an alley scene to shoot, and have found the office, check the streets nearby for suitable alleys.

Some of this you can find out on a first look; some will require you to ask the owner; some will only turn up on a more detailed recce.

Getting Permission

- **Individuals or Small Private Organisations** If the owner is a person whom you can actually talk to – the owner of a small shop, for example – it's much easier to establish a rapport. If they want to observe the shoot or be an extra (and if it's possible), let them.
- **Large Private Organisations** If local staff can't take a decision, you'll need to speak to the PR department (unless you have any other contacts). As long as you're not doing anything that will make them look bad, they will often allow you in. Having some local press coverage will certainly help. What you can get depends enormously on who you talk to. People at ground level are sometimes more sympathetic than someone in a distant faceless office; but if you don't ask, you'll never get anywhere.
- **Public Areas** Many cities now have Screen Commissions, which act as the first point of contact for filmmakers looking to shoot on public property, particularly in city centres. However, they're mostly

intended for professional productions and usually require that you have expensive Public Liability insurance, Risk Assessments and other paperwork – but they also simplify things by acting as a one-stop shop, sorting out all the permissions with other bodies, informing the police and fire brigade and so on. They can sometimes act as a barrier, but may be more understanding for student productions and first time filmmakers. If there isn't a screen commission in the area, you'll have to talk to the local authority for permission; each one is different and you may have to speak to several people to get the permission you need. They're also likely to need you to have Public Liability insurance.

Whoever you talk to, make sure you do so with plenty of advance notice – especially when dealing with large organisations that may need time to filter the request through several layers of bureaucracy. Make sure you're upfront about not having any money – if you fail to mention this point, you may end up with an unexpected invoice after the shoot...

Recce

Once you have found all your locations, check them out in detail. This is called a 'recce,' and on a short film can be done in a day. Day-to-day familiarity won't necessarily give you all the information you need; check out things like power supply and safety regulations. Never assume. If you're employing crew members, bring them along (lighting cameraman, AD and design people in particular). Their experience will help you to find out potential problems and the sort of things you'll need to bring with you.

On Location

While on location, be as considerate as possible. Any rubbish you create should be cleaned up and removed; any damage you make should be paid for. Have a member of crew responsible for fielding enquiries; this is often useful as a delaying tactic in the event of a confrontational person coming along. If you're out in public, you might find yourself needing a few people to keep pedestrians under control; areas in which you shoot can be 'locked off' for brief periods of time, but pedestrians should not be held back for too long; let them go between takes, then lock off again. Be polite if you're doing this, even if people just push past you and walk through anyway.

After the shoot, be sure to send the owners a nice letter thanking them for everything, and a DVD copy if your budget stretches that far; put the relevant name in the 'thank you' section of the credits.

CASTING

Casting your friends and family is easy – they're free, and (usually) prepared to go out on a limb for you. But, more than likely, they're not very good actors. Even if they are, bear in mind that although the idea of making a film sounds glamorous, the reality may involve standing in a wet field in January pretending it's July. Making a film can leave you without any friends if you're not careful. If you do have a talented friend or relative, then by all means use them, but on the whole, friends and family are best employed as extras, crowds, corpses, zombies etc. – anything that needs a warm body but not acting ability.

Real actors are surprisingly easy to find and employ, whether they be drama students looking for experience or professional actors between jobs. Many actors are willing to work for expenses on small productions halfway up the country, because most actors are in exactly the same position as the filmmaker seeking to employ them – they need their work to be seen. And many actors who would seem to have no such need are willing to work for little or nothing if they like the script or trust you.

But you must treat your actors with the respect that you would hope to receive yourself. Simply because they're willing to work for free is no reason to exploit them. If you cannot pay someone a fee, you must still pay them expenses – travel, food and accommodation. This doesn't mean you have to put them up in a four star hotel and have a chef flown in, but putting someone out of pocket when they're giving up their time for free is nothing short of an insult. You may be able to satisfy the accommodation requirement with a sofa, a pillow and a blanket – but a spare bed is better. Another thing that actors appreciate is a DVD copy of the film when it's done. Treat your actors right, and they'll repay you for it on the screen.

Your aim is to find enough people to audition; you should see at least five different performers for each major role. Places to look include local drama groups (consult your library, community centre, theatre, university), drama schools (particularly if they're nearby), personal contacts, and so on. If you want to find people from within the community, many local newspapers will print a story about you and your film, with contact details at the end. Or you can advertise. Some publications charge for this service, but others will provide it for free; be sure to include the relevant dates, the location, and the level of payment you're offering. Casting services exist on the Internet, and local organisations may also have websites and email addresses you can contact. There is also a publication called *Spotlight*, which lists all the actors in the country, with photos, and contact details for their agents, and has a website you can look this up on.

Unless you already know the actors, you should get hold of a photo and CV for each one, which will give you enough information to be able to whittle the numbers down to acceptable levels. Firstly, do they look right for the role? Bear in mind that the photos are not always entirely accurate. What's their experience like? If they've done loads of theatre but almost no film or television work, they are either unsuitable or very keen to gain experience. How old are they? As in any profession, those that do not succeed or have limited ability tend to give it up after a while. If you advertise for young actors, you will get vastly more applications than you would if you were looking for older actors; but the older actors are more likely to be competent.

Auditioning requires a room, a table, some chairs, and a video camera (make sure the actors say their name on camera to help you identify them later). One thing you must not do is audition anyone in your own home. One of the commonest horror stories is of the audition an actor went for at someone's flat which turned out to be run by just the one guy, whose requests seemed a little... inappropriate. So, get an audition room somewhere that isn't going to make the actors worry about their safety, and never audition alone – as much as anything else, the extra sets of eyes and ears will be invaluable.

How you audition people will vary according to what you want from them; if you want someone who can read the lines acceptably well, then that's all they'll need to do. If you want to see how they bounce off other actors, have them come in groups of one candidate for each character. Give them a chance to read for more than one character if possible. Bear in mind that, just as you're sizing them up, they'll be sizing you up. The more professional and accommodating you are, the more you will impress them; having somewhere to serve as a waiting room and giving them tea and coffee tends to help. I like to run my auditions as mini-workshops – get a group of actors together for maybe an hour, do readthroughs, and then experiment to see what they can add to the characters and story; most actors seem to find this approach refreshing after the usual cattle calls, and you can afford to take this time when making a short film with a limited number of characters.

You'll often know if someone is wrong for the role a few seconds after they start talking, but you should still give them a chance. You'll probably have a fairly good idea of who you want to cast almost as soon as the auditions are over, but think it over. Review your tapes. Discuss it with the people who were there with you. Check back over your notes. Choose the person you feel is right, but have a second choice as well; the first choice may turn out to be unavailable, especially if paid work turns up. Make sure they're happy to work for whatever you're offering, particularly if it's just expenses. Finally, once you have your cast confirmed, do everyone else the courtesy of a phone call or email to let them know.

Most agents I've had dealings with are very nice, helpful people. A lot of them will send out photos and CVs of their actors in reply to your ad despite the fact that there's no payment; but by and large, you're a very small blip on their radar. Many of your actors will be happy to deal with you directly; your dealings with agents will probably be minimal. But do be polite. So far as Equity goes, their influence over microbudget productions is limited. If your actors have agreed to work for expenses or a low wage, that's generally the end of it (unless you're at film school, in which case there are agreed rates you should already be aware of).

CREWING

On a feature film, you can expect to have a crew of dozens of people working as a tight and efficient unit. On a short film, you may be able to get away with doing pretty much everything yourself – but you won't sleep much. Have a go at as many of the major jobs as possible to get a feel for them and make yourself aware of what's possible. The list that follows is not exhaustive, nor do you necessarily need everyone – at a minimum you need one person on camera and one person holding the microphone.

– **Producer** Responsible for organising pretty much everything with regards to the production and its subsequent distribution. Read the rest of the book.
– **Director** Responsible for interpreting the script into storyboards/shotlists, the overall 'look' of the film, directing actors and crew during the shoot, working with the editor to get a cut of the film, directing the sound design.
– **Writer** Getting the script done. There's not much they can do on set, except as a consultant.
– **Assistant Director(s)** If you've got more than the most basic crew, you'll need an assistant director (AD). The AD's job is to keep the set running smoothly and ensure that the production stays on schedule. They take the hands-on organisational work off the shoulders of the director, leaving him or her free to concentrate on the creative side. The AD may also be responsible for directing crowds and

extras. Runners report to the AD.

- **Director of Photography/Lighting Cameraman**
A Director of Photography (DoP) designs and implements the lighting for the film, supervises the camera operator, and plans the actual shots with the director. A Lighting Cameraman (or woman) is a DoP who operates the camera as well; you're better off finding one of these for your film, since it means one less crew member. Having a skilled DoP or Lighting Cameraman on your crew is an invaluable aid to an inexperienced director.
- **Camera Assistant** Assistants may be required to take care of focus pulling, setting up monitors, keeping the camera fed with batteries and tapes, cable bashing etc.
- **Sound Recordist/Boom Operator** The Sound Recordist is responsible for ensuring that dialogue is recorded as clearly as possible, and also collects any 'wildtracks' or 'atmos' required (see page 149 for details). While it is possible to keep an eye on the levels meters and hold the microphone at the same time, it's better if you have one person monitoring the sound, and one person, a Boom Operator, keeping the microphone pointing in the right direction.
- **Grip** The Grip's responsibility covers any kind of mobile camera mounting, particularly 'dollies,' which are wheeled carts (running on tracks or tyres) on which the camera and operator sit while the Grip pushes them along. On a low-budget short the person not doing anything else tends to end up pushing the dolly.

- **Continuity (Script Supervisor)** The Script Supervisor is responsible for making sure you don't have continuity mistakes which disrupt the flow of the story, even when scenes that follow one another in the script are shot days or weeks apart. They keep a note of what each character was wearing in every scene, whether they used their left hand or right hand to perform an action, where objects were or how they were handled, and take Polaroids of performers and sets as a reference guide.

- **Make-Up Artist** The Make-Up Artist is responsible for keeping everyone on screen looking as gorgeous or horrible as necessary. If they're doing more than basic beauty make-up, they may need to be paid something to cover the use of materials. Most make-up artists can do minor prosthetic work (bullet holes and burns, for example), but anything larger will require a specialist.

- **Runners** If you have more than a few people, it's useful to have one or two people available to do whatever needs doing – holding reflectors, making coffee, dashing off to buy extra tape stock etc. It's preferable for a runner to have a car because otherwise you'll have to stop the shoot while a key crew member runs off to get that vital widget halfway across town.

- **Stills Photographer** One of the things that's often forgotten in the heat of the moment is that, for any film to sell, there must be stills to go with it. So get someone to take stills (preferably with a digital SLR camera).

- **Composer** Okay, you don't need a composer on set. But if you're going to need original music for your

film, think about recruiting someone now, and
getting them as involved as they want to be. Young
composers might even volunteer to be runners if they
have the time.

- **Production Designer** On a professional production, the Production Designer is in charge of all
aspects of design – sets, props, costume and so on –
and runs the Art Department, with its legions of
Wardrobe Assistants, Property Buyers, Carpenters and
assorted useful people. On a low-budget short, most
of this will be done by you. It's not impossible to find
a Production Designer to take this off your hands, but
the need for a Production Designer implies complicated or large design requirements which are best
avoided on your first few productions.

If you're just starting out, it's perfectly fine to use your
friends to fill crew roles, especially when there's only a
few of you. You might find yourself bargaining with a
facilities house on the phone one minute, and pushing
a dolly the next. You should make sure that someone in
your group can drive – over the age of 25 if you're
hiring vehicles, since hire companies won't insure
anyone younger. It's very useful to have someone with
experience around who can spot disasters before they
happen and give you the advice you may desperately
require. Make contact with your nearest media centre
or filmmaking group and ask if there's anyone who can
help you out, or (even better) if you can volunteer for
someone else's production, get some experience and
end up with them owing you a favour. I highly recom-

mend doing a stint as a lowly runner or assistant; it gives you an appreciation of the process which can rescue you when you make your own film.

Like actors, many crew are willing to work for nothing but expenses, but this only applies if they are in a similar position to yourself – looking to gain experience, develop their skills and build up a showreel. Camera Crew, Editors, Sound Recordists, Make-up Artists – anyone with a creative aspect to their work can be found. But some people are in this business to make a living and support a family; Sparks, for example, are unlikely to give their time for free.

If you're recruiting, places to look include the media centres already mentioned and film schools, which will have a number of students and recent graduates interested in gaining experience. Things like design and make-up will also be taught at local colleges, where students will be just as keen on getting some experience. You can advertise online with organisations like Shooting People and Mandy.com; remember to specify the wages and expenses situation, shoot dates and the part of the country you're shooting in. Crewing often works by means of personal contacts. You'll get more people if you've already made something yourself or have assisted on someone else's production. Just as with actors, respect your crew as you would have others respect you. Expenses are a minimum if you're not simply drawing upon your friends and family, and a DVD copy for everyone is vital for people to be able to build up their showreels.

PROPS, COSTUMES & MAKE-UP

The first thing to do is to find out exactly what you need; break the script down into scenes and make a list of all the props, costumes and special make-up requirements mentioned in the script, and then a list of anything that might be required for set dressing. If you don't have things like costume actually specified in the script, make notes anyway on the sort of things you would like your characters to wear.

When making the list, make sure to note whether or not any of it will need to be dirtied, stained, damaged or destroyed in the course of the story. Say, for example, you have a shirt which must have coffee spilled down it; this is all very well for the first take, but unless that one went perfectly (very unlikely), you will need to go again, and you don't want to wait for the washing machine to finish first. What you do is get 'repeats' of the same item. Three should be a minimum – if you can't afford that, be very, very careful when you shoot.

As with everything else, the best props and costumes are the ones you don't have to pay for. If you have a contemporary story set in locations you already have access to, then you can probably get most of the props and costumes with ease. But a sixteenth century costume drama is going to need an enormous amount of work; don't attempt it unless you have the contacts to make it happen. The film industry is served by a number of specialist props and costume hire companies which are perfectly willing to negotiate a discount, but extremely unlikely to give away anything for free.

If you have a local theatre, it's worth making contact to see if you can borrow (or hire cheaply) anything from their props or costume stores. Getting to know your local theatre is good in more ways than one; there are often local companies and youth theatre groups attached, which can be good for finding actors with some degree of competence; they may have dedicated workshop space and construction staff who can advise you on possibilities for set construction or modification; and they may be willing to let you roam through their stores without let or hindrance. But do be considerate, and willing to offer your assistance to them in return.

For contemporary stories, many actors will be willing to wear their own clothes. Ask them to bring a few possibilities for each individual change, and work together to see what's best. The high street should contain two places which will make your life easier – the charity shop and the pound shop. Charity shops are filled with all manner of clothes and other bits at ridiculously low prices. For any item of general clothing, they're worth a look; hang on to the receipt in case it doesn't fit. Pound shops are good places to pick up bits and pieces, not only for props but for many other things you might need when you're out on location; markets are similarly a good, cheap source. Costume hire shops generally carry novelty stuff rather than authentic looking costumes; they're great for a gorilla suit, but not for a realistic police uniform.

Never underestimate the value of that which others throw away. Check around your contacts to see if there's something they want to offload either for free or a modest price. Do the same with organisations, if they have something you think you might need. Never be afraid to take a peek into a skip to see what potentially valuable item has been discarded (but do ask permission if you want to take anything away).

Using firearms or offensive weapons is a problem, as they can be dangerous to your cast and crew, and be mistaken for the real thing. Before using fake weapons of any kind, contact the police to warn them in advance – they're generally quite understanding and just as star-struck as everyone else. It is illegal to fire even blanks without a qualified armourer on set, and they tend to be expensive.

Make-up

For make-up, you really need a dedicated Make-up Artist, but many things can be managed easily if you don't have one. A lot of people can handle their own make-up, and if not, then what's usually required is foundation (to hide blemishes and conceal the effects of hangovers) and powder to reduce shine and soften the face, as cameras highlight facial reflections very efficiently and make people look sweatier than they really are. You need to be very careful with hygiene when doing make-up, as it's all too easy to give people spots (which are then almost impossible to hide) – brushes should not be used on more than one person without being cleaned.

You might also be able to manage more ambitious

make-up work such as wounds and bullet holes. Morticians' Wax is available from most costume hire shops and can be moulded to create the shape of a wound. Blood can be bought (check to see if it's non-toxic if it has to go in the mouth), or you can make it with golden syrup and red food colouring (cochineal). Use a little coffee powder if you need to darken it and be prepared to dilute it to create various consistencies – test it before you use it!

BUDGETING

A 'Microbudget' short film usually means any short made for less than £500 ($1,000), which seems a lot if you're a student or on benefits. But you don't have to spend it all at once, nor is it necessary to spend that much. Everyone has a range of contacts and opportunities to get hold of freebies, whether it be photocopying and phones at work or access to your mate's handycam over the weekend. Whatever your friends and relatives have, don't be ashamed to ask. They might just say yes.

What follows is a list of things you might have to shell out for. Prices will vary according to region; Londoners in particular will probably find that things are more expensive. Also make sure to find out if VAT is inclusive in the price. In most cases it'll be obvious but always check; professional places always assume you know the real price will be 17.5% higher. For a sample budget at three different experience levels, flip forward to the Case Study at page 236.

- **Audition Room** Meeting rooms at arts centres, media centres, theatres, student unions etc., might cost you £50 ($100) or so if you can't get a freebie.
- **Location Hire** The best locations are the ones you get for free but sometimes there's a location you just have to have. Try not to spend more than £50 ($100), though.
- **Transport** If your actors are travelling from the metropolis you'll be paying (one reason why locals are sometimes better), either for petrol or the train fare. 40p a mile is the rate currently specified by HM Revenue & Customs, a quite high rate intended to cover wear and tear as well as petrol; train fares vary, but you should be able to get cheaper tickets if you book in advance. You might need a van if you have lots of equipment – if you don't know anyone who owns one, it can cost upwards of £100 ($200) to hire one for a weekend so it's probably better to distribute kit among multiple cars unless there's no other option. If you do hire a van, make sure the driver is over 25 and doesn't give their profession as 'actor', 'filmmaker' or anything else that sounds unusual – they probably won't be covered by the insurance.
- **Accommodation** Hotels are the last resort, unless your cast and crew are experienced professionals who expect that level of comfort. If you can't find somewhere among friends and family, a better option is to make friends with your local theatre, which faces a similar problem on a regular basis and might have either their own cheap accommodation or a 'digs list' with special cheap rates.

- **Production Design** Depending on your film, this could be the single most expensive area; even if it's a film with minimal requirements, you might need £50 ($100) for bits of set dressing that help to make a location look real. Costume hire is often the most difficult area – proper realistic costumes might cost upwards of £50 ($100) a day. Time to make friends with the local theatre again…
- **Phones** You're going to be spending lots of time on the phone, and probably calling lots of mobile numbers. Using a pay-as-you-go phone is a good way to waste lots of money; landlines will be less expensive, and you may be able to make free calls at various times; you may be able to make some calls for free using Skype or other VOIP software (if the person on the other end also has the same setup); but the best option at present is a monthly contract mobile with lots of free minutes and free texts which will cover most, if not all of the cost. And avoid faxing wherever possible – only a few organisations still require it, and email is usually better.
- **Photocopying & Printing** It's less necessary these days to print up lots of copies of script, schedule, shotlist etc. to send out to people – just distribute them by email and let them print it themselves. But you'll still need to run off a few copies for use during the shoot, so here's another fiver gone at least (unless you have access to the photocopier at work).
- **Actors** You may often find that actors will work for expenses (travel, accommodation, food), but £50 ($100) a day is a microbudget rate if you find yourself

paying. Equity minimum is very much not a microbudget rate, so don't get yourself in a situation where you'll have to pay it.

- **Crew** Many of your crew will be in it for experience and showreel material, and will only need feeding (and possibly transportation and accommodation). But there's one exception: the seasoned professional who gives your crew the reservoir of experience that just might save the day, especially on a difficult and ambitious shoot. They won't be able to work for free but might be willing to charge half price – this varies between different professions, but £150–250 ($300–500) a day isn't unreasonable. And they might even bring their own kit, which saves you the cost of hiring it.

- **Stock** Tape costs vary between different formats. Mini-DV can be found in many outlets for between £5–10 ($10–20) but in most cases it's better to go to a professional supplier because it's one less level of mark-up to deal with – and better still, you can find incredibly cheap deals if you pay via the Internet. If you're using cards, hard drives or similar options, they should usually come with the equipment, and your costs will be the hard drive space to copy the footage onto.

- **General Supplies** Much of the stuff in the Shopping List on page 80 will cost you money – for example, gaffer tape is around £5 ($10) a roll (get it from a proper hardware store and not a high street store), and all those little bits and pieces add up. Put aside £30 ($60) or so, depending on how long the shoot is.

- **Catering** Lunch and breakfast for a crew of ten people will cost at least £30 ($60) a day, and may require £50 ($100) or more. Costs can be brought down by buying ingredients and making it all yourself (or getting someone to do it for you) but remember: feeding people badly is a false economy.
- **Make-up** Most make-up artists will ask for some money to pay for materials, whether it be the basic ubiquitous powder or the raw materials for horrifying wounds. The amount they will need will vary according to the requirements of the film, but £20–50 ($40–100) isn't uncommon.
- **Kit Hire** Professional hire companies are largely out of reach, so you ought to be using your own kit, borrowed kit, or kit hired from a media centre, especially as they'll usually have subsidised rates. You can often find equipment that costs £100 ($200) per day to hire at a professional place costing a half or a third of that with a concessionary rate. Even so, kit hire can set you back a good couple of hundred, and will likely be your biggest cost if you're not paying cast and crew.
- **Edit Hire** You should be able to keep this cost down to zero by using your own computer at home. A professional edit suite could cost you hundreds, and you simply don't need it for your first few films. What you might have to spend money on is upgrading your system – buying extra hard drive space, for example.
- **Music** You're unlikely to be able to afford either commercial or library music, so forget about it now. Look at the prices on the MCPS website if you don't

believe me. Much better to find a local band or composer and persuade them to give you some music for free.

- **Public Liability Insurance** Far too expensive unless you can get yourself covered by someone else's insurance, or can take advantage of deals with organisations like BECTU or the IAC.
- **Equipment Insurance** Media Centres and local colleges will insure their own equipment, but professional companies often won't. You might have to pay for insurance on top of the listed price.
- **Sending Out the Film** The cheapest method is to post the video on YouTube or a similar service, then send people the URL; but this reduces the quality. DVDs are reasonable quality; a spindle of 50 DVD-Rs doesn't cost much more than £10 ($20), DVD cases can be bought relatively cheaply from professional tape stockists (but don't forget the cost of printing up covers!). Postage and packing might set you back, though – DVDs, even in the smallest possible packing, will be classed as 'Large Letters' by the Royal Mail and priced accordingly. You could spend 70–90p on each one. Making and sending DVDs could easily cost £1.20 ($2.40) per disc; it adds up fast.

PRECAUTIONS

Emergency Services

Most of the time you won't need to inform the police of what you're doing, but bear in mind that if you're depicting any activity that seems illegal or dangerous, 'concerned' neighbours are all too capable of dialling 999 and getting the local armed response unit to scare you half to death. Calling the police and letting them know what you're up to is no more work than a phone call. Make sure you get the name and number of an officer you can contact if difficulties arise. It may also be worth leafleting the local residents to let them know what's going on, especially if you're likely to be shooting at night. If you're going to be setting fires or even just using a smoke machine outdoors, let the fire brigade know. Bear in mind that if they get a 999 call, they are still obliged to attend – but if you informed them beforehand, at least you won't be charged for the cost of the call-out. And most importantly, make yourself aware of the location of the nearest A&E unit, just in case you need to take someone there in a hurry.

Health & Safety

One of the key principles of the English judicial system is that the accused is considered innocent until proven guilty. But not under Health and Safety Law, and with good reason. The onus is on the defendant to prove they took appropriate measures to ensure the health and safety of employees, participants and public; therefore, you are effectively guilty until you can prove yourself innocent. Not that you have to stress yourself out if it's just you and a couple of friends messing around with a camera, of course, but as soon as you start getting more ambitious, take the time to work out all the possible things that can go wrong, and ways of making sure they don't.

Contracts & Legal

On your first few films, you probably won't need to get anyone who works for you to sign a contract; the people you'll be working with should either be friends, people in the same position as you, or at least very understanding about the amount to which you'll be able to remunerate them. And with little or no revenue from your film for anyone to argue about, there's very little potential for anyone to turn nasty later on. On the other hand, you might get lucky and sell the film, in which case you absolutely do need to have all performers (even extras) sign either a release form or a contract, plus you'll need location owners to sign an agreement that allows you to use footage filmed at the location. Sample versions can be found on various websites, including Shooting People (although you have to join Shooting People first – but it's worth it).

Insurance

- **Public Liability** insurance protects you against claims by the public or organisations that suffer injury or damage as a result of your filming, and is often required as a condition of filming at certain locations. You can gain this cover quite cheaply by joining organisations such as the Institute of Videographers or the Institute of Amateur Cinematographers, or

BECTU (the crew union), but it may only cover you and not your cast & crew, should they be responsible for anything going wrong. If you do have to buy insurance, it's best to buy an annual policy rather than a policy just for the shoot, as it'll probably cost the same, strangely enough – it's such a small policy for the companies that minimum premiums come into effect. This can cost close to £1,000 ($2,000), though, so it's not for people without serious resources.

- **Employers' Liability** is a legal requirement for any company employing people, and as such, you probably won't have to buy it as you're probably making films as a private individual.
- **Equipment Insurance** is a separate matter – kit hired from media centres will already be covered, but professional hire companies will require you to get your own, or pay through the nose for their insurance.

Production

ORGANISATION

In a perfect world, the day-to-day running of a shoot is handled not by the director but by the assistant director and his or her team of runners and assistants. In the real world (the one without any money in it), you might have an AD, but you will still be responsible for a lot of what follows. If you're just making a film with your friends on a more informal basis, you don't need to worry about everything – just do what seems sensible. Anything you forget will provide you with an unforgettable learning experience. If you're trying for a more advanced shoot, pretty much all of this will be relevant – something, somewhere on your shoot will go wrong, and having a belt and braces approach will help you cope.

Picking Up the Kit

If you're hiring or borrowing equipment, you'll need to pick it up the day before the main shoot. This can be a major operation in itself, usually requiring two people – one to drive and one to navigate. Make sure you have a comprehensive list of every last piece of kit (down to the most insignificant cable or adapter) so you can check it all off and make sure it was actually there when you picked it up. If not, you may have a nasty surprise when you return the kit and find yourself charged for the missing pieces, which might have been accidentally left out of the kit in the first place. Once you've got the kit home, go through every last piece of it and make sure it's working as expected, especially if it's kit you haven't used before. And unless you've actually watched the batteries being charged, put them on charge yourself.

Movement Orders & Call Sheets

It's your job to make sure that everyone knows where and when to go. Don't rely on them to figure it out by themselves or to follow verbal directions – make maps ('Movement Orders' in professional parlance) with written directions and a route marked out. Remember to add postcodes as people have a tendency to rely on their sat navs. On professional shoots, call sheets are used to tell everyone what's going on in general and any special responsibilities they may have for that day. These need to be prepared every day to reflect the schedule changes which are likely on a long shoot, and aren't usually necessary on a short film as the plan is unlikely to change and a simple schedule along with contact details for everyone is usually enough.

Keep the Receipts

Get receipts for everything, preferably VAT receipts,

which you need if you can claim VAT back. But even more importantly, make sure that the people whose expenses you are paying give you receipts for everything they've bought, as there's no other way of tallying up what you owe them (or being able to have a quiet word about spending too much of your money).

Preparing for a Take

You can't just jump straight in and shoot – for each scene there needs to be preparation:

- **Block** The first step is to 'block' the scene through with actors, establishing where everyone's going to be and what they're going to do. Technical crew need to watch this so they know what they're going to be dealing with.
- **Light** And then everyone gets out of the way so the camera crew can get in and set up lights and the camera.
- **Rehearse** Once the lighting and camera are in position, rehearse the scene and refine the action. As well as getting the actors ready, this allows the boom operator to practice getting the boom mic in the right place, the camera operator can practice any moves or focus pulls, along with anyone else who needs to do anything during the take.
- **Shoot the scene**

The Routine for Doing a Take

So it's time to go for a take...

- **Lock off the set** If you're in a public place, get runners to hold back pedestrians for the duration of the take.
- **Get some quiet** The AD yells at everyone to shut up and stop moving. Absolute quiet is essential.
- **"Playback" (if necessary)** If you need music playing in the background (so people acting or dancing to it don't lose the rhythm), start it now. If dialogue is included in the scene as well, make sure you've practiced the timing to have it switched off.
- **"Roll sound"** (If sound is being separately recorded and required for the take.)
  Sound Recordist reports "Sound rolling."
  Sound Recordist reports "Speed." (Tape recorders take a moment to reach full speed.)
- **"Roll camera"** (people sometimes say "Turn over" instead).
  Camera Operator reports "Camera rolling."
  Camera Operator reports "Speed." (Cameras also take a few seconds to get properly up to correct speed).
- **"Background Action"** If you have extras doing something specific (e.g. dancing), you may want them starting before the actors enter the scene.
- **"Action!"** After "Action!", actors may need separate cues to enter or perform an action. Practice this in advance. On a professional shoot, it'll often be the AD doing this.

The action proceeds. Watch closely until…

- **"Cut!"** Wait for a few seconds after the scene is over to give yourself a little space in editing before you call cut. The camera operator can also call 'cut' if things go wrong on their part. Actors can stop themselves if things go wrong. However, if they're deep into the scene and something beyond their control goes wrong, they'll usually find it irritating to have to stop.

- **Discretely ask the camera operator if that was good** The people you need to talk to most after a take are the actors – but you also need to know if the take was technically okay. So have a brief word (or meaningful look) with the camera operator and sound recordist.

- **Check with the actors** Let them know what you thought of the performance and offer suggestions for the next take; as the takes go on, you may not have much to say, but at least give them some reassurance that things are going well. Be prepared to listen if they have ideas, but be decisive about your response to them.

- **Release any pedestrians you had waiting** Try and do this between takes if possible.

- **Repeat until you've got what you want** Doing only one take is unwise. You should shoot at least one more, known as a 'safety,' just to be certain you've got something. I find that a range of 2–5 takes is about normal, though trickier shots (usually camera moves) can sometimes take 10–15.

Shoot Ratios

The shoot ratio is the ratio of footage shot to the actual length of the film. A ten-minute film edited from 100 minutes of footage has a 10:1 ratio. Shoot ratios tend to be higher on video than on film, since the medium is cheaper; an efficient film shoot might be 6:1, but video shooting ratios can easily creep up to 20:1 or more. Tapes are relatively cheap these days and much longer than they used to be, and you might even be shooting on reusable memory cards, so there's little need to be paranoid about shooting too much. Just bear in mind that it means more work in the edit.

Watching the Take

If you aren't the camera operator and you have a field monitor, you have a dilemma: do you watch the actors or the monitor? Watching the actors will give you a better idea of their performance – but tells you nothing about the framing and look of the shot. The monitor will tell you everything you need to know about the way things look – but may not give you the best view of their acting. Try both and see what you prefer. If you go for the monitor, try and keep it as close to the action as possible so that you can communicate with your actors and camera operator easily.

Backstage

The make-up artist is going to need somewhere to

work, and they're going to need light. Actors will need somewhere to change, and preferably a place they can hang out when not on set. Tea and coffee will have to be made somewhere, usually wherever the kettle can be plugged in. Equipment needs to be piled up somewhere dry. Extras should have somewhere to wait. All of this has to be kept out of earshot or close enough so that people can hear you when you tell them to be quiet.

Closed Sets

On professional shoots, actors who are called upon to go partially or totally naked, or perform sex scenes, are protected by having a closed set – just them and a minimal crew, so they don't feel like they're being leered at by dozens of hairy crew members. This goes for both male and female actors. While it's unlikely that you'll be doing too much sex and nudity in your first few films – because a) it's difficult to persuade people to do that sort of thing, and b) do you really want to get that kind of reputation early on in your career? – you still may end up with scenes where people are down to their underwear or otherwise feel vulnerable. If in doubt, offer to make it a closed set and respect your actors.

Protecting the Footage

The worst thing that can happen to your film is losing or damaging the footage. Make sure there's a designated box the tapes go in while you're out on location, and never leave them lying around. You don't want to go through the experience of ripping a friend's van to pieces because you can't find yesterday's footage.

Make sure that each tape is numbered and labelled as soon as it comes out of the camera, and remember to push the write-protect switch. In the confusion of a shoot, it's all too easy to grab the wrong tape and record over all the hard work you did yesterday.

If you're shooting on memory cards, you will eventually find that these are full and need to be transferred to a hard drive. Make sure you have enough cards to be able to keep on shooting while you do this, and always transfer the footage to at least two hard drives – because one of them will be dropped or be damaged sooner or later.

Sometimes it's necessary to review your footage to see what you shot earlier. This is easy enough if the footage is on cards or hard drives; you can just skip to the relevant file, take a look, and then when you press record again, the camera just records a new file. Not so with tapes – it's all too easy to forget to fast forward back to the correct point to continue shooting, thus destroying hours of work. You also have to be very careful how you cue up the tape to continue recording if you've gone back to look at something – lopping off the end of the last take is bad enough but the worst problem is starting to record too late and causing a timecode break. Some cameras have a function which searches out the end of the last recorded piece and prepares the camera to shoot again – check the manual and make sure you know how to use it.

Nervous!

Before you leave a location, be sure to take one final look round for anything you may have left behind. This is sometimes known as a 'nervous', and has saved many a production from embarrassing slip-ups.

Reshoots & Pick-Ups

Once the shoot's over, it's not always over. In the industry, it's quite common to reshoot sections of a film after the initial edit and a sudden realisation that it just didn't work. Unfortunately, this costs money and is therefore unlikely to be an option for microbudget shorts. Negative Insurance could pay for reshoots in the event of losing the footage, but if you can afford that, you're not shooting on a microbudget. So you'd better damn well get it right…

That said, some things can be done after the shoot, particularly if they are small details like close-ups of a particular physical action or a prop doing something interesting. These are known as 'pick-ups,' and you often find yourself doing a few to correct eyelines or clarify actions or grab stuff that there just wasn't time to do in the first place.

Have a Nice Day…

Making films is supposed to be fun, for you and everyone else. Cast and crew will work better if they're enjoying themselves, especially when the hours are dragging on. Try and keep a good-humoured work environment for everyone, even if you're completely stressed out yourself. But don't let things get slack. Everyone collapsing in laughter at a fluffed line is fine once or twice, but the shot still has to be done. It's a delicate balance sometimes; helping out on someone else's film will give you a good sense of the right kind of atmosphere.

Shopping List

This is a not an exhaustive list; different situations will call for different bits and pieces, and you may not need everything on it – make your own judgements, but be prepared.

- **Car** All this kit needs to be moved somehow…
- **Shotlist, Storyboard, Script** Keep spare copies as someone will lose theirs.
- **Money**
- **Kit List**
- **Map(s)** You never know when you may need to navigate through unfamiliar territory.
- **Gaffer Tape** Why is gaffer tape like the Force? Because it has a light side, a dark side, and it binds the universe together. An essential bit of kit for making sure that things don't fall apart, putting marks on the floor for actors, and so on. Also known as duct tape; hardware stores and camera shops will stock it.
- **Camera Tape** (White electrician's tape.) If you're hiring bits of kit from different places, use this to label

each piece so you know where it goes at the end of the shoot.

- **Lens Cloth & Brush** To keep the camera clean.
- **Stepladder** Handy for putting lights and props in high places.
- **Boxes** Large plastic ones available from pound shops and hardware shops. Not cardboard.
- **Safety Pins, String, Pen & Paper, Marker Pens**
- **Big Bits of Card** To write complicated dialogue on if actors are having trouble with it.
- **Towels** If anyone's going in the water, or it looks like raining, towels are essential.
- **Toilet Roll** Because not all lavatories are civilised.
- **Cleaning Equipment/Products** Some locations have this stuff, but you should be prepared anyway.
- **Refuse Sacks** It's your responsibility to clean up after yourselves. Also very useful as waterproofing, or to black out windows if necessary.
- **Kettle/Gas Stove (& Bottle)**
- **4-Way Mains Adapter** (At least two.)
- **Food & Drink** – Including: munchies (biscuits, chocolate etc.), tea & coffee (with decaf versions of both), hot chocolate, milk, sugar, cold drinks & water (if it's anywhere near summer).
- **Cool Box** For cold stuff.
- **Mobiles** Make sure these are turned off for shooting, but don't leave them behind.
- **First Aid Kit** It's useful to have someone trained in first aid as well.
- **Chairs** Director's chairs are uncomfortable. Folding garden chairs are better.

– **Umbrellas** Large golfing types if possible.
– **Wet Weather Gear**

PERFORMERS

Rehearsal

Rehearsals before the shoot can help enormously, if you have time. Half a day to a day should be enough for most short films. You'll need a room and a few chairs, plus maybe a table and as many props as you have available. Mark out the floor in the approximate shape of the location with gaffer tape or chalk, or rehearse in the actual location if you can arrange it.

You can use this time to go through the characters the actors are going to portray and invent background information that may be of assistance – it can be great fun brainstorming the back-story for a character, even if you have already worked out everything you thought you needed to know. A useful technique is 'hot-seating.' The actor sits in a chair and takes on the role of the character, and everyone asks them questions which they have to answer in character – use this to explore the type of person the character is, what they would do in certain situations, and to get the actor more involved with the character. Encourage actors to take notes about both their characters and the minutiae of performances, as details can easily be forgotten when shooting out of sequence.

The key is to cooperate with the actors, rather than give them orders. Actors thrive on interaction. You must be prepared to give them feedback on their work at the end of every run-through. Pay attention, take notes during the performance, and let them know what you think. "That's fine" or "I don't like that" aren't enough during rehearsal; explain in greater depth what you did or didn't like. Some directors believe that actors are nothing more than sophisticated tools, and to some extent this is true – they are a component of a process which is larger than them, much more so than in theatre. But I find it more useful to think of them as collaborators – people who are there to help you create the story you set out to tell and, hopefully, improve it.

The main reason to rehearse before filming is to save time on set. There will still be on-set rehearsal time, but that's as much for the crew as it is for the cast. You and your actors should be able to approach the shoot with a good idea of how you want to play the scene already lodged in your minds and notebooks.

When approaching a scene, it's worthwhile to get the actors to read it through once without prior preparation (a 'readthrough'), just to see where they take it instinctively. This may not be the way you want to do the scene; subtext may be misinterpreted, lines delivered the wrong way, the scene may be too fast, too slow, too menacing, too fluffy, too static – but instead of jumping straight in to correct them, take the time to find out why it happened. The actors might have found a fundamental problem with the scene – for example, you may have a scene that is meant to be fast and pacy, but the dialogue takes too long to speak and needs to be cut.

Unless the actors have magically created the interpretation you wanted first time – and even if they have – spend some time breaking the scene down and going over it to work out what should be happening on a moment-to-moment basis – what the subtext is, what 'business' (physical actions) they can perform, whether or not the dialogue should be modified, whether anything can be added or subtracted to make the scene funnier, scarier, creepier, colder, warmer, joyful, depressing, or whatever else you think it should be. Let it be a collaborative process, but remember that, at the end of the day, you're in charge and you have the responsibility of steering the scene in the direction you want it to go.

Many people find discussing and describing the nuances of performance difficult. You may feel the urge to demonstrate what you mean, rather than explain, but this is a bad move. It's a rather patronising way to explain something, and can be insulting. It also doesn't work as well; if an actor arrives at the correct performance under their own steam and with your guidance, they will know exactly why they're doing everything. But if you demonstrate something to them and try to skip over these stages, then they're just puppeting what you're doing, making for a phonier performance. Instead of demonstrating, think instead about rephrasing what you're trying to say, or working backwards to a point in the discussion before confusion arose, and deal with the underlying problems rather than trying to paste a demonstrated action onto the performance.

On Set

The first thing to do on set with the actors is to 'block out' the scene – deciding where people will be and what movements they will make around the set. Bear in mind where the camera is going to be and what sort of shots you're going to be using. If you were able to rehearse in the location, it will speed up this part of the process; in many sets and locations, however, this won't be possible, and you may have to adjust performances to suit the environment. Once the actors are fine with the scene and the crew have had time to light it, it must be rehearsed again for camera movements and any other technical requirements; this is not the time to make major changes to performance.

During shooting, you need to make the actors aware of shot size and framing. In a long shot, actors need to be aware of their whole body and what it's doing, while facial expressions can be a little more exaggerated; in a close-up, they need to be careful not to overdo facial expressions, while at the same time they have the full responsibility of carrying the story and need to be at their best.

In dialogue scenes, you may not have all characters in shot at once. Technically, the people who are out of shot don't need to be there, but try and keep them around to deliver their lines as it will assist the performer who's on camera. This is known as 'lines off' or 'reading in'. However, don't bring an actor onto set if this is all you want them to do. When shooting phone calls between two locations, a member of crew can fill in the lines off for the performer who's supposed to be on the other end of the line.

Since sound cannot be recorded when there's loud background noise going on, actors will often find themselves having to pretend to shout over the sound of a crowd, or loud music, or airplanes taking off, or the end of the world or whatever. This is not a natural thing for people to do; they tend to naturally recede back to a more comfortable level. So, if possible, turn on the music or get the crowd to talk for a while and have the actors practice the right level at which they have to pitch their voices. When actually shooting, keep an ear on them to make sure they keep up the right volume – it's very easy to slip, so just give them a gentle reminder if you need to.

Something to watch for is complex movements that have to be repeated in every take; is the actor reproducing the same movement each time? Are they getting the timing right? It's impossible to be perfect in every performance, but if they are doing wildly different things in each take – causing you major continuity problems – you'll need to take them aside for a moment and communicate this problem to them and find some way of overcoming it – possibly simplifying the action, or a moment of rehearsal to clarify it, or cutting it out altogether.

Extras

Extras don't need as much attention, and the job of directing them is often handed over to the AD. Their job is usually just to be there, but you (or the AD) do need to spend a moment to explain what's happening in the scene, and what they're required to do. You also need to make it clear that they must not look at the camera – the last thing you need to discover in the edit is an extra staring down the lens and then guiltily looking away.

Children & Animals

It's probably best not to. Children have limited attention spans and are rigorously protected by employment laws (although if it's your younger brother or sister on a small shoot during the holidays with very short hours, few are likely to complain). Animals are also protected by law, and cannot be forced to work; some animals may be able to do simple things if they think they're playing, but others will be difficult to persuade to do anything at all.

CAMERA

Before you shoot anything, familiarise yourself with the camera. If you've never used the particular model before, go through the manual page by page to make yourself aware of its abilities – and whether or not it still works.

Things to Avoid

– **Automatic Functions** Most cameras come with

little helpers like autofocus and auto-aperture — which have a nasty habit of adjusting themselves unpredictably and ruining your shot. You need as much control over your camera as possible, so locate anything automatic and switch it off.

- **Digital Zoom** is pointless — it looks horrible and if you really need the pixellated effect you can do it in an edit suite and have greater control.
- **Gain** A way to increase the brightness of a shot electronically. However, it makes the picture grainier and of lower quality and it's a lazy way to avoid lighting a scene properly. It's mainly intended for documentary use, when you won't always have a chance to put up lights.
- **Effects** (e.g. fades) Most of these are unnecessary because they can be done better and with greater control in the edit suite — and if you do them in camera, you'll be stuck with them later on. Not wise.
- **Time Stamp** There's nothing worse than trying to edit with a time stamp indelibly marked on the picture. Turn it off.
- **Long Play** If you use this feature, you might get more footage but it'll be of lower quality. If you need to shoot more, buy more tapes or get a bigger hard drive.
- **Mixing Tapes** Cameras tend to get used to the brand of tape they use, and suddenly using tapes from another manufacturer can cause problems. So select one kind of tape and stick to it.

Lens

Not all lenses are the same; they vary according to how 'wide' or 'long' they are.

- **Wide angle lenses** pack more into the frame, and make objects smaller, making it seem like everything is further away. In extreme cases, they distort the picture visibly, making objects bulge out towards the viewer and seem more three-dimensional. They're often the only choice for shooting in small spaces as they'll pack all of the surroundings in. They also have a large 'depth of field'; everything, or almost everything, will be in focus.
- **Telephoto lenses** (also known as 'long' lenses) are the opposite: they pack less into the frame and therefore things look much closer, which can be a problem in a small space as you'll hardly be able to see beyond a small area. They also look flatter, and a long lens will have a shallow depth of field; focus will have to be adjusted carefully to get a sharp picture. Longer lenses are commonly used in professional filming, where the shallow depth of field gives a more pleasing look.
- **Zoom lenses** are found on virtually all video cameras, and can move between wide-angle and telephoto, making it appear as though you're moving closer or further away from the subject. There will be almost always be a rocker switch marked 'W/T' (Wide Angle/Telephoto) which allows you to zoom in and out. On cheaper cameras, you may only be able to do this at one speed; on better ones, you should be

able to 'feather' it and have greater control. Zoom lenses on video cameras rarely go to the extremes on either end; the telephoto side can't achieve as shallow a depth of field as a dedicated telephoto lens, nor can they go as wide. A common add-on is a wide-angle adapter, another lens that fits onto the end of the first. You can get very good results, but you may not be able to keep focus when zooming through them and some can cause vignetting.

Lenses should be cleaned with calotherm lens cloths (available in camera shops), or the sort you use to wipe your glasses (so long as the cloth is clean). Dust and marks on the lens are often invisible when shooting, but show up later when watching the film on a monitor.

Focus

Most cameras have a focus wheel on the lens which you can adjust manually. This is known as 'pulling focus' when you do it in the middle of a shot. In order to get perfect focus, you should zoom all the way into your subject, focus on them there, then zoom out. The subject now remains in focus at every stage of the zoom.

Aperture/Iris

The 'aperture,' also known as the 'iris,' is the gap through which light passes into the camera after being focused by the lens. It can usually be opened wider or closed down to allow more or less light through, brightening or darkening the image. On video, you can usually judge the correct setting by eye with the viewfinder or a monitor. It's vital to get this right because too much light results in areas of the screen 'bleached out' with no detail left, whereas a picture that's too dark looks grotty and suffers from similar loss of detail. You can't fix this in an edit suite afterwards – you absolutely have to get it right in camera.

Another effect of adjusting the iris is a change in the depth of field. If the iris is closed down, then a lesser portion of the lens is being used to admit light, reducing overall picture quality, but increasing depth of field. Conversely, opening up the lens will decrease the depth of field. This isn't usually a problem with basic video cameras, but will be noticeable when you move to professional equipment.

Shutter

The shutter is a device which opens to allow light onto the chip that detects the image, and closes down between frames, in order to split a constantly moving image into separate frames for recording. The duration of time the shutter is open affects the quality of movement on the screen; if the shutter speed is lower, it allows more time for objects to move – and so fast motions tend to blur. On high shutter speeds, the shutter opens for less time; movement no longer blurs, and fast moving objects stay solid. A common use of high shutter speeds can be found in coverage of sports like skiing, where the subject moves fast but needs to be filmed clearly. Generally the shutter speed should be kept at 1/50 unless absolutely necessary, since messing with the shutter also affects the brightness of the image. If you do need to change it, some cameras will have a 'sports' preset, but use a manual control if possible. Beware of fluorescent lights, which tend to flicker when you film them at a high shutter speed.

White Balance

The human eye is better at adjusting to different lighting conditions than the camera. Light that you think is white may become pale blue or pale orange when the camera sees it. This is because of the different temperature that light sources burn at; the hotter they burn, the bluer the light, and the colder, the more orange. 'Daylight' has a colour temperature of about 5600 degrees Kelvin and looks blue, while 'Tungsten' lights (normal light bulbs) come in at roughly 3200K and look orange.

To adjust to this, you need to 'White Balance' the

Figure 4 The White Balance Symbol

camera, and you must do this every time you reset the camera or the lights. Place a piece of white paper (or a white shirt, or white whatever) a few feet away from the camera, making sure it's lit by your light source. Zoom all the way into the piece of paper until it fills the frame, then press and hold the white balance button. The white balance symbol will flash in the viewfinder until the process is finished, and then turn solid. Daylight and Tungsten lighting are so different that you may have difficulties if both types of light are present in a scene. See page 129 for more information.

Filters

Some cameras have filters built into the lens mechanism and some filters screw directly onto the front of the lens. You may also be able to get hold of a 'matte box' which fits on the front of the lens and can hold multiple filters as well as having a larger and more effective lens hood to prevent flare. If you're about to go out and buy something that will screw onto the front of the lens, make sure you know the diameter of the lens ring – this will be in the manual but should also be written on the lens itself.

- **UV** Usually screws onto the front of the lens and is a basic filter to protect your main lens from dirt and scratches as well as a device to exclude UV light, too much of which can create an unwanted blue haze.
- **ND** (Neutral Density) This is the equivalent of

putting shades on the camera and is often an internal part of the lens itself. Direct sunlight can be too much for a camera even when the iris is closed as far as it can go, so having an ND filter to cut down the light levels can be very handy on a sunny day.

- **Polariser** Probably the best filter of all. Polarisers only allow through light that is 'polarised' – moving in roughly the same direction. In practice this means three things: the glow you get from diffused light is reduced; colour saturation is increased; and, most amazingly, reflections in windows and other reflective surfaces are sharply reduced – if you use a polariser when shooting through a car window, the obscuring reflections disappear as if by magic. But there's also the saturation effect; not only will colours be more vibrant, but there will be greater definition within the colour area, capturing details you wouldn't otherwise have seen. This is especially useful when the sky is in shot. Polarisers can be revolved to exclude light coming in at different angles; you'll need to turn it to select the correct angle for any given lighting condition.

- **Grads** Graduated filters have a gradually increasing level of colour across their width and are mainly used to apply a filter to one part of the picture, often a very bright sky needing to be darkened. They come in various different colours depending upon the effect you want.

Inputs & Outputs

- **Video Out (Composite)** This will usually be of the

BNC or phono type. It will usually be used to send analogue video out to a monitor so you have a better picture to look at than the viewfinder can provide. If you want to output your video camera to your TV or video recorder at home, you will generally find you will have to plug the outgoing leads into a SCART adapter, which either comes with the camera or can be found in an electronics store.

- **S-Video Out** Usually a 4-pin DIN type plug, this analogue signal offers a better quality picture than a composite signal and can usually be plugged into a SCART adapter for playback on a normal TV.
- **Component Out** Sometimes found on HD or higher end cameras, this offers the best possible picture quality in an analogue signal but not all TVs will accept the input.
- **SDI/HD-SDI Output** This is a high-quality digital signal, and rarely found except on top-end equipment or professional HD cameras.
- **Audio In** Not all cameras can accept incoming sound from an external microphone, but you should try and get one that does. The best audio leads are 'balanced' 3-pin XLRs (see Sound for details), though it may be a phono or minijack on cheap cameras.
- **Audio Out** Again, XLRs are nice, but on most cameras these will be phonos and colour coded: LEFT AUDIO – Red, RIGHT AUDIO – White.
- **AV Out** Some cameras will have an AV out socket, a minijack output which divides into three phono plugs – the red and white ones for audio, and a third yellow one for composite video.

- **Headphones** This will usually be a minijack, but sometimes a full ¼″ jack or phono. Make sure you get headphones to match the socket.
- **DV Out** DV cameras should come with a 'DV Out' socket, which will send video and audio information through a 'Firewire' directly to a computer-based non-linear editing system. The benefit of this is that the signal does not have to be translated from digital to analogue, and will be preserved at highest possible quality. The 'DV Out' socket will also sometimes act as a 'DV In' socket, allowing you to use the camera as a record deck. Due to EU tariffs, cheaper cameras in Europe may not be able to do this – make sure you find out before you buy.

For more information on exactly how some of the video connections work, see page 161.

Widescreen

There's a good reason for widescreen: take a look at your field of vision. One eye might see a roughly round image, but two eyes together see an oval. You see the world in widescreen all the time. However, widescreen isn't as simple as pressing a button and having a wider picture; for a start, you need be aware that there's more than one widescreen ratio.

The way 16:9 works for TV and video is by adapting the same trick used for Cinemascope: the 16:9 image is squeezed into a 4:3 frame when recorded, and when played back on a 16:9 TV or monitor, is unsqueezed again.

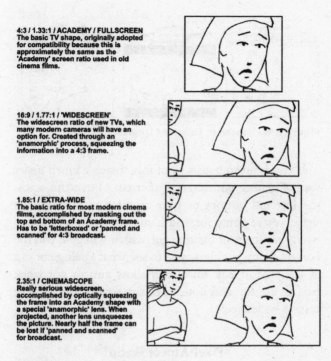

4:3 / 1.33:1 / ACADEMY / FULLSCREEN
The basic TV shape, originally adopted for compatibility because this is approximately the same as the 'Academy' screen ratio used in old cinema films.

16:9 / 1.77:1 / 'WIDESCREEN'
The widescreen ratio of new TVs, which many modern cameras will have an option for. Created through an 'anamorphic' process, squeezing the information into a 4:3 frame.

1.85:1 / EXTRA-WIDE
The basic ratio for most modern cinema films, accomplished by masking out the top and bottom of an Academy frame. Has to be 'letterboxed' or 'panned and scanned' for 4:3 broadcast.

2.35:1 / CINEMASCOPE
Really serious widescreen, accomplished by optically squeezing the frame into an Academy shape with a special 'anamorphic' lens. When projected, another lens unsqueezes the picture. Nearly half the frame can be lost if 'panned and scanned' for broadcast.

Figure 5 Widescreen Diagram

However, this means that when you play the same footage back on a 4:3 TV, you will see the squeezed, anamorphic image – everything will look taller and thinner than it should. Most editing systems are now capable of unsqueezing 16:9 or changing it into letterbox format for ordinary TVs; unfortunately, the method used to get 16:9 on non-professional DV cameras isn't perfect and loses a little quality.

Figure 6 Widescreen to Fullscreen Diagram

If you want to bypass all of this, there's a much easier way of getting widescreen: gaffer tape. Put strips across the top and bottom of your monitor to simulate the shape you're going for, and frame accordingly (alternatively, use strips of lighting gel, which will give you the correct frame but allow you to see what's being cut out as well). Most edit suites will allow you to put black bars at the top and bottom of the screen. Hey presto: instant widescreen.

Pixel Aspect Ratio

The sneaky trick of recording a 16:9 image in a 4:3 space is achieved by changing the shape of the pixels themselves. Normal 4:3 pixels are themselves not perfectly square – they have an aspect ratio of 1:1.07; but in 16:9, they are stretched to 1:1.42, meaning you need not record any extra information to create a wider screen.

HD formats were originally supposed to not have this problem, having pixel aspect ratios of 1:1. Unfortunately, the need to get the data into a smaller space meant that many HD formats ended up using the same trick, this time with a pixel aspect ratio of 1:1.33 for most formats that do this, allowing them to throw some picture information away.

This issue becomes especially important in postproduction, when you may need to get the settings in your editing software right, or else the footage will get stretched or squished the wrong way and end up looking seriously weird.

Timecode

Timecode is a counter which is recorded invisibly between frames, but which identifies and labels every single frame – vital if you want to find anything when you're editing. The camera should have a tape counter on the side if it has timecode, and you'll see it there. It appears in the format HH:MM:SS:FF, e.g. 10:34:22:24, and can be preset to begin at any point you wish. Hour numbers on each tape you shoot should be different so that an edit system doesn't get mixed up between the tapes; if shooting on memory cards, you can either let the timecode run on, or reset it for each card – just so long as each frame has a unique identifying number. The convention is that tape 1 begins at 10:00:00:00, tape 2 begins at 11:00:00:00 etc. If the tape is longer than an hour (as many DVCAM tapes are), you'll need to set each tape to start at whatever the next available hour number is. Many Mini–DV cameras have timecode but the starting value cannot be set by the user. This makes Mini–DV less convenient to use in the edit suite, though not impossible.

Power & Batteries

You'll almost always be running your camera from batteries. Always carry more than you think you'll need; you'll almost certainly end up using them. Batteries for video cameras are all rechargeable, but older nickel-cadmium batteries might suffer from what is called the 'memory effect'; they must be fully discharged before being recharged, or they will not fully recharge. More recent Ni-Cad batteries are supposed to be free from this problem, and lithium batteries have always been able to recharge fully from any state of discharge. You should make yourself aware of how long the batteries last, and how long they take to recharge; get them charged up before you go. If using batteries in a field monitor, be aware that they'll run out far faster than in anything else – run the monitor from a socket unless you have no other option. This does, however, make a monitor a good tool for discharging batteries quickly if needed. Cold can severely reduce battery life, so try and keep them wrapped up warm if you're shooting in winter (or any refrigerated area).

Interlaced & Progressive Scan

While modern video systems are wonders of technology, they are still stuck with the legacy of the past, and one of these legacies is Interlacing. Interlacing was a solution to a problem that television had while it was originally being developed: the phosphor dots on the screen that made up the image wouldn't glow for long enough to be able to stay on screen for a full frame; they could only last for half a frame.

The solution was to divide each frame into two halves by first showing all the odd numbered lines (1, 3, 5 etc.), allowing them to form an image, and then showing all the even numbered lines (2, 4, 6 etc.), and allowing them to form the next image. Dividing a frame into 'fields' like this got past the problem; but because each field is filmed after the other, it effectively doubles the frame rate and makes movement look very different, generating the typical crisp video look.

A great deal of effort has been made to try and turn Interlaced video into something that looks more like film; one field can be copied onto another, or the two of them can be blended; best of all, modern cameras (especially HD ones) often have the option to shoot 'Progressive Scan', in other words to shoot each frame as a whole without fields, replicating the rough frame rate and visual quality of film.

Formats

Analogue formats are now effectively dead except as legacy and archival systems; if you're starting to make films now (and indeed for the last several years) then you'll probably never encounter an analogue video format. The main difference in formats these days is between Standard Definition and High Definition. It used to be the case that filmmakers could happily forget what SD was because they simply didn't need to know when starting out, but the advent of HD presents so many options that you really should try and get your head around all this stuff.

Standard Definition

'Standard Definition' formats – those in use since the 1960s or 70s – come in three basic flavours, and the one you use depends on where in the world you live. In North America, Japan, and parts of South America, the format is NTSC, which has a screen size of 720×480, and runs at about 30fps (it's actually 29.97, just to make things absurdly complicated). In the UK, Ireland, most of Europe, most of Asia, Australia and New Zealand, the format is PAL, with a screen size of 720×576 and a frame rate of 25fps. There's also SECAM, used in France and the former Soviet Union, which has the same dimensions and frame rate as PAL, but has a different colour system. But since people tend to shoot PAL and only transfer to SECAM for broadcast, it's not of much relevance to us.

Most people reading this book will be shooting PAL, and that'll be the same basic screen format regardless of what tape format you use – VHS, DVD, Mini-DV. DVCAM, Beta SP, Digibeta, DVCPro and others all record the same size frame at the same frame rate – unless you get the NTSC versions, of course.

Standard Definition is already fairly complicated. With the advent of High Definition, you might have thought that manufacturers would want to simplify and standardise so that we all use the same basic video format. Of course, you'd be wrong…

Name of Format	Compression Rate	Sample Rate[2]	Other Formats That Can Be Played Back[3]	Manufacturer	Possible Tape Lengths[4]	Notes
DV/Mini-DV	5:1	4:1:1	-	various manufacturers	Mini-DV: 60, 63, 80, 83; DV: 124, 180, 186, 276	Now the basic consumer format. The sound and picture quality vary enormously depending on the camera. DV is a version with larger tapes (the same size as standard DVCAM), but otherwise identical to Mini-DV.
Digital 8	5:1	4:1:1	Hi-8, 8mm	Sony	Uses Hi-8 tapes	Lost out to Mini-DV when Sony realised they were making way too many digital tape formats. Very hard to find.
DVCAM[5]	5:1	4:2:0	Mini-DV, DV	Sony	Mini: 12, 22, 32, 40; Standard: 34, 64, 94, 124, 184	Near as dammit broadcast quality, and the commonest semiprofessional format (for the time being, anyway). Some cameras (e.g. PD150/170) use the same size tapes as Mini-DV.
DVCPro[1]	5:1	4:1:1	Mini-DV, DV, DVCAM	Panasonic	Medium: 12, 24, 33, 46, 63, 66; Large: 64, 66, 94, 126, 184	Offers comparable quality to DVCAM but hasn't taken off in the same way.
Betacam SP	N/A	N/A	Betacam	Sony	Small: 5, 10, 20, 30; Large: 60, 90	The only analogue format in this list – little used for filming now but still accepted as a delivery format.
Betacam SX[†]	10:1	4:2:2	Betacam SP	Sony	Small: 6, 12, 22, 32, 62; Large: 64, 94, 124, 184, 194	Beta SX uses a codec based on MPEG-2, accounting for the high compression rate. It can't match Digibeta for quality, although it is a bit cheaper. Hard to find, though.
Digital S	3.3:1	4:2:2	VHS, S-VHS	JVC	10, 34, 64, 104, 124	Digital S is an excellent format – comparable to Digibeta – but very hard to find outside universities and colleges.
DVCPro50[†]	3.3:1	4:2:2	Mini-DV, DV, DVCAM, DVCPro	Panasonic	Uses the same tapes as DVCPro, but they last half as long	Like DVCPro but with twice the data rate, and very close to Digibeta in terms of quality. Cheaper to get hold of than Digibeta but harder to find.
Digital Betacam[†]	2:1	4:2:2 (Note: bit depth of 10 as opposed to 8 for all others)	Betacam SP	Sony	Small: 6, 12, 22, 32, 40; Large: 34, 64, 94, 124	Digital Betacam (or 'Digibeta') has been the default broadcast quality standard for a number of years now. Many festivals and TV stations accept Digibeta as a delivery format.
MPEG IMX	6:1, 4:1 or 3.3:1	4:2:2	Betacam SX	Sony	Small: 6, 12, 22, 32, 60; Large: 94, 124, 184	Very nearly as good as Digibeta, but not much used in the UK. However, the format can also be recorded onto XDCAM and other tapeless systems, and record in 25p – but you might as well get HD if you want all that stuff.

Compression of 3.3:1 or 2:1 causes little or no deterioration in the signal, but anything more can lead to artifacting. Betacam SX is an exception because of the codec used.
[2] Sample rate is explained in the Digital Video Sample Rates section, below. 4:2:2 is broadcast quality.
[3] Some decks (but never cameras) may be able to play back other formats. Not all models have this feature.
[4] Some tapes have 2-4 extra minutes at the end. However, some tape manufacturers now include this in the overall tape length.
[5] DVCAM cameras and decks can record DVCAM onto Mini-DV/DV tapes, but they only last about 2/3 as long as they do when recording Mini-DV/DV.
† These formats have two sizes: a small (or medium) size for camera tapes, and a larger one for mastering. Cameras can only use the small size, while decks can use both.

Figure 7 SD Formats Table

High Definition

The first problem, before we even get to formats, is that there's more than one kind of HD. A lot more than one kind. There are three basic variables that you can mix and match to get a variety of different HDs...

– **Screen Size** is the first variable. There are two main screen sizes: 1280×720 (known as **720**), and 1920×1080 (known as **1080**). Some cameras and screens can handle both; some can handle only one. And some cameras (notably those made by RED) can shoot at even larger screen sizes.
– **Frame Rate** is a legacy variable that depends mainly on whether you live in an NTSC or a PAL/SECAM country (regardless of the fact that you're not using any of those formats). So you can get either **25** or **30**fps (or **50** or **60** if interlacing).
– **Interlaced/Progressive** is still available as an option, depending on whether you want the footage to look like TV or like film. The letter **i** denotes interlaced, and **p** denotes progressive. When shooting Interlaced, the frame rate is usually listed as the number of images captured – so 60 instead of 30, 50 instead of 25.

So, you may find yourself shooting at **720 25p** (the smaller screen size at 25fps and progressive scan), or perhaps **1080 60i** (the larger screen size, interlaced and at a frame rate appropriate for North America), or any one of the many combinations possible.

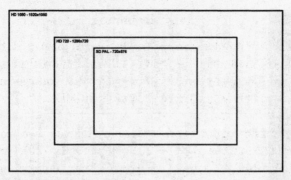

Figure 8 Formats Scale Diagram

And then once you've figured all that out, you can start worrying about all the individual formats. Bear in mind that nearly all of them can now be recorded on more than one kind of media- cards and hard drives are a possibility as well as tapes.

Digital Video Sample Rates

As you're probably aware, digital audio is recorded by sampling an incoming signal thousands of times a second (44,100 times for CD quality – 44.1 kHz). Digital video does the same thing in a slightly more complicated way. The video signal is usually split into three parts – one for Luminance (brightness) and two for Chrominance (colour). The human eye sees less colour detail than it does brightness detail, and therefore digital video formats sample colour at a lower rate. The broadcast standard for sample rates is defined as 4:2:2. The three digits mean:

Name of Format	Formats[1]	Bit Depth	Pixel Aspect Ratio	Data Rate[2]	Sample Rate	Other Formats That Can Be Played Back	Manufacturer	Media[3]	Notes
HDV	1080i, 720p	8	720p: 1:1 1080i: 1.33:1	1080: 25 mbps 720: 19 mbps	4:2:0	Mini-DV/DV, DVCAM	Sony, Canon	Mini-DV tapes, XDCAM discs, SxS cards, hard drives	Records onto Mini-DV tapes at the same rate, making it a very easy format to transition to. But regarded as marginal for broadcast purposes.
ProHd	720p	8	1:1	19 mbps	4:2:0	Mini-DV/DV, DVCAM	JVC	Mini-DV tapes, hard drives	This is HDV with JVC branding and an improved version of 720p. Despite the low data rate, often better quality than HDV.
AVCHD	1080i, 720p	8	720p: 1:1 1080i: 1.33:1	25 mbps	4:2:0	None	Sony, Panasonic	AVCHD Optical discs, memory cards	An optical disc based consumer/semipro format, comparable to but technically better than HDV. Discs can play back on Blu-Ray players.
XDCAM HD/EX	720p,1080i, 1080p	8	1.33:1 or 1:1	18/25/35 mbps	4:2:0, 4:2:2	XDCAM	Sony	XDCAM Discs, SxS cards (as XDCAM EX)	An improvement on HDV. The EX version, recording onto cards, has an HQ mode allowing for the higher end settings seen here.
DVCProHD AKA DVCPro100	720p, 1080i, 1080p	8 or 10	720: 1.33:1 1080: 1.5:1	100 mpbs	4:2:2	Mini-DV/DV, DVCPro, DVCPro50	Panasonic	DVCProHD tapes, P2 cards, hard drives	Cheaper and virtually as good as HDCAM. Varicam is a name for the top end versions. Can shoot real slow motion.
HDCAM	1080i	10 or 12	1.33:1	185 mbps	3:1:1	Some Beta formats	Sony	HDCAM Tapes	The first major HD format and professional only.
HDCAM SR	1080i	10 or 12	1:1	440 mbps	4:2:2, 4:4:4	HDCAM	Sony	HDCAM SR Tapes	A development of HDCAM, now used for high end drama & TV but mostly studio based.

[1] Not all screen sizes can be recorded by all cameras, and constant innovation means that things like 1080p are occasionally added as time goes on.
[2] Compression rates aren't as useful for comparing HD formats as they are for SD formats as the type of encoding can make a massive difference. Data rate gives a much clearer idea of the comparative quality of HD formats.
[3] Note that the recording media you use can determine what screen format you can record – check what the system is capable of before you jump in.

Figure 9 HD Formats Table

4: Luminance (Y)
2: 1st Chrominance channel (Cr)
2: 2nd Chrominance channel (Cb)

And what do the actual numbers mean? It's a ratio: for every four samples of Luminance, you're going to get two samples in each of the Chrominance channels. So each colour channel is recording half as much information as the Luminance channel. Why does it start at 4? It's just a convenient number. Just think of it as four parts of brightness to two parts of each colour channel. Different formats will have differing ratios, such as 4:1:1 (only a quarter as much colour as brightness!), 4:2:0 (better than 4:1:1, not as good as 4:2:2 but please don't ask me why) or even 4:4:4:4 (i.e. all sampled at the same rate, plus there's a fourth channel for 'alpha' information, which denotes how transparent parts of the screen are if the image is to be placed in front of another).

Formats using 4:1:1 or 4:2:0 will probably be perfectly fine for most microbudget filmmakers, but you should bear in mind that chromakey (bluescreen or greenscreen) won't work as well with these formats, because it depends upon the quality of the colour signal in order to distinguish background from foreground. If you want keying to look good, you have to use a 4:2:2 format or better.

There's one other factor: bit rate. Most digital formats use 8-bit encoding, but Digital Betacam (and some HD formats) use 10-bit encoding. This means that there are two more digits available to record each piece of information, giving four times as many numbers to describe those pieces of information, providing for much greater subtlety and depth.

Monitors

Many cameras have an LCD screen which flips out from the side, and can be reversed so that you can shoot yourself and see yourself at the same time. This is great for 'video diary' shots, but LCD screens of that size are almost useless for showing true contrast, brightness or colour, and can be almost invisible in direct sunlight. They're best as a framing guide.

Plus, if you're shooting on an HD camera, there's an extra problem: the LCD screen (and usually the viewfinder as well) are generally only SD quality, meaning that you're not seeing all the pixels that you're recording – and most importantly, you can't tell if the picture is in focus. Many cameras have a 'focus assist' option to help get around this, and these work in a variety of ways – but it's a workaround at best.

For a better idea of what the picture really looks like, plug in a 'field monitor'. These vary in size from the tiny (6″) to full scale LCD monitors. The settings on the monitor need to be calibrated carefully to make sure the picture you're seeing is accurate. Calibration requires your camera to be capable of outputting colour bars (some have a hidden mode which can be discovered with a little bit of Internet research) and that your monitor has a 'blue only' switch. It works like this:

- Set your camera to output colour bars.
- Turn Colour (Chroma), Brightness and Contrast down to zero.
- Turn up the Brightness until you can just about see the difference between the two bars on the right hand side.
- Press 'blue only' and turn up the Chroma until the colour bars appear as alternating blue and black bars, with the leftmost blue one just very slightly brighter than the other three, which should themselves be of equal intensity. Turn off 'blue only' when this is done.
- Turn up the Contrast until the white bar seems to jump out from the others a teensy bit (very subjective, I know, but you should find this happening somewhere in the lower mid-range).
- Turn off the colour bars.

You should now be seeing a very accurate representation of the true image – but since the appearance of the screen depends on the light falling on it, you'll need to recalibrate every time you move the monitor into a substantially different lighting environment. One common error to watch out for: plugging the input into the output socket. You may still get an image but it'll look very, very wrong and leave you tearing your hair out in frustration; check the plugs at the back. You might have a choice about what kind of connection you can use – look at the section on page 161 for more information on the various different types of video connections.

Bars & Tone

If your camera has colour bars (and you're recording onto tape), make sure you record 30 seconds of these at the start of every tape, as you may find that your edit suite (or more likely, someone else's edit suite) isn't set up quite right and will interpret your images with slightly wrong colours – but colour bars will allow an editor to calibrate the settings on the edit system to counter this. If your sound recordist has a sound mixer, ask them to send some 'tone' to the camera while you record bars (see page 144 for details). This will allow the same calibration process for audio. And make sure you've set your timecode correctly before you record bars and tone, or you'll have to do it all over again. In this day and age, bars and tone aren't as vital as they once were to ensure technical quality, but at the very least you'll get past the dirtiest part of the tape which can often have flaws that will render your footage useless.

180° Rule

Also known as 'crossing the line.' This is one of the most fundamental but easy to break rules of camerawork. Simply put, if you're filming two people, you need to keep the camera on one particular side of them, because if you move it to the other side, the mind is unsettled by the cut.

Imagine you have two characters: Mr West and Ms East. Draw an imaginary line between them, running

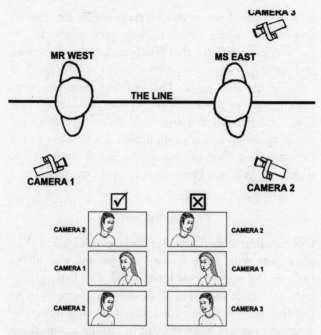

Figure 10 Crossing the Line Diagram

West to East. Say the camera is south of that line; it can cut between shots favouring either Ms East or Mr West, over-the-shoulder shots even (Cameras 1 & 2 on the diagram), but what you cannot then do is cut to a camera position which is in the north (Camera 3). That's crossing the line. Partly, it's a problem of the viewer suddenly seeing what seems like a reversal of the positions of the two characters, and partly it's a problem of the sudden change of background to something previously not established. The problem can easily be solved if you have a shot during which the camera moves from south to north; but once you're in the north, you've still got that line between the characters, and cutting to a camera position in the south would be crossing the line again. The problem becomes more complicated as you put more characters into a scene. Even experienced directors and camera operators can screw up when it gets complicated. It's possible to use the unsettling effect of crossing the line deliberately, but make sure you first know how to avoid the problem.

Composition

Composition is the choice of visual elements and their placement within the frame – where you put all the stuff on the screen so it looks good. The basic guidelines are much the same as in stills photography – it's just that you have the added fun of moving objects or a moving camera, allowing you to change composition during shots. Composition is entirely subjective, and no 'rule' can ever be 100% correct in every situation, but some things definitely do look better and the following are a series of guidelines to help you out.

– **Drawing Attention** One of the basic purposes of good composition is to subtly draw the eye's attention towards the point of interest in the picture. The eye can only look at one thing at once, and will be less comfortable with a composition which has two points of interest. For example, shots in which two people look at each other, both in profile, are relatively rare; if we want to show two people talking to each other, we usually use over-the-shoulder shots and cut between them every time we want the point of interest to change.

– **The Rule of Thirds** The most basic and useful rule of composition. Imagine a series of lines dividing the screen into thirds, both horizontally and vertically (or better still, look at the diagram). All you need to get something that looks better than a random choice is to place important elements of your image somewhere on one of those lines. So a pair of eyes might go on the upper horizontal line, someone looking off into the distance in a long shot might be placed on the left vertical line and a horizon will almost always want to be placed either one third or two thirds of the way up the frame. It doesn't matter what the subject is – the image will usually look more balanced if you place it somewhere on one of those lines. Incidentally, when we speak of a 'balanced' composition, we don't mean a composition which is symmetrical – we mean one in which the elements of the composition are pleasing to the eye. Perfect symmetry in an image can look very mechanistic and unnatural, although that might be exactly what you were after in the first place.

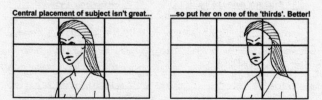

Figure 11 Rule of Thirds Diagram

- **Headroom** Beginners instinctively put the face central in the frame. Unless the face is already filling the frame, this can leave a rather large and empty looking space above the character. Instead, you need to put the head higher in the frame and leave a strip of 'headroom' above them unless you're close enough to have the top of the head going off the top of the frame.
- **Converging Lines** There are many things that get smaller as they vanish into the distance, such as roads, corridors, the streaking of stars in hyperspace and so on. The 'vanishing point' where the lines converge should be placed with care and usually looks best when placed with respect to the rule of thirds. It also draws the eye down the line of perspective and is a good trick to draw attention.
- **Natural Framing (Frames within Frames)** Another cute trick is to use elements within frames that create frames themselves. A tree trunk and spreading branch might create a nice little border to a rural image, or someone might be standing behind a window, isolated in a tiny frame within the main image. Whatever you use, bear in mind that all the

Figure 12 Headroom Diagram

other guidelines may well apply to the frame within the frame – rule of thirds, headroom etc.

- **Focus** Placement is not the only tool for composition. It's also possible to draw attention by narrowing the depth of field (by placing the camera further away and zooming in). The eye will be drawn towards whatever part of the image is in focus. A focus pull can then be a good way to change the object of interest.
- **Camera Height (High & Low Angles)** One of the most important choices you can make is the height at which you set the camera, because it has huge implications for the relative power of characters within the frame. A low angle makes people look bigger and more powerful; a high angle makes them look smaller and less powerful. Setting the camera height at around eye level puts us on an equal footing with the character, but bear in mind that this is the most common setting and, if you do it just as a default, it can get a bit boring after a while.
- **Verticals** A particularly common mistake is to place a vertical element (e.g. a tree) behind an individual. This gives the unpleasant impression that something is sprouting from the top of their head and should be avoided. Two such lines might make them look positively satanic.
- **Relationships** If two characters are put together in a frame, it draws them together; if they are kept in separate frames, even if they are physically close, it seems to put some space between them.
- **Looks & Implications** The amount of space you

leave above, below, or to the side of a character or object can say a lot about what else is going on outside the frame. If you leave a vast amount of space beside a character, the audience will often think something's about to come in from that direction. More simply, if characters are looking in a certain direction, you can place them to either the left or the right of the frame to suggest the space they're looking into. This is a common technique when two people are looking at or talking to each other.

- **Widescreen** Widescreen is great for landscapes, which is why westerns and road movies often use it. However, faces are more vertical than horizontal; a 4:3 frame allows you to go close on a character and have them fill the frame, but in widescreen formats the same shot size will leave space at the side – the framing effects can be very nice, but not everyone likes it (Fritz Lang's opinion was that it was only good for coffins and snakes). Another thing that widescreen can do is pack more characters into a frame. If you're filming scenes where characters are sitting or standing beside each other, you can accommodate more of them at the same shot size than you could with 4:3.
- **Safe Area** Not everything you see through the camera will actually appear on your TV! Since TVs vary with quality and age, video is recorded with a slightly bigger frame than it actually needs, just to be on the safe side. But what you see in the camera eyepiece is the full image without the crop which will eventually result. The part of the image guaranteed to be seen on all screens is known as the 'Safe Area,' and

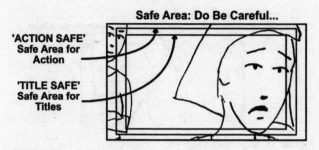

Figure 13 Safe Area Diagram

you may have an option on your camera which marks this out on the viewfinder; if not, a field monitor will show you what the image will look like when it's cropped (and a good one will have an 'underscan' button which will show the whole image without the crop). To be safe, don't put anything important right at the edge of the frame. Of course, when you see the image on a computer screen – on YouTube, for example – you'll be seeing the whole image without any cropping. So you always have to be a little careful…

– **Lenses** Your choice of lens (or your choice of how far to zoom in) affects the visual quality of the picture. Wider lenses allow for a frame with more visual information packed in, and have a larger depth of field; this makes them a more naturalistic way of presenting things. More extreme wide lenses have the effect of creating disturbing images, the subject seems to bulge out towards us as it grows closer. Longer lenses flatten out the picture and make the depth of

Vignetting: sometimes a problem when using wide-angle adapters

Figure 14 Vignetting Diagram

field shallower, making the image more beautiful, due in part to the out-of-focus areas of the screen. If you're using more than just the standard zoom lens on your camera, watch out for an effect called 'vignetting', where the edge of the lens becomes visible in the frame. This, unsurprisingly, is something you want to avoid.

Eyelines

One of the trickiest things to do when filming actors is to get their eyelines right. From the simple question of 'do they look to the left or the right of the camera?' to subtle graduations to make it look like they're eyeballing different objects or people within a single shot, you need to be aware of what shots are going to be next to each other in the edit, and where people will be looking in all those different shots. Making a mistake with an eyeline can make an actor look like they're addressing the window when they're supposed to be staring daggers at someone in the middle of the room.

Camera Movement

Moving the camera should only be done when there is motivation for the move. Having the camera move for no apparent reason, or not as part of an overall style, is distracting. Any camera move (except zooming or very limited handheld work) absolutely has to be carefully planned because it takes far more time to accomplish than the same shot done on a tripod. But dammit, it looks good and it's well worth learning how to do. Here are some things to bear in mind:

- **Tripods** The default camera mounting for most situations, and primarily there to stop the camera from moving. But they also enable the most basic form of movement: panning (left/right) and tilting (up/down). An otherwise unmotivated pan or tilt can be used as a way of getting into or out of a scene. Don't use a stills tripod as a substitute – they're not designed to take the weight of most video cameras.
- **Tracking vs. Zooming** I usually prefer tracks, because they feel like a more natural movement – the perspective changes and you actually feel like you're moving, whereas zooming looks mechanical and unnatural. However, zooms are often useful as a very slow movement into or out of a frame; the change can be barely visible, but still gives a powerful effect.
- **Towards or Away?** Tracking/zooming toward a subject has the effect of drawing the audience closer. Look at me! it shouts, partly because we're all programmed to pay attention to objects approaching

119

us (especially if moving at speed), and partly because there's less to look at in the frame. Tracking out tends to make a character look lonely and less powerful, isolated and vulnerable. It's also a good way to close a scene or the film itself; the extra visual information entering the frame makes it look very profound. Just remember that you have to light all the extra information.

- **Dollies** In the industry, tracking is literally done on tracks. These are laid out by the grip, who then pushes a 'dolly' (a mobile camera mounting) back and forth on them. This can be expensive, but simulating it is surprisingly easy; gaffer taping a camera tripod to a pram chassis is a great trick, and hand-holding the camera while sitting in a wheelchair is another good one, although it's not always very smooth. These are fine by themselves over smooth floorings; on other surfaces, cardboard or plywood sheeting can be useful to make a smooth 'track.'

- **Jibs** If you're very lucky, you might be able to get hold of a 'jib,' a counterweighted mini–crane which can be massive or might only raise the camera a couple of metres. This allows you to move the camera in all kinds of directions while still being able to tilt and pan. Plus you might even be able to mount the whole thing on a dolly. I wouldn't recommend using one of these on your first shoot because they add a degree of complexity which will slow filming down to a crawl; plus, you've got a long stick with a camera on one end and heavy weights on the other, which can be a safety issue if you're not looking where it's going (I've hit my head on them far too often). But if you're moving on to more advanced stuff, it's certainly worth giving it a try.

- **Handholding** Allows you to do whatever you like, but has an additional effect: because it's not a straight-line geometric movement, and because it's naturally a bit shaky, the overall field of vision is wider, and more akin to the way your eyes work; it makes the subject feel more natural. But it can distract from the subject, and takes practice to do well: you still have to compose your shots and doing that on the fly is harder. It makes sense to plan a handheld camera move in as much detail as a dolly shot.

- **A Neat Trick** It's possible to track back from a subject while simultaneously zooming into it (or the other way round). While the subject will appear to remain static, everything around it will change according to the changing properties of the lens – seeming to be stretched or compressed in a very eye-catching way. Famous uses of this: done fast in *Jaws* (Roy Scheider sees the shark) and done slowly in *Goodfellas* (Ray Liotta, sitting in a diner, realises he is about to be executed by the mob).

Cheating

Actors and props don't always have to be left in exactly the same place when you move the camera to a new angle. Very often, it will be impractical or time-consuming to do so. For example, the wall behind a character may not be properly dressed, but 'cheating' the actor round a little to edge out the offending section of wall will not offend the eye when you cut the sequence together. The only consideration is: 'will it be noticeable when we cut it together in the edit?' If you can save time and effort by cheating, do so.

Filming Computer Screens

CRT computer monitors do not run at the same frame rate as TV and Video, and will therefore appear to flicker when filmed. There are several ways of dealing with this:

- **Use an LCD Monitor instead** Because it's the simplest solution and CRT monitors are getting rarer and rarer anyway. LCD screens have pixels that continually luminesce, and therefore don't flicker.
- **Use a Phase Converter** A box of electronics which will adjust the frame rate of the computer monitor, but also costs you money.
- **Reset the Monitor** Most video cards these days can set the frame rate of the monitor to match that of the camera (set the monitor to run at 100Hz to match the 2-field 25fps frame rate – presuming the monitor can cope!).
- **Reset the Camera** Professional cameras can some-times be adjusted to cope – check the manual to see.
- **Cheat** If all else fails, film computer screens as cutaways and use an LCD screen to get the image.

Filming Stills

These days, it's possible to put still images into your film by scanning them and importing the resulting image (preferably a .jpg) directly into the computer. If you do this, remember to scan at high quality (300 dpi or greater) to give yourself more flexibility in the edit – you never know, you might end up using only a part of the image, and if you scanned it in at low quality (or compressed it too much), you'll end up with something nasty and pixellated.

This method works great as long as you don't try much in the way of movement. Subtle zooms will often be okay, but anything more complex will need a lot of work to make the move look natural, and most editing programs aren't capable of this subtlety. You can take the image into an effects program like After Effects to get the move, but it may be easier to film it during production. Professionals will be able to afford specialist companies to do this 'rostrum' work (which is why Ken Morse has his name on so many credits), but a cheap version can be done by pinning (or Blu-tacking) the still to a wall, lighting it evenly and then performing whatever camera move is required with the equipment at hand.

Camera Insulation

If you're in a very quiet environment, you may be able to hear the whirring motors of the camera. In this case, it's time to get someone to sacrifice their jumper or jacket and use it to 'blimp' the camera. In the event of rain, you'll find that, even if you have an umbrella over the camera, it will be wise to wrap it in a refuse sack anyway. Rain can easily dribble in despite the umbrella holder's best intentions.

Camera Care

- **Condensation** When moving from a cold to a warm environment (e.g. from a cold exterior to a heated swimming pool), water may condense on the inside of the camera. Some cameras will flash up a warning light when this happens; if it's not there or you don't pay it heed, the camera will at best be clogged up by the tape getting wet, and at worst become an electrical hazard. To avoid this, acclimatise the camera slowly; wrap it up in a black sack or put it in its case, and allow it to sit for fifteen minutes to reach the ambient temperature.
- **Dust and Sand** Cameras are vulnerable if these get inside the casing; if this is likely to happen, wrap the camera up well and keep a brush handy to clean the damn stuff off.
- **Clean the Heads** The record/playback heads in your camera will probably get dirty after a while – to make sure you're still recording good footage, buy a head-cleaner tape and use it as directed.
- **Butterfingers** Dropping a tape-based digital camera can knock the record heads out of alignment, meaning that the camera will now be recording

footage which can only be played back on those misaligned heads – any other camera or deck will see blocky, distorted pictures. If you drop the camera, record something and check the footage back on another player as soon as possible. If it's damaged but you have to keep shooting with it, be certain to copy the footage onto another tape before you send the camera off to be fixed, otherwise you'll lose it permanently. This mostly happens to Mini-DV cameras because they're usually smaller and easier to drop.

LIGHTING

Lighting has three basic purposes:

- **Illumination** Getting enough light onto the subject so that the camera can record a good image.
- **Modelling** Getting the right combination of light and shade on a subject gives the eye and brain enough information to deduce the third dimension – no small trick when the image exists in only two dimensions.
- **Aesthetics** Creating mood, emotion, and other aesthetic considerations. Or just making it look really cool.

Hard Light/Soft Light

Light comes in two basic flavours, and you'll often need to use both when lighting: hard light is directional, and throws a distinct shadow; soft light bounces around in all directions, throwing an indistinct shadow (if any).

Soft light is less powerful when coming from the same source as hard light, because so much of it is heading off into other directions – half the intensity or more can be lost. In nature, the hardness or softness of light depends upon the size and distance of the light source. Light spreading from a distant light source will seem soft; nearby light will seem hard. But if a light source is larger than the observer, less of the overall light will be seen, and that which is will be shining directly at that observer – therefore seeming more directional. Thus the sun, while distant, emits comparatively hard light.

Soft light can be created in a number of ways. The simplest is to bounce it off a light coloured surface, scattering it; walls, floors and ceilings are all usable but specialised reflectors are often used (see the section on page 135). Another way is to 'diffuse' the light. A kind of paper called 'trace' can be pegged in front of the light; or taped onto a window through which hard light is shining. Normal paper is no good for this, because it will burn when placed too close to a hot lamp. Photographic shops and media centres should have supplies. Smoke machines are also good – pumping lots of smoke into the air and wafting it about until it is finely distributed will diffuse all the light in the scene (but make sure the smoke detectors are off). And finally, you can stretch a stocking over the lens, diffusing the light coming into the camera. This sort of thing tends to get used for close-ups on an individual subject, because it's indiscriminate about what it diffuses. A combination of soft and hard light is usual in most scenes. Faces are flattered by soft light, but may need a little hard light to add definition. Hard light is good for backgrounds, especially when you're on a longer lens, putting them a little out-of-focus.

Three-Point Lighting

The basic textbook lighting setup. The three points are three light sources, which happen to correspond to the three basic purposes of lighting:

- **Key Light** A bright, hard light usually positioned in front and slightly to the side of the subject. Provides the main **Illumination**, but throws some nasty hard shadows.
- **Fill Light** Also in front of the subject, and towards the other side, should be a diffused light source throwing a softer light onto the subject. This eliminates as much shadow as possible (as a softer light, it won't be throwing much shadow itself) and flatters the subject a little. Variations of fill light fulfil the **Aesthetic** purposes of the lighting (or, more simply, these are the lights you use to make people look pretty).
- **Back Light** A light source from somewhere behind and above the subject adds a little light to the rear of the subject, distinguishing it from the background. This rounds out the subject and gives it a bit of **Modelling**.

While this is mostly used only for interviews, it's still a good starting point; the basic ideas of key light, fill light

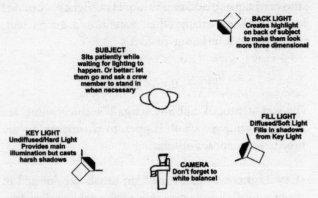

Figure 15 Three Point Lighting Diagram

and back light form the bedrock of more complex setups. Bear in mind that all of the light sources can come from reflectors (a reflector with a shiny surface will reflect hard light rather than soft light, so even a key light can be created if reflecting a powerful enough light source). Another interesting thing is that the lighting style of Film Noir (harsh edges, shadows everywhere, high contrast between light and shade) can be easily produced by switching off the fill light.

Available Light

You can save yourself a lot of time, money and stress by using the sun as a light source. However, the sun is vastly more powerful than any film light and creates the following problems:

- **Exteriors are Too Bright** Direct sunlight is usually too much for a camera. Use a Neutral Density (ND) filter to cut down the overall light level.
- **Exteriors with Too Much Contrast** The difference between light and shade in direct sunlight is vast, and beyond the capabilities of most cameras to deal with. But you can easily deal with this by treating the sun as a key light, and using a reflector to turn the same light into a fill light, bringing the shadows up enough for the camera to cope with.
- **Interiors with Blown Out Windows** Shooting towards a window through which the sun shines is tantamount to filming into one of your lights, and you get the same effect: it burns out on the screen. ND gel on the window or more light within the room will help.
- **Movement of the Sun** You will have to compensate for this, or else the lighting will change between your shots and will look strange in the edit. Shoot wide first to get the master, which will show the largest amount of area the sun is shining on. Then do your closer shots, in which you can exercise more control over the lighting with reflectors and adjust to the changing position of the sun while concealing the change.

Colour Temperature

The hotter a light source, the bluer the light it will give out; the colder, the more orange. Light sources are conveniently split into two groups – Tungsten (orange), so called because this is the element used to make the filaments of light bulbs, and Daylight (blue), which includes the sun but also 'daylight-balanced' lights.

The camera can adjust to either of these with the white balance control (see page 92), but when both types are present in a lighting setup, you have to take some action to sort it out. This is done with gels; rolls of translucent plastic sheeting which come in a variety of colours for cosmetic and effects purposes, but can also change the colour temperature of the light coming through them. A blue gel turns tungsten light into daylight and an orange one turns daylight into tungsten.

Gels can be clipped (with wooden or metal pegs, not plastic ones because they'll melt) onto the barn doors of a light; if you have the sun outside, you can put orange gel over the window to turn it tungsten and match your interior lighting.

Not every environment in the real world is naturally so balanced. There are little discrepancies everywhere – in a single room, direct sunlight may come from one window, and reflected sunlight from another, which has a slightly lower colour temperature. Man-made lighting has created such mixes all over the place. You may approach a ticket office in a train station with the sun to one side and tungsten (or fluorescent, or both) coming from the inside of the booth. So sometimes you have to live with it, though it'll help if you can mute the contrast.

Fluorescent Lights

Fluorescent lights are neither tungsten nor daylight; instead of coming out blue or orange, they have a greenish tinge (making your actors look unwell). The white balance control can adjust to this, but the same problem of mixture with other light sources remains. Gels are available to modify lights to match fluorescent light – 'plus green' to modify daylight and tungsten, and 'minus green' (actually pink) to modify fluorescent to tungsten. But mainly, the best approach is not to mix fluorescents with anything – either use fluorescents on their own and colour balance to them, or switch them off and use other lights. And fluorescents have a second problem: they flicker, sometimes visibly, but often at rates which will show up on camera – another reason to avoid them whenever possible.

Types of Lights

Lights are measured by their wattage; light bulbs at home are either 40, 60 or 100W, while a standard fluorescent tube is about 70W. Film lights can go up to 18,000W (18kW) or more and can almost replace the sun sometimes, although you're unlikely to use anything that powerful on a short film.

Domestic lights are usable only if you have nothing else; you can get larger bulbs to go with them but bear in mind that they really aren't meant to cope with higher wattages. Theatre lights (PAR Cans) are of marginal use, since they are designed for the eye rather than the camera. What you really need are film lights, which can be found at media centres, colleges that teach the subject and professional hire companies.

The basic film lights are known as Redheads (800W) and Blondes (2,000W/2kW), which tells you something about the people working in the industry in the early days. Redheads come in packs of three and are standard interview equipment; Blondes are a higher-powered accompaniment. Neither have fresnel lenses, but they're excellent lights to work with when you're learning the basics. Lights with fresnels come in various wattages and have many names, the commonest being 'Mizars.' If they're available, get them.

Very small lights (100W or thereabouts, sometimes called 'birdies') are good if you need to put in a little highlight to make things more interesting; 12V battery lights are handy for this kind of work, especially at night, and are also good for wrapping when it's pitch black outside and you've just turned all the other lights off to cool down (which you must do as they will be far too hot to touch immediately after use).

Daylight balanced lights of the HMI or MSR type are available from professional suppliers. They both have fresnel lenses, but HMIs are older, bulkier, heavier, and they flicker; it's best to get the 'flicker-free' variety which are more expensive but less of a headache. MSRs are more expensive still but a lot less hassle. You'll need a dedicated stand to hold each one, since they're all quite heavy. Each comes with a 'ballast,' a transformer which amplifies the power from the ring main and must itself be turned on before the light can operate.

While these lights may be very expensive, they are twice as powerful as tungsten lights of the same wattage – it's worth getting hold of a 1.2 kW MSR on more advanced shoots if you can manage it. This is the maximum size you can safely run off a domestic ring main, and it makes an excellent key light for most situations. On night-time exteriors it can be invaluable, and when placed outside a window can turn a night interior into a day interior.

A favourite for most people is the 'Kinoflo' type. This uses a bank of fluorescent tubes which have been balanced to either tungsten or daylight (and should be easily swappable). They provide a very flattering soft light which makes for an excellent fill and can even be used as a key if you have the larger kinds.

Features of Lights

- **Spot/Flood** Film lights usually have a control which allows you to 'spot' or 'flood' the light. This will make the light more directional (spot) or make it spread out more (flood); it also changes the area the light shines on, and the intensity.
- **Fresnel Lens** A 'fresnel' lens on the front of the light increases intensity and makes the light more directional. This is a scaled-down version of the lenses used on spotlights, and assists greatly in making the light controllable. Lights without a fresnel are basically naked light bulbs with only a reflector at the back, and therefore less efficient. An 800W open-face Redhead might be outperformed by a 650W fresnel-equipped Mizar.

– **Barn Doors** Most lights come with four flaps on the front which open outwards to let light out. They can be used to control light, closed down to get rid of flare, or turn the light into a thin bar of illumination – handy for little cosmetic touches.

Lighting Accessories

– **Lighting Stands** Basically, tripods with poles on them. It's a good idea to have a few stands spare, as these can be used to hold flags, polyboards, gobos and other assorted odds and ends aloft. You can also get a kind of stand called a 'polecat,' an extendable pole with rubber 'feet' on each end which can be wedged between floor and ceiling (or two walls). Clamps can then be used to hang lights from it.

– **Clamps** The 'Italian clamp' consists of a grip which can be applied to any surface (or slid onto a stand), and a mounting for lights. Another kind is known as a 'magic arm' and is jointed to allow enormous flexibility of positioning. They're mostly useful for lighter bits and pieces; small lights, flags etc.

– **Flags** Any large, flat object light enough to be easily moved around which you can use to block out any unwanted light. If the light from one lamp is going into the wrong place, you can put an edge on it by 'flagging it off.'

– **Gobos** Light on its own can sometimes be boring. One way to make things more interesting is to interpose a 'gobo' between the light and the subject. A gobo is anything that breaks light up and puts a natural-looking pattern onto the subject. A favourite is a small tree branch gaffered or clamped to a stand.

Increasing/Decreasing Light on a Subject

If you decide you need to make things brighter or darker, there are five basic options:

- **Walk the light in or out** (ensuring that it's switched off first). Bear in mind that the amount of light hitting a subject will decrease exponentially the further away the light is – taking it out to twice the distance will mean that a quarter of the light falls on the subject, rather than the half that you might have expected.
- **Spot or flood the light** This is a pretty fine adjustment but it may be all you need.
- **Open or close the aperture on the camera** Not advised due to the effect on picture quality and depth of field – it'll be a major job to adjust everything.
- **Remove/replace diffuser** Although this will have an enormous effect on the amount of light hitting a subject, it will quite possibly screw up the overall lighting setup.
- **Turn the light a little** This moves the subject closer or further from the brightest part of the light's output; the centre. This can cause problems elsewhere in the lighting setup which will need to be rectified.

Reflectors

Reflectors are a basic but handy tool for the

microbudget cinematographer, and can easily be scrounged or made. The professional kind are usually referred to as 'lastolites' (after one of the companies that makes them) and are a circular frame inside which is stretched reflective fabric; this frame twists and folds into a smaller shape for storage. They usually have a white side and a silvery side; the latter reflects light more directionally and provides harder light. Some might have a gold foil surface which is used for reflecting a warmer light onto a subject.

Polyboards (great big sheets of polystyrene) are available in the industry as 8′ by 4′ sheets, and usually painted black on one side for negative bounce. They're not terribly expensive and the same material is often used as insulation in building. It's possible to scrounge or buy from builders' yards. It can be cut down to smaller sizes for more finicky work – a 4′ by 4′ shape is common.

You can make a reflector quite easily. You need a white sheet, something flat (or a frame of some sort), and wooden pegs to clip the sheet on. If you need harder light, clip kitchen foil on instead. Better still, use both – one on each side. Black drapes are something that theatres and other public venues are most likely to have; borrowing them is a matter of making friends with your local theatre people. Of course, the material can be bought, but will tend to be expensive.

Flare

Lenses sometimes catch the light in such a way that it

bounces around inside the lens, producing 'lens flare,' familiar to filmgoers as pretty multicoloured circles but more usually an annoying patch of light on the screen. The light that causes the problem must be 'flagged off.' Place a flag between the light that's causing the problem and the camera, and carefully adjust to make sure that the flare is removed but no interference with the lighting setup has been made. You can also use the barn doors to do the same thing, but this is more likely to have an effect on the lighting setup.

Shooting At Night

There are two types of night for lighting purposes: 'real' night, without any light source (other than stars and moon, which are too dim to be of practical use); and the sort of night-time you get in cities, where artificial lights of all kinds abound. To make shooting 'real' night a possibility, take the biggest light you have and place it very high up behind the subject (out of a window or on a big stand), make sure it's got blue gel over it and then colour balance your camera for tungsten light. Everything becomes rather blue and monochrome – which is what your eyes see under moonlight.

Recreating artificial light is fairly easy; if it's already there in the environment (like street lights) you can use reflectors just as though it were available light. Otherwise, use your lights to mimic whatever would normally be there. Some cameras will come with lights mounted on top; these are intended for documentary use and not much good if you want naturalistic light.

Out in the wilderness there are unlikely to be sources of power. In the industry, generators ('gennies') are used; but the smaller versions you might consider for use on a microbudget production are often very unreliable. Some hardware hire shops carry them, but they're not intended for film use; you'll have to check the power output and match it to the requirements of your lights carefully. You'll also need someone to look after the genny and keep it safe – the job of a spark. So generally, it's not recommended.

Day for Night for Day for Night...

Sometimes it's not possible to shoot at the time of day indicated in the script. Night scenes are a particular problem – expensive, annoying and always too slow. But there are ways to get around this...

- **Interiors** Relatively easy to fake. If it's light outside and you need a night scene, just cover up the windows with whatever's available (black sacks, polyboard, mattresses etc). If it's dark outside but you need to do a daytime scene (a common problem if shooting during the winter months), take your biggest light (a daylight balanced HMI or MSR if possible, a blue-gelled Blonde if not) and put it outside the window as a key light to replace the sun.
- **Exteriors** It's tougher, but it is possible to shoot night scenes during the day using the venerable technique of 'day for night.' The old fashioned technique will have you white balancing for the normal exterior

followed by a special blue filter (or a bit of blue gel gaffered to the camera) and slight underexposure can often work, as long as the sky isn't in shot and you didn't need to see working streetlights. If you have more experience with postproduction, you may be able to create this effect purely while grading, even turning a sunny day into a dark night.

Safety

Sticking a bunch of extremely hot lamps with electricity running through them up onto high stands, which are sometimes more wobbly than we'd like, creates a number of health and safety issues…

- **Heat** Lights are too hot to touch. When turned off, they need time to cool down (a good fifteen minutes or so). You must take pairs of heatproof gloves with you because you'll probably have to adjust gels clipped to barn doors, and barn doors get hot too. Some smoke detectors will set off a fire alarm if a hot light is placed beneath them. You may notice a bit of smoke coming off a light when you turn it on; this is probably dust burning off, and nothing to worry about.
- **Light** When turning lights on, shout "eyes!" as a warning. Lights should, wherever possible, be used above or below eye level, since they can dazzle or damage the eyes of performers. Children are easily distracted by bright, hard lights; softening the lights you use on them will help to avoid both dazzle and loss of concentration.

- **Power** Domestic ring mains are only capable of bearing so much – 13 amps per power point (not per socket!). To find out the amperage of a light, divide the wattage of the light by the voltage of the power supply (230V in the UK – it used to be 240, but we're now standardised with the rest of Europe). Redheads: 800W/230V = 3.48 amps. Blondes: 2000W/230V = 8.69 amps. So the formula is: Wattage/Voltage = Amperage.
- **Water** Electricity and water do not mix, although HMI/MSR daylight balanced lights can get hot enough to make drizzle evaporate the moment it hits them. But in worse conditions, they will need to be protected, the same as other lights. Cables should be kept dry in all circumstances, especially where they join to other cables. Some of the plastic boxes you might be using to carry props or goodies are useful as a basic 'umbrella,' while wrapping them in bin bags or cling film is another method.
- **Topple** If lights are up high on stands, weight the stands at the base with sandbags or stage weights, or anything else that is particularly heavy. And you must never put a light onto a stand for which it is not intended.

SOUND RECORDING

When shooting film, sound is recorded separately from the picture, meaning that they will have to be synchronised in postproduction; every shot is marked with a clapperboard (known as a 'slate', although they're plastic these days) which visibly makes a sharp sound to allow picture and audio to be matched. On video, sound is recorded directly onto the same tape, and automatically synched. A slate is only required if you need to have a visual marker for each shot, or are using two cameras and want to record the sound onto just one of them. But otherwise, recording sound for video requires exactly the same care and attention as it does in film, and should be the job of at least one person throughout the shoot.

Digital/Analogue

If sound is recorded analogue, it will be laid down as a waveform; if it's recorded digitally, then the sound will be sampled thousands of times each second. The practical difference is that analogue sound needs to have input levels set very carefully – if it's too quiet, the sound will be lost in hiss ('noise floor') and be useless. Digital formats effectively have no hiss (unless they're copying from an analogue format, in which case the hiss will be reproduced perfectly). They usually have a control which allows you to select a sample rate: 36 kHz (which allows some formats to record four tracks), 44.1 kHz (CD sample rate) or 48kHz. The higher the sample rate, the more information is encoded, and the more space that information takes up; therefore the tape will run faster, and won't last as long. It's best to record at the highest quality possible, but bear in mind that some people have customary sample rates – composers in particular prefer 44.1 kHz because they usually have to output their work to CD, so you may have to request 48 kHz masters from them.

Cables & Inputs

Sound can be carried on two types of cables – 'balanced' or 'unbalanced.' Unbalanced leads (like phonos or minijacks) carry the signal upon two wires (positive and negative). But over distances of more than a few feet they pick up radio signals – mobile phone pulses, local cab firms and sometimes Radio 4, all of which will make the sound unusable. Balanced leads, called XLRs (or cannons), have three wires in each cable and through some clever trickery make radio interference cancel itself out. Most consumer cameras will have no sound inputs at all, apart from sometimes a single unbalanced minijack. Higher-end consumer cameras and all professional cameras will have two XLR inputs. Many microphones will only plug into an XLR. Outputs also vary; on some professional equipment, it is assumed that the camera will not be used for playback, and outputs do not exist. On consumer equipment, there are usually two phonos.

Headphones

Incoming sound should be monitored at all times – you don't record the pictures without looking at the viewfinder or the monitor, so how can you record sound without listening to the headphones? The camera headphone socket is often a minijack, but on some models may be the larger ¼" jack. Make sure you get the appropriate set of headphones, although a pair of earplugs from a Walkman can be good enough if there's nothing else. It's always better to have head-phones designed to exclude outside sound if at all possible. In the event of problems with the main audio outputs (if the camera has any), it is also sometimes possible to output the sound from the headphone socket if you're desperate.

Input Levels

Cheaper cameras will not allow you the chance to adjust the input level coming in from the microphone. In fact, many will automatically change levels when they get too high, causing an unpleasant change in the sound quality. However, better cameras allow you to manually set the input level with the 'gain' control. This has to be checked and adjusted before each take, no matter how fiddly the position of the level meters and the gain control. The worst thing is levels constantly at maximum (visible on the meter as solid bars all the way to the top or needles jammed all the way to the right), that means guaranteed distortion. The 'peak' should be about two thirds of the way up on most meters, unless they're dials with needles in them, in which case you want to be peaking between four and five. Before a take, be certain to ask a performer for a 'level' – get them to read their line in the same manner as they're going to perform it and adjust the input levels until you've got something usable. If there's a camera

PAUL HARDY

rehearsal going on, try and use that to get your levels, as it saves time. If you want to know more about levels and metering, pop ahead to the section on page 185.

Sound Mixers

If you don't want to rely on the input levels of the camera, you can use a separate sound mixer to pre-adjust the levels first. The mixer will be able to output a 1kHz test signal (called 'tone') which you use to set the input level of the camera to the appropriate position, after which you put gaffer tape over the dials to ensure they aren't jogged. Analogue cameras should have the levels adjusted so that the tone hits 0dB; digital cameras should have tone adjusted to −18dB. Once the levels are set on the camera, the mixer has complete control over the sound and should set levels exactly as described in the previous section – only it'll be easier because you won't be trying to squeeze past the camera operator all the time. Tone is also useful for one other purpose – the beginning of every tape should have thirty seconds of 'bars & tone' recorded on it, and the camera operator may ask you to send tone to the camera to do this (see page 110 for more details). This acts as a reference signal to allow an editor or dubbing mixer to transfer the sound without setting their own input levels too high or too low.

The mixer should have XLR inputs and outputs as standard, a headphone socket and levels meters. It'll also have things like attenuators (which cut input levels drastically – good for noisy environments), bass cut (handy for places with lots of outside noise coming in as a bass rumble), and a teensy onboard mic for the sound recordist to record little messages to label things like atmos and wildtracks. Most mixers run off batteries to avoid the hum you sometimes get from an AC mains power supply, and usually they'll be adapted for professional rechargeable batteries. Some run off ordinary AAs and last only about ten hours (i.e. one day), so carry lots of spares. Some mixers can also provide phantom power (needed by dynamic microphones – see below), but there are several kinds of this and the wrong one might damage the mic – always consult the manual and don't risk it if you don't know what you're doing.

Microphones (Mics)

Most cameras come with an on-board microphone (written as 'mic,' pronounced 'mike'). These are only good as back-up, because the mechanisms of the camera and handling noise are easily picked up, and also because the camera may simply be too far away from the subject to pick up good quality sound. But if your camera has no other sound inputs, then that's what you're going to be using.

If your camera has inputs, you can use a separate microphone. Microphones are defined by the method through which they pick up sound and the directionality of the sound they record.

– **Method** Two main ways exist to pick up sound –

'dynamic' or 'condenser'. Dynamic mics use a mechanical process, and do not need batteries; condenser mics use an electrical process, and need on-board batteries (or 'phantom' power from a sound desk – if you're being loaned a condenser microphone from a musician or a recording studio, make sure they give you one that carries batteries).

– **Directionality** Hand mics used by presenters and singers (like the Shure SM58) are designed to pick up sound from in front of the microphone and partly from the sides in a sort of heart shape ('cardioid'). These are okay, but they do pick up extraneous noise from other directions. It's better to have a directional microphone which picks up sound from directly in front; these are long and thin in shape, usually mounted on a pistol grip, further enclosed within a rigid cylinder called a 'windshield' and, in windy weather, a big furry sock called a 'windjammer'. These are the microphones seen on professional film shoots mounted on the end of a long pole called a boom. Most media centres that hire video equipment should have one available for you to use (the Sennheiser 416 is the usual workhorse). If you can't get this, then a hand mic, a broom handle and some gaffer tape can make a substitute.

Radio mics are useful when there's no other way of recording the sound; for example if the angle is too wide, or if the camera is moving so much that a boom would get in the way. The actor wears a tiny microphone concealed somewhere on their front, wired up to a transmitter hidden under their clothes. The sound recordist carries the receiver, which is plugged into the mixer or camera. They take time to put on, often pick up the rustling of clothes and are known for being more trouble than they're worth. But sometimes there's no other way.

Recording Clean Dialogue

The job of the sound recordist is mainly to record clean dialogue. Everything else – from the sounds of an explosion, to the sound of a car revving up, to the sound of a crowd in the background, to the minutest tinkle of glass hitting the floor – can, if necessary, be recorded at another time or added in postproduction. The sound recordist is well within their rights to ask for an extra take if something went wrong during a shot, no matter how good the actors' performances were. Things to watch out for include:

– **Mumbled, incoherent or overlapping dialogue.**
– **Traffic noise** (cars, trains, airplanes etc.).
– **The crew.**
– **Wind** (atmospheric or otherwise).
– **Radio mic interference or clothes rustling.**
– **Spectators shouting "cut!"**

Sometimes you need sound going on in the background. People may be required to dance to music, in which case you need to be able to play it on set ('playback'); if there's dialogue during such a sequence, it's best to have playback when you start the shot so that the performers can get the rhythm, and switch off the music as soon as anyone is supposed to speak. If you have to shoot inside a moving car or any other environment which has continual sound, try and keep the mic as close to the performer as possible; radio mics are especially useful here as they will always stay the same distance from the subject no matter what the size of the shot.

Boom

One of the commonest errors seen in films is when the boom pokes into the shot. To deal with this, the boom operator must ask for a frameline from the camera operator before the shot begins – simply a matter of putting the boom closer and closer to the subject until the camera operator says it's in shot, after which the boom operator knows the precise limit of the frame. The boom can be held above, below, level with the subject – just as long as it's out of shot and pointed at the sound source. If there are several performers, this may involve some careful movement to keep up with the current speaker – the boom operator must make use of camera rehearsals to get this sorted out. The cable of the microphone should be twisted around the boom by spinning the pole and allowing the cable to wrap around it as you do so; a loose cable is at best annoying and at worst a safety hazard.

Wildtracks & Atmos

Soundtracks are built up of many elements besides the dialogue, but you can save yourself time, stress and money in postproduction by recording some of them on set. Specific sounds to be recorded are known as 'wildtracks' – 'wild' because they are not recorded at the same time as the picture. These may include the sound of a car engine, the bark of a dog, the scrape of a chair, an airplane landing, the background buzz of conversation in a pub; if you think you need something and it's available on set, get it while you have the opportunity. List the sounds you want along with your shotlist. For an example, flip forward to page 227 in the Case Study.

'Atmos' must be recorded in every room or location that you shoot in. This consists of everyone staying silent while the sound recordist gets 30 seconds of the background sound of the room. This is vital for sound continuity when you edit (see page 179). For both atmos and wildtrack, the sound recordist should label the takes verbally, since finding the material you want can be tricky when there are no visual cues.

Postproduction

EDITING

When we say we're making a film, we usually refer to the actual shoot, but this is misleading. Because all you're doing during the shoot is gathering the material you need to make the film – it's only during the edit that you really start making the film and finding out whether or not it is going to work.

But, despite its importance, editing should not call attention to itself. The audience must remain unaware of the tricks played upon them because if they become aware of the editing, their attention is no longer on the story.

Editing, on professional productions, is a collaboration between an editor and the director; the editor operates all the technology while the director supervises the process. You probably won't have this luxury when making a microbudget film, but it is helpful to have someone in with you or to have sat in with someone yourself.

Logging

Logging is a tedious job that TV companies delegate to

work experience people, but it's absolutely vital to your edit. If you don't know where everything is, how are you going to put it in the film?

- **If you shot onto cards or discs or a hard drive** you'll first have to 'ingest' the footage, importing it into the editing system. You'll usually find that each take has been recorded as a separate file, unless you just kept the camera rolling, in which case you'll have to separate the takes yourself by 'subclipping' (see below). With the takes already separated, all you need to do is watch them and make notes to distinguish them and decide which ones are worth using; either in a 'notes' section on the edit software, or by changing the filename to reflect the contents of the take – e.g. *'1-3 mcu tk2 ok until aborted due to laughing'* gives you a quick way to refer to the second take of the third shot of scene one, shot as a Medium Close-up, some of which is usable until the point at which the actors ended the take early by corpsing.
- **If you shot onto tape** then you need to capture the footage first. If you never intend to edit the footage elsewhere, then capture each tape as a whole; if you intend to do further work elsewhere (and will therefore need to recapture the footage later), capture each take separately as timecodes can slip when recording whole tapes. If you've captured each take separately, then just label each one appropriately inside the edit system; if you captured the whole tape, you'll need to divide it down into 'subclips' which contain individual takes, a process which most edit systems should support.

What's absolutely vital is knowing what was going on in each shot – what was intended, and the way it actually turned out; if an actor fluffed a line; if they did something particularly brilliant; if the lighting was slightly off; the size of the shot, and anything else you may notice. Sitting through the footage and getting to know it more intimately usually helps spark off ideas for the edit itself.

Offline & Online

Traditionally, video editing is divided into two stages: offline and online. These can be translated as 'rough cut' and 'final cut.' On professional productions, the offline stage is usually done on a cheaper system, so you can spend more time on it without bankrupting yourself. Then, for the final version of the film, the edit is recreated or adjusted on an online system, which usually costs vastly more money.

The steady increase in computing power has blurred this distinction; the same system can often be used for offline, sound mix and online, and this is common for home editors. No matter what system you're on, the first job is to edit the film together from beginning to end as you originally intended. This is the 'first assembly'. It may be a bit rough, and will certainly be too long by at least a third, but you'll quickly see what needs changing. Make notes. Work out what's wrong with it. Come back with fresh ideas and re-edit it. Recut it again and again until you have it down to length. Let other people watch it and give their opinions, but exercise judgement – not all the advice you get will be useful. Don't be precious about your camerawork; a shot that you love may be getting in the way of the scene. A lot of editing is about thinning down all the bits you love and selecting the ones that actually work, even if they weren't the very best takes.

Editing with Coverage

If you've shot coverage, there's an easy way to get an edit of a scene and build up a quick first assembly. Lay down the master shot first, then go back to the beginning of the scene and edit in the angles on individual characters or groups of characters, or any cutaways you may need. This also works if you have only two angles on, for example, a conversation between two characters. Lay down one side of the conversation as a whole first, then insert the other side wherever necessary.

Shot Length

It doesn't take the eye long to get bored with a shot. If you give the audience a master angle to watch for a large part of the scene, attention can rapidly drop away. Similarly, a person speaking for longer than a few seconds doesn't need to be left on the screen all the time; reaction shots can be cut in (especially when the reaction of a character is more important than the line itself), or a cutaway could be used. A little practice should give you a sense of when a shot has outstayed its welcome.

Hard Cuts & Soft Cuts

Making a cut in both sound and picture at the same time is known as a 'hard cut,' and is rather abrupt. You'll be able to make smoother edits if you stagger the cuts on picture and sound. Say, for example, you have a conversation between two people, during which you need to cut from one to the other. With hard cuts, you can only cut the picture between words or speeches, because the sound would otherwise be disrupted. Instead, try cutting from one character to another before they've finished speaking – but allow the sound of their speech to continue, and only cut to the sound from the second angle when the second character speaks. This is a 'soft cut,' which is less obvious to the viewer and gives you greater freedom to choose when to cut.

Match Action

A vital trick to make cuts smoother and less obtrusive is to cut on action. So long as the performer has been doing similar things in each take, you can cut from one shot in which, for example, a character is rising from a chair, to another angle where the character is completing the same action. Exact timing will need some work, but you can create the feeling of a smooth, single motion while cutting to a very different angle or shot size.

Even if you don't have the same subject in frame, it's possible to cut on a common movement within the frame (remember the bone turning into a satellite in *2001: A Space Odyssey*?), or similar camera movement –

or, of course, opposite movements (e.g. one person goes left; cut to another person going right. Or the camera tracks in; cut to a shot where the camera tracks out).

Jump Cuts

The opposite of Match Action is a cut to the same frame on a character without cutting on any kind of continuous action. Instead of seeing a continuity problem, the eye reads it as a brief jump in time. As such, it can be a great way to skip over dull moments in a performance. Violating reality in this way is jarring when done only once, but when it becomes a style – either throughout the film, or within a scene – the viewer accepts it readily.

Another kind of jump cut, and one you should use sparingly (if at all), is a sudden series of cuts to smaller shot sizes. It does the same job as a zoom or a track but is very jarring and an incredibly powerful way to grab the audience's attention. And usually it's too powerful. Shoot something else as a backup if you decide to use this technique.

Cutting to Camera Movement

Cutting to and from camera movement can be tricky. Cutting into the middle of a fast movement (or from a fast movement to a static frame) grabs the attention, and while this can be used effectively to draw the audience's interest, it may disrupt the flow of a scene if used haphazardly or in the wrong place. Cutting from one kind of movement to another can also be jarring, especially if the two movements are at substantially different speeds. If you want to cut to a movement, try cutting to it shortly before it begins, so that the eye has a better chance of going along with it.

Extension/Compression of Time

Time is rarely quite what it seems in films. It's possible to speed things up or slow them down to a tension-dripping crawl.

- **Compression** You can shorten scenes (and thus speed things up and prevent boredom) while still apparently showing a complete event. For example, a character has to walk from the middle of a room to a door. If you show them starting to walk, then a cutaway of something else, then them reaching the door, you can get through the action in a fraction of the time it would actually have taken.
- **Extension** The commonest example of this is the ticking clock scene, where something is about to explode, and we cut to and from the timer as the heroes make frantic attempts to save the world – and somehow the timer takes twice as long to reach zero as the numbers ticking down would seem to indicate. Extending an action depends either on using cutaways to drag things out, or showing the same action repeated from different angles (so the audience don't perceive it as repetition), or a combination of both.

Transitions

When you cut to a new scene, the viewer needs a moment to realise where (and when) the new scene is taking place, particularly if the new location is unfamiliar. Therefore, it's common for scenes to begin on a wider shot or a shot which locates the scene in time and space (an 'establishing shot') before going in closer to concentrate on the subject. You can turn this on its head and conceal the nature of the location until later in the scene if you want to trick the audience for a moment – then use the reveal for a joke or a moment of insight.

A common trick is to use dissolves, wipes, or a brief fade to black between scenes; these can quickly get tiresome, so use them sparingly, if at all. Their main use is to imply the passage of time.

To make cuts between scenes more interesting, you can make the images (or sounds) on either side of the cut have some relation to each other. You can do this to give information, keep the plot moving, or just for a nice visual moment. Some examples:

- **Moving the Plot Forward** Someone asks a question at the end of a scene. Someone, maybe even the same someone in the next scene – possibly years distant and thousands of miles away – answers it.
- **Passage of Time** The camera ends a scene on a shot of a house. Cut to a shot of the house derelict, years later.
- **Exposition** The scene ends with the hero being shown a mug-shot of the villain. Cut to the villain in disguise

– now we know how he's getting through security.
– **Visual or Conceptual Link** A character gets into a car and drives away. Cut to a shot of a child riding a tricycle before panning up to show the person waiting for the character in the car.

Of course, any of these can be played as their opposites, or used to trick the audience.

Pacing

Pacing is a subtle and subjective art which depends to a large extent on the material originally shot. What I can say for sure is this: it's a lot easier to make a fast-paced film than a slow-paced one. A fast paced film is created by cutting out lots of material in the edit, allowing you to manipulate the pace through editing (as long as you have enough material to edit with – a fast paced film often needs more footage than a slow paced one!). A slower pace depends more upon what you shot because you probably won't be cutting as often. And during the shoot you don't usually get the chance to go back and try again in a couple of days when you've figured out how to do it better (a luxury editors generally possess). Plus, of course, a slow pace can easily turn into a boring pace, or be the result of not having enough footage to edit with. A slow paced film can be fascinating, or, as Sergio Leone showed us, absolutely dripping with tension, but keeping it interesting is a lot more difficult than it looks.

Either way, music can be key. A long boring shot can

become tight and tense just by sticking a dance track on the top, and throwing in some gentle Bach can easily smooth out a slow-paced film and help the audience get past the fact that the picture isn't cutting as often as usual.

Regardless of what pacing you prefer, you would be wise not to keep your editing style at the same pace throughout the film. A sudden burst of speed can grab the audience's attention, a slow rise in pace can draw them in gradually, and a slackening off after a tense moment will let them get their breath back – but a constant pace just becomes repetitive.

Preroll

When a tape recorder is ordered by an edit controller or a computer to play a piece of footage, it doesn't start at the beginning. It nips back to a few seconds before that point, and then starts playing, in order to get the player up to speed and working smoothly. However, if your timecode is discontinuous, the system may become confused and get trapped rewinding and fast-forwarding to find a non-existent timecode. You can also get this problem if the required material is too close to the beginning of a tape (another reason to record bars & tone at the start of each tape, as gives plenty of space for preroll). Some systems allow you to reduce preroll time in order to solve these problems, and a non-linear suite may allow you to digitise 'on the fly' without needing to look up the timecode; but sometimes the problem can be insoluble without copying the material to another tape.

Types of Video Connections

Once you reach the editing stage, you may have to send video signals around on cables, and if you do, you need to know what the connection is doing to your footage – some of it isn't pretty. The actual cable itself often doesn't matter as they're all metal wires cased in plastic, and you can sometimes cut the plug off and solder on a different one if necessary. What matters is the information you send down the cable.

– **Composite** The most basic analogue video connection, which can be carried on a single cable of the BNC, phono or MUSA type, and is also the method by which analogue TV signals reach you at home. The problem is that Luminance (brightness) and Chrominance (colour) are carried on one cable, sacrificing quality. Colours may bleed and you might see some weird primary colour artifacts turning up. Use this for monitoring on location and maybe in the edit suite if there's nothing else.

– **S-Video** stands for Separated Video. S-Video is an analogue signal that separates the luminance and chrominance, thus preventing most of the degradation. It usually travels down its own special connector, a 4-pin DIN plug, but can sometimes be found travelling on two separate cables.

– **Component** consists of one luminance channel and two chrominance channels which are always carried on three separate cables. You'll usually only find component on professional broadcast equipment, and it's as good as you can possibly get with analogue connections. If SDI isn't available, use this to send video to the edit system in preference to anything else, and use it for monitoring if you want an absolutely accurate picture. These days, you'll often find Component outputs on HD equipment as well, mainly used for monitoring.

- **Firewire/I.Link/IEEE 1394** The standard digital consumer AV connection comes on its own special kind of (expensive) cable in 4-pin and 6-pin flavours. 4-pin connections fit into cameras while 6-pin plugs fit into computers and can carry power as well. It's the standard consumer level DV connector, and SD video signals you send down it will always be compressed. HDV signals, which can also use this connector, will be even more so (but no more than they already were).

- **SDI** (Serial Digital Interface) This professional level digital connection is as good as it gets – uncompressed video which can be interleaved with audio if required. It travels on a single cable, usually BNC, but you're unlikely to find it outside the more advanced professional edit suites. If it's there, use it!

- **HD-SDI** is the HD equivalent of SDI (again using BNC cables), and is mostly found only on professional equipment.

- **HDMI** is the consumer HD cable, carrying video and audio. It isn't often used for editing purposes, but your computer's video card may have an HDMI output. The cable isn't tied down to any single format and can be used for a wide variety of signals.

– **Audio** If you're moving audio around separately, it's always preferable to use 'balanced' XLR cables rather than 'unbalanced' cables for reasons which are explained on page 142, and you'll need one for every separate channel of audio – generally two at a time but some formats can carry four channels. Of course, Firewire SDI and HD-SDI can carry audio along with the picture but many professional suites choose to use XLRs anyway.

Linear & Non-Linear

There are two fundamental types of editing systems:

– **Linear** uses two VCRs to copy shots from one tape onto another. The tapes can be analogue or digital, so this isn't, strictly speaking, the 'analogue' way of editing, but it is nevertheless largely obsolete. It suffers from a serious difficulty: once an edit has been completed, it is impossible to add a shot or a scene somewhere in the middle without wiping over something that was there before.

– **Non-Linear (NLE)** works by 'capturing' the footage onto a computer, where it can be manipulated without the need for any of it to be copied over or destroyed. The editing is done on a timeline which graphically shows the sequence of shots. Most will allow you to manipulate the sound in the same way as the picture, and produce a reasonable sound mix. They should be able to play back digitised footage and the timeline on the screen, though more complicated effects will require the computer to do some 'rendering' before it can show you anything. We'll assume that this is what you're using – indeed, if you're starting your career now, you'll probably never encounter anything else.

Hardware

Many people these days use their own computer. Obviously this is more convenient but unless you're stunningly rich, you'll be restricted to using your camera as the playback and record deck and going into the computer via Firewire, which means that Mini-DV or HDV will probably be the highest format you can cope with. Putting together a computer for editing isn't as simple as just going into a shop and buying the latest model – you need to be very specific about what you're looking for, and a generic PC usually isn't enough. Here's a few things to consider:

– **Mac or PC?** Macs are generally better as computers and will often come with many of the required features as standard, or as an option you can select when buying the computer. If you can afford it, Macs are definitely recommended. However, the cheaper PC, while not as stable or reliable, is capable of doing much the same thing as long as you're willing to get a screwdriver out and add a few bits and pieces.
– **Processor/Memory** Get the fastest possible processor and as much memory as you can afford. While slower processors might be able to run the

software adequately, they'll take forever to render even the simplest effect, and extra memory will speed render time significantly.

- **Graphics Card** Don't rely on a graphics chip built into the motherboard if you can help it – get a separate one, although don't go overboard; expensive graphics cards are designed for 3D games and not for the simpler task of rendering 2D video. If possible, get a card that can drive two monitors to expand your desktop – editing programs take up a lot of space on the screen and two monitors makes editing a lot easier.

- **Sound** A good sound card is essential, as is a good set of speakers; standard PC speakers aren't all that good at lower frequencies, and how can you mix sound if you can't even hear it properly?

- **Storage** Your drives need to be at least 7,200rpm, if not better, and you should store your footage on something other than the system drive. DV and HDV footage takes approximately two gigabytes for every ten minutes, and it's all too easy to fill up 100GB while making a complex ten minute film (those rendered effects have to be stored somewhere!). Internal drives can be bought with enormous capacities, but for greater ease you can get external drives which connect to a Firewire socket so you don't have to rip the system apart every time you add a bigger drive.

- **Capture Card** The best option is to make sure the motherboard at the centre of the system already has a Firewire port, but you can get separate cards very cheaply if this isn't the case.

Software

Software is another vexed question. It'll be one of the most expensive items on your shopping list and by far the most important choice. Software gets updated far too often for any advice to remain valid for long, and this is nothing like a complete list, but here's a few of the current candidates:

- **iMovie** Comes for free with Macs and mainly good as a cutting tool. It can't do a whole lot else. Everything about it is simplified and easy to use, so it's a good way to learn the basics of editing or do a quick rough cut, but it's not a realistic substitute for a full-scale editing system.
- **Adobe PremierePro** Premiere is cheaper than most systems and often the default choice, but was developed from a consumer product and suffers from this; it does, however, tie in very neatly to Adobe's other products, which are much better.
- **Final Cut Pro** Apple offer this versatile, reliable and rather damn good system, but only on the Mac. If you have a Mac, this would almost certainly be the best choice as it's been steadily gaining ground in popularity and quality for quite some time.
- **Avid** The advantage of Avid is that they make the standard NLE systems you'll find across the industry and throughout the world. They also make a package more on the consumer level (Avid Xpress Pro), and learning how to use it will stand you in good stead in most edit suites. The disadvantage is the cost

– huge in comparison to either Premiere or Final Cut Pro.

Editing Procedure

The various software packages you might use have many common features, but not all systems support every function – some need add-ons, and some are simply incapable. Check the system before you begin. You may need to set the system up to accept the correct type of footage – the usual options include 'DV PAL' or 'DV PAL Widescreen' if shooting 16:9, and then a plethora of options for the various HD formats – make sure you select the right one if you're shooting HD.

– **Digitising/Capturing** The first task is to get the footage into the system. If you filmed onto cards, discs or hard drives, this is a simple matter of importing the files. If you shot onto tape, you'll instead have to go through a process known as 'digitisation' or 'capturing.' Digitisation can be done 'on the fly,' simply pressing the relevant button to start and stop as the tape plays, or (if the tape format has timecode), you can type in the 'in and out points' and let the computer do it itself. 'Batch digitising' or 'batch capture' is a process where you give the information on multiple clips to the computer and let it get on with it by itself, only changing tapes as necessary (thus saving huge amounts of time). Some systems take advantage of a function in the Mini-DV format which allows them to record each shot as a separate file – this saves time but is no substitute for proper logging. Some systems allow you to digitise at different rates of compression; the more compressed a file is, the lower quality the image will be, but the less space it will take up. But if you're coming in via Firewire, you're stuck with the one compression rate. If you can, digitise all the footage at the lowest quality possible at first to save space on the disks (something that's more an issue with HD); later on, you can redigitise the material that survived into the final cut at higher quality (but only if you have timecode – if you don't, you won't be able to find the footage with the necessary accuracy).

– Digitising/Capturing Audio If you're capturing with Firewire, you'll find that you won't be able to adjust the levels of audio and video as they come in, and if you had your camera set up correctly in the first place, this should be fine. But if you're working with analogue inputs or with SDI, you will have the option to alter these input levels. Video generally isn't too much of a problem – you have to screw up your camerawork quite badly to generate footage that doesn't look okay at the default input settings – but audio can sometimes be difficult. This is where the bars & tone you recorded at the start of the tape can come in handy (you did record bars & tone, right?) as this provides a reference signal you can match your system to. Simply play the bars & tone back and adjust the audio input settings, so that the levels match the setting you used when you recorded the tone in the first place – so long as you recorded your sound correctly, it should sound fine when digitised.

- **Organising Footage** 'Clips' of digitised material are stored in 'bins,' folders you can open to access the clips contained inside. Organise bins according to scenes, so that all the clips for a single scene can be found in the same place. If your film contains only one scene, create bins for each camera angle instead. When you add a clip to the timeline, you can usually select which part of the clip you want to lay down rather than having to add the whole thing and trim it later.

- **Editing in the Timeline** The timeline is where you actually do the work, laying down shot after shot. The workings of the timeline vary between the different software packages, but you should be able to both overlay shots on top of old material, or splice in shots, pushing aside the old material. You will also be able to trim or extend the beginning and end of every clip on the timeline to make adjustments – you should be using this facility every time you perform a cut so you can get it absolutely right.

- **Widescreen** All systems support the 16:9 widescreen format and can read anamorphic images correctly, but you'll have to make sure that the right option is selected. They will then show you the picture in the correct aspect ratio while still holding it in memory as an anamorphic image. When you output, you may get the option to convert the picture to a letterbox image which can be viewed on a standard 4:3 screen, or you may have to apply a squeezing effect across the whole film. If you want to use 16:9, make sure you find out what the system can and can't do.

- **Audio Editing & Mixing** A non-linear system should give you at least two tracks of audio to play with (i.e. a stereo pair, although you don't have to use them as a pair if you don't want to), and most will allow eight or more. However, there are sometimes limitations on how many you can play out at once. They are manipulated in much the same way as video tracks, with the exception that you may be able to change volume, pan, EQ or other settings. A useful feature, if you have it, is 'audio scrub,' which allows you to drag the mouse across an audio clip at any speed and hear a frame or so of the audio at preset intervals, so you get a sort of sampling of the audio every time you move the mouse up or down the timeline.

- **Importing/Exporting Files** Since you're working on a computer, the NLE system should be able to import a wide range of video, graphics and audio file formats, turning them into clips which you can then incorporate into your film. You should also be able to export the film as any one of several kinds of video file; if you do so, make sure you know exactly what kind of file you need down to the most minute setting. Incompatible video files can be a major headache.

- **Saving Projects** The edit is saved as a complete 'project,' incorporating the current timeline and state of clips and bins. This is not transferable between different software packages, but you should have the option to produce an Edit Decision List (EDL) instead, which is a text file containing basic information about the edit. This can be imported to another system and used as the basis to redigitise the necessary footage.

- **Mastering to Tape** is a simpler matter on some systems than others. Some allow you to watch the edit on a monitor as it plays, which allows you to plug in a VCR or camera and record it at the same time. Others find this a bit of a stretch, and require that you render the whole edit before you can play it all back in one go.

- **Safe Area** As with cameras, your NLE system will display the whole image rather than the image that will result when cropped by a standard TV. You should be able to switch on a 'safe area' guide, which will outline the safe area, so you know whether or not your film will actually be visible when people watch it at home.

- **Autosave** One final piece of advice: NLE systems have a habit of crashing from time to time, though much less than they used to. All NLE software should have an autosave option which you must activate – it may be annoying to have to pause every ten minutes as the project is saved, but that's better than losing a day's work when the system goes down.

Effects

Most NLE systems will present you with a limited range of effects, which you can use to modify your edit.

Some will need to be rendered while others can be played out in real time without rendering, but will usually need to be eventually for output. Some common effects include:

- **Fades/Crossfades/Dissolves/Wipes** Most of these are fairly simple – you should be able to set them to any length and to start at any point in relation to the actual cut, but make sure there's enough spare footage on either side of the cut to make the effect possible. Some systems might have fades and dissolves set to look more like optical film fades and dissolves. I think they look better, but make your own mind up before you use them.
- **Freeze Frame** Most systems allow you to specify a single frame and make a still image of it – essentially another clip in which every frame is a copy of the original. But watch out for the field options – you might only be able to make a still from one field, or you might be able to create a composite of both. You should also be able to import graphics files from outside and turn these into stills clips.
- **Titles** Most systems have some sort of titling facility, generally fairly basic, allowing for crawls and title rolls. Plug-in titling systems usually offer more choice and flexibility. Note that the safe area for titles is slightly smaller than the safe area for picture; the title tool should show you how close to the edge you can safely put your titles with a 'title safe' box.
- **Colour Correction/Colourisation** (Grading) Being able to change the colour levels is a very useful

tool; you might have presets that allow you to make colour footage black and white, or sepia, or correct a shot you forgot to white balance (but don't rely on this!).

- **Flips & Flops** Reversing the picture either horizontally or vertically can be useful if you've made a slight mistake with regards to the 180° rule. Beware of things that could give away the trick, like street names, newspapers and number plates.
- **Slow Motion/Fast Motion** Computers can speed up footage very easily by cutting out frames. Slowing down footage is more difficult. The computer will create 'inbetween' frames to stretch out the footage, but the resulting image will still have a stepped quality.
- **Resize** Making footage smaller or subtly zooming in can often be useful (but don't zoom in too much unless you really want it to look all pixellated and horrible). You should also be able to resize both horizontally and vertically – handy for weird effects but on some systems the only way to turn 16:9 anamorphic footage into 16:9 letterbox footage.
- **Keying (Chromakey and Lumakey)** The system can be set to 'key out' a particular colour (commonly blue or green) or brightness level, replacing it with other images Using these effects, however, does depend upon the quality of the footage being used – the bluescreen needs to be evenly lit with as little of the background colour reflecting onto the subject as possible.

For more accomplished work you'll need a separate package such as Adobe After Effects or Shake. Learning how to use these programs can be tough but well worth it if you have the time. If you do use them, remember to export the video files 'full frames' and uncompressed or else you may be losing information you'll never get back.

Monitors

If you're in a relatively professional edit suite, you should find that it comes with a very large broadcast quality monitor which will need to be calibrated exactly the same as a field monitor (see the section on page 108). This is useful, as the size of the image on an edit system can be quite small and it's easy to miss things that will show up later on – especially tiny details like pieces of equipment left in the back of shot which will be especially embarrassing later on. Many NLE packages now allow you to switch to a full screen view for playback, which can help, but if it can't do this, you may be able to connect an ordinary TV to your system. This is easy if your computer has analogue outputs or HDMI out for HD, although you may need to pop down to an electronics shop to buy some adaptors. If you only have a Firewire output, you'll need to use a camera or a special converter to create an analogue signal the TV will understand. Make sure your TV has a compatible input socket before you try this. You'll then have to calibrate the TV by eye, since the user will almost certainly have it set up wrong.

But you should avoid relying solely on the image on the computer screen. Computer monitors use progressive scan by default (see the explanation on page 100) and interlaced footage will have a 'film effect' on it whether you like it or not – and it's all too easy to forget that the footage is still interlaced and will still look like video in the end (and may even have had the fields accidentally reversed). Plus it's very difficult to properly calibrate a computer monitor, as they tend to have rather idiosyncratic controls intended for the comfort of the user rather than accuracy in video applications – so if you can watch the picture on a broadcast monitor, or even on a field monitor plugged into the computer, you'll have a much better idea of the final image quality.

Whichever monitor you get to use, take a look at the film with the brightness turned up. People have a nasty habit of doing this to their TV, so if your film has errors too dark to see at the correct brightness level they may still show up when someone plays the film at home.

Film Look

Everyone seems to want their video to look like film, but it's never as simple as just applying an effect. Film has a greater contrast range than video which can never be completely mimicked, but good lighting can make a big difference, as does taking care with the depth of field. Video is often shot on the wider end of the zoom lens and therefore completely in focus, while a more common choice in film is a shallower depth of field with slightly out of focus objects behind and in front of your subject. You can get this in video by shooting on the longer end of the lens (zoomed in with the camera further away), although this does change other lens properties as well. Getting things slightly out of focus can be aided by diffusion – using a smoke machine or (less subtly) a stocking over the lens are good tricks. Careful grading to improve contrast can also help, and there are effects and plug-ins which can add film grain or film damage to your footage, if that's what you need.

The main problem, though, is interlacing (see the explanation on page 100), which is what creates the sense of crisp, clean movement in video. The easiest way to deal with it is to use a camera that can shoot progressive scan, but this isn't always possible. If you're stuck with interlaced footage, the first method to get a film look is to copy one field over the other, resulting in a constant image in both fields. The only problem with this is that you're throwing half the information away; making horizontal lines in the image look stepped rather than constant. Another method if you have more advanced software is to blend the two fields together, keeping most of the original image and achieving the necessary film look. However, this results in some blurring and can look a bit odd when there's a lot of movement in the image, especially movement filmed at high shutter speeds – the two blended fields create a double image which looks like strobe lighting. Some software can compensate for motion within frames and generate good solid frames in most conditions; Magic Bullet (a set of plug-ins for Adobe After Effects) is very good at this.

Feedback & Test Screenings

At some point – maybe after your first assembly, maybe after the second cut – you have to show your edit to somebody. This is even more vital if you're not working with an editor, who can give another point of view during the edit. These early viewings should be with small numbers of people rather than a full audience because an audience will be in more of a socialising mood and expect to be entertained, which they won't be when they see your half-finished early cut. Whoever you get, be very, very careful how you treat their advice – not all of it will be useful...

– **Screening to Non-Filmmakers** What you're trying to find out is their general impression rather than any specific points. They may not be able to compensate for the lack of polish in unfinished films – to them it'll just look like a bad film. The main reason to show it is to find out whether or not your film makes sense; they may not be able to tell you why something's wrong but they'll feel that something's not right even if they don't know why. Then you can start to track down the problem and come up with a solution. But beware the opinion of the loved one who doesn't want to hurt your feelings – it's rarely useful unless they're filmmakers themselves and know how important feedback is.

– **Screening to Professionals** Expect lots of specific information but bear in mind that they can sometimes be more interested in their own specialism than in whether or not the film works as a whole. They may love or hate something that the general audience will never even notice. But their perfectionist standards are well worth aspiring to, so pay close attention anyway.

– **Screening to Cast or Crew** Your cast and crew have preconceptions that will deeply colour their opinion of the film (as does anyone who has read the script). They're likely to be enjoying it more because of happy shared memories of the shoot than because of any inherent qualities in the film itself, and access to the script means they'll understand things that a fresh viewer might not.

Once the film is more or less finished and reasonably well polished with temp music and a bearable sound mix, a test screening before an actual audience will tell you a great deal about whether or not you've made a good film (as well as telling you what a video projector does to the picture quality). Local film clubs are a good outlet for this since they're less picky about what they show than full scale film festivals, but they can sometimes be harsh and unhelpful. Some audiences are very vocal with their opinions, but most will be scrupulously polite when talking to you face to face, and you'll have to listen out for the subtext ('I like the pacing' is often a good sign that your film has some major shortcomings). If possible, watch the audience while the film is running – they may well give away their reactions far more openly while they're absorbed in the film. Those making comedies have an advantage since the audience either laughs or it doesn't although if it doesn't, it may just be the wrong kind of audience. For everyone else, polite applause after the end of the credits is often a good sign that the audience weren't impressed, although that's not a hard and fast rule; however, if you hear loud applause as soon as the credits begin, then you've got a guaranteed happy audience. If they applaud again at the end of the credits then you can probably get drunk for free that evening. Isn't film-making great?

SOUND EDITING & MIXING

Sound can enhance your picture edit, make cuts smoother, introduce tension where there was none, make an unreal environment pulse with life – but it's harder work. The ear is better able to detect mistakes and discontinuity than the eye. Eyes can be switched off by shutting the eyelids, and suffer no feelings of discontinuity if you quickly flick them from side to side. But the ears cannot be switched off, nor are they directional in the same way that eyes are. Creating sound continuity within a scene is vital for preserving the illusion of reality and, along with a clearly audible dialogue track, is the most basic aspect of sound mixing.

Types of Soundtrack

While working on your picture edit you'll be laying down sound as you go along, no doubt jumbled up to fit into whatever space is available on your system, which may or may not have as many audio tracks as you need. But all your sounds should fall into the following categories:

- **Dialogue** A clean dialogue track is essential. No background noise, all lines as audible as possible. If the dialogue isn't clean, you may need to re-record some lines (see the section on ADR on page 184), but this is almost impossible if you have no money.
- **Sound Effects** These can come from wildtracks recorded during production, or you can get them from CDs.
- **Temp Music** Anything you grab from your music collection to edit the picture to and give your composer a guide. If you're not distributing, or if the copyright is easily gained, this can even be your final music track.
- **Atmos** In every scene, lay down a continuous track of the atmos you recorded for the scene. This will cover any gap or dodgy cut in the other tracks and preserve sound continuity.

On a professional production, these tracks will be taken to a specialised dubbing studio for mixing once the picture edit is complete. Naturally, this is hideously expensive. You will be much more likely to be mixing your sound with whatever facilities are present inside your own computer.

Adjusting Sound Quality

Some important things you should be able to do are:

- **Echo (Repeat) and Reverb** Sound has a habit of bouncing off hard surfaces and reflecting back to be heard again. This can create echoes, which can be reproduced electronically. In film, echoes are generally limited to psychological effects and simulating the effect when you couldn't get it on location. A much more important result of sound bouncing off surfaces is 'reverb.' In a more enclosed environment, sound bounces so close to the source that the repeated sound is neither distinct nor separate from the original sound; we hear the sound seem to continue for a time. This effect can be best observed by going into a church and clapping, then going out into the open air and doing so again – note how much longer the sound carries on inside the church. Reverb gives every room its own sound quality. Soft surfaces absorb sound; hard surfaces reflect it, so the kind of furniture or the number of people in a room can change the quality of the reverb. If your sound is recorded on location, then it's usually accurate to the original ambience of the room. But additional sound effects, ADR or background music (music heard by the actors in the scene), must be matched to the kind of sound you had on location. Reverb effects can sometimes be found inside NLE systems, but you're more likely to need a separate piece of software to do it well.

- **EQ** stands for 'Equalisation,' a system allowing the different frequencies of sound within a track to be made louder or quieter as you wish. Sound is made up of vibrations in the air; the more vibrations there are per second, the higher pitched we perceive the sound to be. For practical purposes, the useful range is 80Hz to 12kHz. Outside of this, sound can be heard, but only barely. A trumpet can range between 200 and 800Hz, and a human soprano voice goes from about 250Hz to 1.2kHz. You may have EQ controls that can only change the levels of a pre-selected range of frequencies, or you may be able to select the frequency to be adjusted. These controls can usually be found inside non-linear editing systems, and for linear systems on the sound desk that comes with the system (if there is one). If, for example, you want to make a voice sound like it's coming through a telephone, cut off everything below 150Hz and above 3.6kHz.
- **Compression & Normalisation** Sound levels from dialogue have a tendency to vary a great deal during any given speech, which causes problems in the mix as you might find yourself unable to hear certain sections while others may drown out everything else. A 'compressor' can smooth out the loud bits by subtly turning levels down when they breach a certain 'threshold.' This can make the voice seem closer and more intimate, very useful for things like whispering and voiceovers but the main use is to bring a troublesome signal under control. You'll be able to set the threshold at which the compression cuts in, the

amount of time it takes to respond, the amount of time it takes to switch off again, the ratio by which it reduces levels once is has responded, and there should also be a gain setting allowing you to bring the whole signal back up a bit once the levels have been smoothed out. Compression is subtle but the effect can be amazing. Computers may also be able to 'normalise' a sound file or a clip within a non-linear editing system; this brings quiet bits up as well as turning the loud bits down and is a rather less subtle tool – it's better to get to know your compressor since you'll have a lot more control over what's happening.

– **Stereo** A sound coming equally from both speakers will be perceived as coming from a point inbetween the two, and you can place sounds anywhere between those two speakers with a 'pan' control. Audio tracks on NLE systems tend to come in pairs that have been preset to be panned to left and right (e.g. track one is usually panned left, and track two is usually panned right). If you've recorded in mono (as you should if you've been using an external mic) then copying the audio so it exists on two paired channels will create the impression that the sound is coming from the centre of the stereo field, because having one channel panned left and another panned right creates the balance necessary to get the sound in the centre of the stereo field. And if you import a piece of sound that already has stereo – e.g. a piece of music – then sending it to a pair of tracks should preserve any stereo effects on the track.

Recording ADR and Voiceovers

If sync sound wasn't recorded on location, or the actor's voice was indistinct, then it's possible to re-record the dialogue, pasting the new dialogue track back into the soundtrack, a process also known as 'looping.' But it is very difficult to recreate the original sound quality of the dialogue without professional equipment, so cheap ADR usually sounds wrong and distracts the audience. But if you're mad enough to try, or if you need to record voiceovers you didn't get during the shoot, plug in a microphone and get the actors to record their lines in time to the edit by digitising or recording the audio while playing a copy of the edit on a DVD. They'll need a few tries to get the timing right. You'll have to be careful with 'plosive' sounds (e.g. Ps and Bs), which cause a small burst of air to rush out from the lips, causing a horrible 'pop' if it hits a microphone. To stop this, either record 'off-axis,' pointing the microphone at the performer from just off to their side, or place a 'pop shield' between the performer and microphone – a pair of tights stretched over a small frame a few inches diameter across does the trick (and if you buy the real thing that's basically all it is).

Foley & Sound FX

There are three ways to add sound effects: record them on location (always preferable), copy them from a sound effects (SFX) album, or record them during postproduction.

Effects recorded specifically during postproduction are known as 'foley,' 'footsteps' or 'spot effects.' Recording a sound effect is a fairly easy thing to do, but takes skill and a surprising amount of time and effort (or money) to get right if it isn't the actual sound recorded on location.

For those of us with less skill or money to spend, there are CDs available which contain vast numbers of sound effects. Some of these are available in music shops, but they are not copyright-free. The real ones are usually only available by mail order, and tend to cost more (upwards of £30 ($60) each), but the extra money pays for copyright clearance. Some media centres and postproduction companies may have their own collections you can take advantage of if you're using their facilities (as they're usually the only ones who can afford to buy full sets).

If you do not intend to distribute the film, have a look through your film collection for sounds that seem appropriate – this is a good way to get unusual atmos sounds such as foreign cities and strange environments. The Internet is also a source for sound effects, but not quite as useful as you might think. Online sound effects libraries are often cut-down versions designed to sell CDs, and sound quality may be deliberately degraded to dissuade people from using the effects – but still, you can sometimes find just the thing you're looking for.

Sound Levels – What are They?

– **Levels are not Volume** The 'level' of audio is NOT

the volume. It's the level at which the sound is being recorded, or has been recorded. Volume is a separate control which can then adjust what goes out to the speakers; if you turn the volume down to zero, the levels meters will still be bouncing around exactly as before. Fiddling with the volume won't actually change the levels, so set your volume somewhere in the middle (wherever is comfortable) and never touch it again.

– **Levels are not Loudness** The level does not always reflect how loud a sound is. It's a measurement of the average voltage of the audio signal, whereas loudness itself is very subjective. Low frequencies will seem very high on the meters but may not register quite as loud to your ears; heavily and carefully compressed sound may seem perfectly fine on the meters but distinctly louder to the ear – a trick used by broadcasters to make adverts sound louder while still conforming to broadcast specifications.

– **Levels are not Decibels** The numbers written on the meters are not the same as decibels, even if dB appears somewhere on them. The actual scale will vary according to what kind of meter you're looking at.

Types of Levels Meters

It's absolutely vital to monitor your audio via levels. But do you think that makes it simple? Nah...

– **VU** (Volume Unit) An analogue meter that's generally cheaper and less sensitive – they simply show a rough idea of what the sound is doing at any given moment but are perfectly good for practical purposes. Can be either the needle kind or a barograph. You're less likely to encounter them but the scale they use often gets used in Digital Meters – this is the one where 0dB comes about two-thirds of the way up the scale.

– **PPM** (Peak Programme Meter) Another kind of analogue meter, usually needle-based and often found on portable sound mixers. As well as being more accurate and expensive, they're designed to fall away slowly from a peak, making it easier for the user to spot the peak in the first place. The peak should be between 4 and 5. PPMs can also be found in professional dubbing studios, where it's absolutely vital to get levels right for broadcast.

– **Digital Meters** will be found on any digital audio equipment, including your computer. They're extremely precise since the sound is now an absolute set of numbers rather than a vague waveform, and precision is vital because digital sound is very unforgiving when it comes to clip distortion. Handily, they often leave a little line at the point of a peak so it's easy to spot. Digital Meters place often 0dB at the top, though some have other scales for comparison.

Clip Distortion

When you exceed the size of signal the system can cope with, the tops and bottoms of the sound waveform are 'clipped' off, damaging the waveform and causing 'clip distortion.' In analogue equipment, you have to be quite harsh to get this to happen (levels solidly all the way to the top) since the analogue signal is fairly fluid in the first place, but digital equipment is almost guaranteed to start clipping the moment you hit the top, due to the sheer precision of the signal. There will usually be a big red light there to tell you the peak has clipped – if it only flashes on for a fraction of a second, you might get away with it, but if it keeps going on and off then the signal is clipping away madly (and your ears will confirm this).

How to Do the Final Mix

You should leave the final mix until you've absolutely finished the picture edit (reaching 'picture lock'). Then, once you have all the elements of your soundtrack available, including the music, you can get started.

– **The Main Purpose of Mixing** is to make sure the levels in the film are peaking at a roughly constant level (though they can vary, particularly for quieter moments). Your mix will be played out on many different systems (hopefully, anyway), which might not be as accommodating as your computer. You need to make sure your levels never get too high that they suffer from clip distortion, nor become so low that they cannot be heard or are lost in hiss when copied to analogue formats. I've found that keeping peaks roughly around −12dB on the digital meter scale is fairly safe. Bear in mind that levels are additive – the more you pile into the mix, the higher the levels will go. Bass sounds have higher levels than treble sounds and may push levels up out of proportion to their actual loudness.

– **Set Up the System** First of all, you need your level meters activated and placed somewhere on the desktop that's easy to keep an eye on. Make sure they're set to stereo if that's only an option. Then pay some attention to your speakers – they have to be set to exactly the same volume throughout the mix or you won't be comparing like with like (check the NLE's own volume setting, the computer's volume setting, and the dials on the speakers themselves). Switch off any EQ adjustments within the computer's own main settings, or similar things on the speakers; if you mix with bass boost switched on there's no guarantee your mix will sound the same on another set of speakers. To make things worse, standard PC speakers are often none too good, often with very poor response on low frequencies. If you can get better speakers, do so.

– **Work through each scene in turn** Make sure the atmos is continuous throughout, then figure out what's the most important thing for the scene – dialogue? Music? Sound FX? Whatever the loudest part of it is, make sure that it's peaking at a roughly consistent level and sounds good when it does so. If the level of a given track isn't roughly consistent, you may need to vary the levels from moment to moment – most NLE systems should allow you to do this by creating 'keyframes' for the level settings on the time-line, which can then be set at whatever level you wish, and varied over time (you can even create fades and dissolves this way, though most systems allow you to generate these faster as effects). Once the main track sounds good, layer in everything else and make sure the overall levels are peaking in around the right place, or not much lower (although of course if there's not much sound other than distant background noise, you don't have to bring that up – you just have to get it sounding right in relation to the rest of the sound-track). After that, it gets subjective – whatever sounds good is good. The trick is to balance things out so that it sounds real and continuous; remember, the ear is harder to fool than the eye and any discontinuity will sound odd. As well as levels, it's wise to pay attention to the tonal balance. If there are other sounds such as music playing at around the same pitch as the dialogue, they may make it difficult to be heard – you'll need to reduce the levels on one or the other. Wise composers write their music around this problem.

– **Finally...** Listen to the mix on different systems and in different formats before you send it out anywhere.

Mixing Stereo

Stereo is never as useful on the small screen as it is in the cinema because the speakers aren't far enough apart on the small screen to allow subtle distinctions. Your music should be kept in stereo but most of your sound should be panned to the centre and will be perfectly happy there. If you have two characters on different sides of the screen you might want to pan them to either side, but don't pan more than 50% if the subject is still within the frame. Panning a sound all the way over to one side or the other should only be done when the source is off screen – TV speakers, unlike cinema speakers, cannot be physically placed behind the screen and, therefore, any sound panned 100% to left or right will sound like it's happening off the edge of the picture. Surround sound has now become possible on some NLE systems, but the fun of placing sounds all over the room may well distract you from the basic point of sound mixing. Learn to mix an acceptable soundtrack in mono and stereo before you mess with surround.

A Few More Tips

– **Drawing Attention** Sound can help to draw attention to a particular object, person or event in the film, just by having it a little louder than everything else. Similarly, you can de-emphasise something if you wish to. For example, if a character's attention wanders, reduce the volume of the person talking to them. The audience will understand what's going on without needing to be told.

– **Semi-Detached Sound** Sound doesn't need to come from within the frame. You can often use a sound effect to signify that something has happened off screen (especially something you couldn't afford

PAUL HARDY

to film). Nor does sound have to be the exact appropriate noise for any given moment – you can do a lot
of comedy by using inappropriate sound effects.

- **Noise & Silence** A quiet soundtrack can work just
as powerfully as a loud one. If a character is creeping
down a sewer with gun in hand, loud noises all around
would be a waste when you could have just the atmos
from the scene, a few quiet footsteps to go with the
character, and then the squeal of a rat when the character reacts to a noise. A sudden sound appearing at
such a moment of tension can be devastating.
- **Low Frequencies**, as has been mentioned, are more
powerful than high frequencies. This means they're
usually all that survives of a sound if it's had to pass
through a wall, for example if music is coming out of
a club. EQing out the high frequencies is always a
good way to make something sound like it's
happening outside.
- **Pops** can occur at the points where individual pieces
of sound begin and end, especially if you're cutting
into the middle of a sound. To stop this, put a 2-frame
dissolve effect over the beginning and end of every
sound clip (as long as that doesn't get in the way of
the sound itself).

MUSIC

Uses & Styles

'Background' music is music heard by the characters. It
will have to be carefully adjusted to make it sound like

it's being played in the appropriate location; music heard outside a nightclub, for example, will have to be EQed so all that remains is the thumping lower registers. Organ music from a cathedral will need reverb. One problem is that the recording quality of most music is so high that it may put the sound you recorded on location to shame – when you add music, it may sound more real than the dialogue of the characters speaking. You will usually need to take out some of the lower frequencies in order to make the sound just that little bit tinnier than the voices in the room, making it sound more like it's coming from a source somewhere in the location.

Sound not heard by the characters is known as 'incidental' or 'featured' music. This has a multitude of uses, from the big movie that plasters a lush orchestral score everywhere, to the art-house flick with a single recurring theme that pops up sparingly. The main purpose of music is to assist with the emotional delivery and pacing of any given scene.

Music can also be useful to mask problems. The continuity of music will tend to smooth out jagged edges, change the tone of a scene, speed it up or slow it down. And never underestimate the power of letting the music suddenly stop; a great tension getter.

Composing & Recording

The reason to go to a composer rather than your own music collection is because the composer (and the relevant musicians, if any) will own the copyright to the work and (hopefully) be willing to let you use it without cost. Be honest with your composer about what you need for the music. Tell them as early as possible. If you can, let them in on the editing process so they can see what you're up to. Once you have the picture edit locked down, go through the film scene by scene and discuss what it needs in terms of music. Give them a reasonable amount of time – a few weeks at least. They should be able to deliver the music on any format you like, but make sure it's uncompressed and at 48kHz for maximum quality.

Contact local media centres to see if they include recording studio facilities where you can get hold of relevant contacts. Community-based recording studios may also have what you're looking for. Universities often have student music societies where you can find musicians, and local bands may be glad of a chance to put their music on a film. It's probably easier to work with a composer who has access to recording equipment, and the keyboards and sequencers needed to put together a soundtrack from scratch.

Copyright

There are three kinds of rights inherent in any piece of music:

- **Composition** Whoever wrote the music (including the lyrics), initially owns the composition rights. It usually gets assigned or licensed to a music publisher.

The copyright eventually expires, usually seventy years after the death of the composer (or the last surviving co-writer).

- **Recording** The recording of any given piece of music belongs to whoever made the recording, and this is usually a record company. Recording rights expire fifty years after the recording was first exploited.
- **Performance** The performance of an artist is also protected by copyright. Usually, the performers' rights in a piece of music are dealt with by the record company who made the recording, but sometimes it is necessary to get separate permission.

If you intend to send your film to a festival, sell it to TV or a website, or exploit it in any other way, you will need to have secured the right to do so from each of the copyright holders. Anyone you send your film to for these purposes will ask you to sign a form saying that you have done so because they don't want to get sued. Getting hold of the rights can be surprisingly easy; an organisation called the Mechanical Copyright Protection Society (MCPS) keeps details on who owns what rights and is often given the job of collecting revenues, making the process relatively simple – if you can afford it. If you can't, the MCPS should at least be able to tell you who owns the rights, and as long as they don't belong to too many people or companies it can sometimes be possible to get rights for film festivals just by asking nicely. They're less keen on giving out the rights to anything you're likely to make money on, of course. Whatever happens, make sure you've got the license agreement in writing or else it's worthless.

Library music is music written specifically to be used in productions of various kinds, and there's more of it than you can possibly imagine, ready made for all kinds of genres and uses. But none of it's for free. The MCPS are in charge of administering it and they do not negotiate. A minute or so of music usually eats up the best part of a hundred pounds, so it's very much not a cheap shortcut.

Be Warned

Music is the most vicious, unforgiving and complex part of copyright law. Many things you might think are in the public domain are actually copyrighted and will have to be paid for if you use them – such as 'Happy Birthday,' for instance. And the definition of music is far broader than you might think – if an actor in your film whistles or hums a recognisable fragment of a copyrighted tune, you may need to pay the composer of the music for the right to use it. And you'd need to pay the actor for the right to use their performance of it. And any music you accidentally record on location will have to be cleared as well. It doesn't matter that you didn't intend to 'copy' it – if it turns up in your final film, you have to pay for it. It's a lawyer's dream and our nightmare, so do yourself a favour and get to know some musicians.

Mastering

There's just one more thing to do – create the master copy of the film. You may be making your masters for more than one purpose:

- **The Master Copy** You'll need to have at least one master which is the absolute, perfect, highest-quality possible copy there is. This is your primary resource for making future copies. This could be a tape copy or a file copy.
- **Sending to Festivals** You may need to make tape copies for festivals (as many still prefer this) – you might get away with just running the film off to a Mini-DV tape, or you may need a proper broadcast master (see below). If you shot on HD, you may need to downconvert the film to SD so they can play it.
- **Uploading** If you're putting your film on the Internet, you'll need to create a lower quality (and therefore smaller) copy that can be watched online – full quality video may take forever to download.
- **Back-up** It's always wise to have another copy of the Master, preferably kept elsewhere or on another system, so you can get the film back if you lose the original master. With more and more films being finished purely as data files, this is becoming more and more important.

Mastering to a File

You should export the film from your NLE to either an

AVI or a MOV, as these are the most common formats and can be read by virtually anything, including DVD Authoring software. When exporting, make sure you don't just use default settings – set things up yourself to make sure you get the right kind of file.

- **Format** The file format will depend on what you want to use the file for – AVI and MOV (Quicktime) are good for archiving and high quality, MPG or M2V will denote an MPEG-2 file that can be added to a DVD, although the DVD Authoring software should be able to do the conversion itself. An MP4 will be an MPEG-4 file, often used for uploading to the web as it's capable of much better compression than most others.
- **Codec** The Codec is the algorithm that compresses video data into a smaller space. It's a separate issue from the actual file format, and many codecs are actually the same on different formats. Saving with no codec means no compression, and a massive file size; if you shot in DV, then DV-PAL will match the quality of the original footage but prevent the file from being too massive; HD formats will also have their own codecs that match the original format they were shot on; and if you're looking to create a file for uploading to the web, H.264 does an excellent job of preserving quality while keeping file size to a minimum.
- **Quality** Many codecs allow you to adjust quality, but remember that higher quality means a larger file size. Keep this at maximum unless file size is an issue, e.g. for online use.

- **Screen Size** Make sure you've got the screen size you want – 720×576 for PAL SD, or the relevant HD screen size. It's also possible here to 'downconvert' the file to a smaller size – bringing an HD file down to an SD size, or reducing an SD file down to a typical downloadable size of 320×240.
- **Field Dominance** This is a crucial factor – if you have interlaced footage, it's possible to mix up the order in which fields are displayed, and that makes a horrible mess when played out. For DV, Upper field/Odd numbers should be selected; for HDV, Lower field/Even numbers should be selected.
- **Pixel Aspect Ratio** This can also be changed at this point, something which is easy to get wrong but which may need to be changed if you're downconverting your video.
- **Colour Levels** If you have this option, select RGB if the file is one you want to do effects work on; select 601 if you're outputting the video just to watch.
- **Audio Codec/Compression** Audio takes up very little space, so there should be no need to compress it – keep this switched off.
- **Audio Sample Rate** Keep this high – 48kHz.
- **Audio Bit Depth** Keep at 16 bits.

And whatever you do, make sure you don't just save it in one place, as hard drives do eventually die and you don't want to lose your only copy.

Creating a Broadcast Master

If possible, make two master tapes – one to put on the shelf and leave alone for archiving, one for actually making copies from.

- **Select a Format** For SD, Betacam SP or Digibeta are the best options – they're easy to get duplicated and almost any festival or broadcaster will require them if they choose to screen your film. DVCAM is a good substitute which is widely accepted. HD formats should be mastered to whatever format you shot with, although you can of course downconvert to SD if necessary (and you may well need to as not every distribution outlet takes HD). Whatever it is, it absolutely has to have timecode.
- **Stripe the Tape** In order to start recording at precisely the right timecode, the tape will need to have timecode already on it, so you'll need to prerecord this. The general convention has the programme starting at 10:00:00:00 (ten hours) on the tape, but you need a couple of minutes before this for other bits and pieces. The record deck will allow you to start recording timecode from any preset number you wish; 09:58:00:00 is a perfectly good start point. Record enough of this (with just a black screen for video) to last the entire film.
- **Set Correct Timecode on the Timeline** Have the timeline start at 09:58:00:00 and budge your film up so that it begins at 10:00:00:00 (of course, there's nothing wrong with using these settings throughout your edit).

- **Add Bars & Tone** Bars & Tone consists firstly of Colour Bars, much the same as a good camera can create (these should be available somewhere in the NLE – make sure they're the ordinary 75% intensity rather than 100% and don't use SMPTE bars unless required to do so) and secondly 1kHz calibration tone, exactly the same as from a sound mixer (which the NLE should be able to create as a clip – make sure it does so at a level of −14dB). Put a minute of bars & tone between 09:58:30:00 and 09:59:30:00. It doesn't strictly matter how much there is, just as long as there's enough for an engineer to make any necessary adjustments to their equipment.
- **Add Clock or Leader** For the last 30 or so seconds before the film, you need some kind of countdown which hits zero at 10:00:00:00 – or at least it would, but you should keep the screen blank after 09:59:57:00 (because if the master is used for broadcast, they need a blank gap just in case they press 'play' a bit too early). This countdown can be in the form of a 'clock' (an actual clock face) or a 'leader' (numbers counting down) although the clock is more normal for broadcast. At 09:59:57:00, put a 1 frame 1kHz audio 'pip' (i.e. just 1 frame from the same clip you used to make the tone) to mark the last frame that your clock or leader is visible.
- **Record to Tape** Each system gives the process a different name (Avid, for example, calls it 'Digital Cut') but you should be able to set your NLE to record the master from beginning to end without any further intervention from you. Ensure that the record

deck is set to 'remote' rather than 'local' (the commonest and most annoying reason why the process doesn't work first time), watch the film as it's laid down just to be certain, and then watch the tape back again once it's finished – this is the final definitive master of your film and if there are any errors, they'll be on every subsequent copy.

– **Label the Tape** On the cover of the tape, write down the timecodes where bars & tone appear and the level you set the tone at, and then the timecode where the film actually starts.

DISTRIBUTION

Festivals & Competitions

Festivals are places to be seen and inform the industry that you have arrived. Or at least, that's the theory. The reality is that short film festivals are chock full of shorts all competing for attention and most of them don't get very much; you probably won't even get any decent feedback. On the other hand, it's worth it to see how many festivals will actually take your film in the first place. Make sure you target the ones who'll actually accept the film (a comedy festival isn't interested in horror unless it's funny) and be aware that anything rooted too deeply in your own culture may not work in another country (British comedy, for example, is regarded by many as an acquired taste they'd rather not acquire). Some of these festivals are competitive, and give out awards. Getting an award is great fun, but not a life-changing event; many of the awards on offer won't cause a single eyelid to bat within the industry. But it's good to have on your CV.

The best thing you can do at festivals is network. Find out who people are and what they do, and make them aware of who you are and what you can do. Get to know how the industry is structured and what might be expected of you. See who's interested in your work and wants to get to know it better. Find the people at your level or a little above who you can get experience from by helping. Find people whom you can give experience by allowing them to help you.

In this country, Encounters (Bristol, November), the Edinburgh International Film Festival (August) and many others accept shorts. There are good lists of festivals on at www.screendaily.com and www.britfilms. com/festivals. Among these are a number of international festivals which you can apply to, most with bilingual application forms. Many of these (and some British festivals) are served by a web application service called Withoutabox which saves you having to fill in all those forms (www.withoutabox.com).

TV

Theoretically, all channels are open to submissions, but terrestrial channels tend to show films they've made themselves or bought in from abroad. You're much more likely to make a sale to one of the non-terrestrial channels. Of course, if your short film is particularly suited to the theme of an individual channel, you will have a much greater chance of a speculative sale.

If you sell your film to TV, you'll need to provide a broadcast quality copy and sign a contract which will probably mean giving up all TV rights to it for a number of years, in territories which, apart from the UK, may include the Republic of Ireland and the whole of Europe. The money is unlikely to remunerate you fully for all the time and effort you put into it, but the main thing is the kudos of getting a TV screening.

Cinema

Cinema distribution is limited, but from time to time someone attempts to match shorts up with features, just like the old days. The catch with cinema distribution is that you have to have the film transferred to 35mm, and usually pay for it yourself. It's an expensive process which is difficult to get discounted down to microbudget levels. Also, ten minutes is the absolute maximum length that is accepted, and shorter is definitely better in this case. Payment is likely to be non-existent; a cinema release is better for your reputation than your pocket.

Internet

Probably the easiest way to get your film distributed, and the widest audience you are likely to find, is on the Internet. Since it takes so long to download video, the Internet is a medium where the shorter type of film has come into its own, and you don't even have to go through an application process any more – just throw it up on YouTube or Google Video or whatever, sit back and see if anyone watches it. And of course, that's the problem – will anyone watch it? There are thousands upon thousands upon thousands of films going up all the time, and only occasionally do they achieve more than a few hundred hits, whether or not they're any good. Not to mention that you're competing with videos about incredibly cute cats. This is where having a web presence of your own helps, such as your own blog or a busy MySpace/Facebook/LiveJournal page that you can use to get people to watch the film.

Some sites do discriminate, though, and you may find it more useful to get your film onto a site that people will go to specifically to watch short films – if your film gets past the application process, then you know you're in good company. If you do get in, you'll probably be asked to sign over non-exclusive Internet rights – non-exclusive because the idea of exclusivity on the Internet is a bit bizarre. If you already have a TV sale, they may put it on their website and pay you a bit extra as well. You will normally have to deliver the film on broadcast quality videotape; the company will have the film transferred and encoded themselves.

Delivery Stuff

– **Stills** If you want to sell a film, you absolutely must have a good selection of stills, preferably both black & white and colour. Frame grabs aren't enough.

Professional photographers are usually expensive, so get a friend to do this, using a Digital SLR camera rather than a compact. You need shots which tell the story and set up the main characters. What you don't need are shots of the crew doing their jobs or arsing about.

- **Music List** To avoid getting sued by the owners of the music, everyone who might distribute your film will want a list of all the music used, along with who owns it, and an assurance that you have gained the necessary rights.

- **Tapes** You'll have to provide tapes. Standard procedure is to send a DVD copy as your application, and some will be able to use this for presentation as well, but not many – usually only small film clubs. Most will require some sort of broadcast quality tape, though the definition of broadcast quality varies. Beta SP or Digibeta are normal. Not many festivals or other outlets yet accept HD formats, so you may have to downconvert your film for distribution – although this will of course change as time goes by.

- **Video Cover** It helps if your DVD has a nice cover. People are a little more likely to pick up an attractive piece of packaging than they are to pick up something with a photocopy jammed in the front. But don't get hung up on it; use a simple, expressive visual idea which gives the hook of the story. Get to know programs like InDesign and Photoshop and put together something tasteful and simple rather than cluttered and shouty.

Case Study: *Blood Actually*

INTRODUCTION

This is a sample set of documents that might help you while you plan your own short film. I've used a short film script that I've already filmed, and which you can find online at www.pocketessentials.co.uk/ bloodactually. *Blood Actually* may or may not be to your taste, but please don't judge it by either content or quality – the important issue is the planning required to get it through preproduction, production and postproduction.

I've included information on how the film could be produced under three different production models, but please remember that these aren't necessarily what would happen in real life. Most microbudget shorts will be a mixture of approaches.

- **Level 1: Total Beginner** This filmmaker has never made a film before, but is wise enough to try something as simple as possible, mainly as an editing exercise to get an idea for how the process works. They'll have minimal equipment, almost no money, and friends and family as both cast and crew. The final film will probably only be seen by cast, crew, friends and family.
- **Level 2: Somewhat Experienced** The second level

filmmaker has made a film or two and gained some contacts through a local media centre. They've probably done a course to help them get the hang of more advanced equipment, including some lighting gear. They're using friends for crew, but their friends are also more experienced, and they've got hold of the cast from a local theatre group or student society. It's just about possible that the film will be good enough for distribution, but still unlikely.

- **Level 3: Almost Professional** The final filmmaker has made half a dozen or more short films and is growing in confidence, experience and contacts. The true cost of the film will be beyond the microbudget level but this filmmaker has learnt to reduce costs and should be able to get by. Professionals have been found for some crew roles and greater care will be taken with the technical side. The cast are professional actors, possibly up from London. The final film has a distinct possibility of distribution (if it's any good – shooting at this level is still no guarantee of the quality of the script or that the film will actually work!).

Please note: the inclusion of these documents does not give or imply any permission to shoot your own version of *Blood Actually*, which remains under copyright. Go and make your own mistakes on your own film – you'll learn a hell of a lot more.

OUTLINE/SUMMARY/SYNOPSIS

Blood Actually is a short romantic comedy about a vampire

who seduces her prey in a shady bar, takes him outside to drink his blood, but quickly finds that he's also a vampire with the same intention; after a moment of extreme embarrassment, they strike up a nervous conversation and are clearly attracted to one another. He introduces himself as Orlok, and she introduces herself as Daisy. He can't help but laugh at her name, and, mortified, she makes to go. Bitterly regretting his mistake, he calls after her, stumbles out an apology and asks if he can call her. Hope rises in her heart once more and she says okay.

SCRIPT

Notes

This is a shooting script rather than a spec script, and has scene numbers to make it possible to plan the production. Scene numbers have nothing to do with the beginning and end of a dramatic scene; they're purely about the physical location of the action.

Remember to make sure every page has a page number as it's all too easy to get the pages mixed up while photocopying them. The first page is a title page. This might seem like a waste of paper but remember, you may have to send your script out to competitions and production companies where it'll be one script among many. So create a clean, simple title page to give basic information like the name of the script, the name of the writer, contact details for the writer, and a copyright notice. Some people include the draft number and a date for the draft, but this is optional.

Blood Actually

by

Paul Hardy

Paul Hardy
18 Any Road
Any Town AN9 2YH
07xxx xxxxxx

INT. TRENDY PUB - NIGHT   1

Red wine pours into a glass in a crowded pub. A hand passes
it to one of the young and lovely people chatting,
drinking, flirting and eyeing each other up.

A BLACK HAIRED WOMAN looks up from her drink. Across the
pub, she sees a BLACK HAIRED MAN enter the pub and look
about, checking the place over.

She gives him an up and down study. Nice.

He notices that he's being watched. Gives a slight smile.
He knows how good he looks.

SLIGHTLY LATER   2

The pair lean against a wall with drinks, talking and
laughing as they chat each other up.

He does a magic trick with his phone, making it vanish.
Then borrows hers and rings his number; she jumps as she
feels it vibrate in her pocket, pulls it out and laughs at
the trick.

She picks up her bag, still laughing, and heads for the
toilet. She pauses by the door and looks back at him. He
takes a drink, grinning and knowing he's got her.

INT. TOILET - NIGHT   3

Women chat in the toilet. The Black Haired Woman stands in
the corner, checking hair and makeup. ANOTHER WOMAN has the
only mirror and applies mascara.

                         ANOTHER WOMAN
               Do you want the mirror, love?

She smiles, shaking the head as the other woman leaves.
She licks her lips. Then checks her teeth.

Her incisors protrude half an inch from her other teeth.
She strokes them with her tongue. Closes her mouth again.
She smiles to herself.

EXT. ALLEYWAY - NIGHT   4

The black haired couple walk away down the alley, still
flirting. She lifts his arm onto her shoulders and he turns
in to give her a kiss, stopping their walk.

She kisses back and they turn round a corner at the end of
the alleyway. He pushes her against the wall. Leans into
the side of her face and runs his lips down to her neck.

His own neck faces her with an invitation. Her teeth extend and she prepares to bite.

But he pulls back and his own vampire teeth glint in the darkness. He hisses and plunges to her neck as she does the same to him.

They gum on each other for a few seconds. Then frown, realising something's wrong.

They pull back from each other.

>   BLACK HAIRED WOMAN
>   Oh... you're...

>   BLACK HAIRED MAN
>   Yeah. I usually hunt here on Friday
>   nights?

She puts her hand over her mouth.

>   BLACK HAIRED WOMAN
>   Is it Friday? I'm so embarrassed...

>   BLACK HAIRED MAN
>   You didn't get the rota?

>   BLACK HAIRED WOMAN
>   I did, I did, I just - I must have slept
>   two days in a row. I'm so sorry...

>   BLACK HAIRED MAN
>   You're new at this, aren't you?

She nods. Uncomfortable silence.

>   BLACK HAIRED MAN
>   You were really good.

>   BLACK HAIRED WOMAN
>   Oh, thank you! And that thing with the
>   phone was really, you know...

More embarrassed silence.

>   BLACK HAIRED MAN
>   I'm Orlok. What's your name?

He extends his hand.

>   BLACK HAIRED WOMAN
>   No, you'll laugh.

>   BLACK HAIRED MAN
> I won't.

>   BLACK HAIRED WOMAN
> It's not very "children of the night".

>   BLACK HAIRED MAN
> I promise you I won't laugh.

She builds up to it for a moment.

>   BLACK HAIRED WOMAN
> I'm Daisy.

He tries to stifle the laugh but fails. She seems
crushed. Now he's embarrassed.

>   BLACK HAIRED WOMAN
> Well, I, I won't keep you from hunting...

She walks off.

>   BLACK HAIRED MAN
> Uh, Daisy?

She looks back.

>   BLACK HAIRED MAN
> I've still got your number on my phone -
> I'm think we should, you know... because
> we don't want to have any more scheduling
> problems... can I call you?

She fills with a sudden hope.

>   BLACK HAIRED WOMAN
> Okay.

They walk away from each other, looking back over their
shoulders as they go, catching each other's eyes and
looking away again.

CREDITS

INT. TRENDY PUB - NEXT NIGHT   5

They sit in a booth together, holding hands. Pull out to
reveal all the other people in the booth are corpses with
bloody necks.

STORYBOARD

Notes

There's a key choice for any filmmaker: do you shoot coverage and leave some decisions until the edit, or do you precisely plan out each shot you need? You usually end up doing both, and that's what's happened here. The early parts of the film are relatively prescriptive about what needs to be seen, with the exception of some shots which are designed to create material for mood-building montages, and of course the biting has to be exactly as storyboarded. But the dialogue scene that takes up the last two pages of the film is done almost entirely through coverage.

Figure 16 Case Study Storyboard

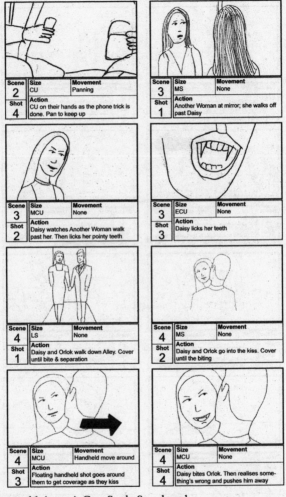

Scene	Size	Movement
2	CU	Panning
Shot	Action	
4	CU on their hands as the phone trick is done. Pan to keep up	

Scene	Size	Movement
3	MS	None
Shot	Action	
1	Another Woman at mirror; she walks off past Daisy	

Scene	Size	Movement
3	MCU	None
Shot	Action	
2	Daisy watches Another Woman walk past her. Then licks her pointy teeth	

Scene	Size	Movement
3	ECU	None
Shot	Action	
3	Daisy licks her teeth	

Scene	Size	Movement
4	LS	None
Shot	Action	
1	Daisy and Orlok walk down Alley. Cover until bite & separation	

Scene	Size	Movement
4	MS	None
Shot	Action	
2	Daisy and Orlok go into the kiss. Cover until the biting	

Scene	Size	Movement
4	MCU	Handheld move around
Shot	Action	
3	Floating handheld shot goes around them to get coverage as they kiss	

Scene	Size	Movement
4	MCU	None
Shot	Action	
4	Daisy bites Orlok. Then realises something's wrong and pushes him away	

Figure 16 (cont.) Case Study Storyboard

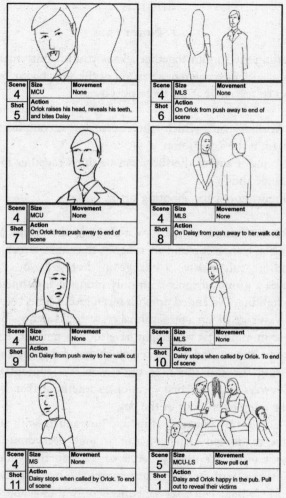

Scene	Size	Movement
4	MCU	None
Shot	Action	
5	Orlok raises his head, reveals his teeth, and bites Daisy	

Scene	Size	Movement
4	MLS	None
Shot	Action	
6	On Orlok from push away to end of scene	

Scene	Size	Movement
4	MCU	None
Shot	Action	
7	On Orlok from push away to end of scene	

Scene	Size	Movement
4	MLS	None
Shot	Action	
8	On Daisy from push away to her walk out	

Scene	Size	Movement
4	MCU	None
Shot	Action	
9	On Daisy from push away to her walk out	

Scene	Size	Movement
4	MLS	None
Shot	Action	
10	Daisy stops when called by Orlok. To end of scene	

Scene	Size	Movement
4	MS	None
Shot	Action	
11	Daisy stops when called by Orlok. To end of scene	

Scene	Size	Movement
5	MCU-LS	Slow pull out
Shot	Action	
1	Daisy and Orlok happy in the pub. Pull out to reveal their victims	

Figure 16 (cont.) Case Study Storyboard

SHOTLIST

Notes

Putting the shotlist together allows you firstly to make an 'at-a-glance' reference version of the storyboard, but also to rearrange it for three purposes:

- Working out which shots can be accomplished within the same setup.
- Seeing if any of the shots can be done together in a single shot.
- Figuring out the shooting order.

The most fundamental is working out the setups. So long as you're looking in roughly the same direction without too massive a change in shot size, you can cover a group of shots with only minimal adjustments to lighting. I've ended up with seven setups here, below the average of ten a professional crew could attain – but bear in mind that you might have to do a unit move to get to the second location (which we did indeed do during the real shoot, as there were no appropriate alleyways near the first location), something that will take a big chunk out of the day.

Once you know the setups and how much work you have to do for each, you can arrange everything in shoot order. It's usually better to start on the widest shot of a setup because that requires the most lighting work (which will afterwards need only minor adjustments), and also because it gives the actors a chance to get through the first few imperfect takes while they're

Scene	Shot	Size	Camera Movement	Actions	Dialogue	Performers	Notes
1	1	CU	None	Red wine pours into a glass, then handed over.	None	Barman, Extras	Slow motion if at all possible. Titles can run over this shot too.
1	2	Wide	None	The crowd in the pub drinking, looking around, flirting	Ad libbed for guide track	Extras, Daisy	This shot is intended to create enough material for a montage of the people in the pub, getting lots of details of them sneaking glances around.
1	3	MCU	Panning around	Camera floats around pub crowd as they look around and flirt.	Ad libbed for guide track	Extras, Daisy	
1	4	MCU	None	Daisy looks up, noticing Orlok as he enters. She makes eye contact.	None	Daisy, Extras	
1	5	MS	None	Orlok enters, looks around, makes eye contact with Daisy, walks out of frame.	None	Orlok, Extras	
2	1	Wide	Slight push in	Wide on Daisy and Orlok. Cover scene.	Ad libbed for guide track	Daisy, Orlok, Extras passing in fg	Extras in fg just wipe frame and make it look more crowded
2	2	MCU	None	Cover Daisy for scene.	Ad libbed for guide track	Daisy, Orlok, Extras passing in fg	Extras in fg just wipe frame and make it look more crowded
2	3	MCU	None	Cover Orlok for scene.	Ad libbed for guide track	Daisy, Orlok, Extras passing in fg	Extras in fg just wipe frame and make it look more crowded
2	4	CU	Panning	CU on their hands as the phone trick is done. Plan to keep up.	Ad libbed for guide track	Daisy, Orlok, Extras passing in fg	Extras in fg wipe frame and conceal the disappearance of the phone
3	1	CU	Pan	Another Woman at mirror: she walks off past Daisy.	"Do you want the mirror, lover?"	Another Woman, more extras, Daisy	
3	2	MCU	None	Daisy watches Another Woman walk past her. Then licks her pointy teeth.	None	Daisy, Another Woman	Vampire teeth req'd for Daisy
3	3	ECU	None	Amy walks across the dance floor towards Daisy and licks her teeth.	None	Daisy	
4	1	LS	None	Daisy and Orlok walk down Alley. Cover until bite & separation.	None	Daisy, Orlok	Handheld shot
4	2	MS	None	Daisy and Orlok go into the kiss. Cover until the biting.	None	Daisy, Orlok	Handheld shot
4	3	MCU	Handheld move around	Floating handheld shot goes around them to get coverage for a montage as they kiss.	None	Daisy, Orlok	Handheld shot. The intention here is to get a variety of material so that a montage of the kissing can be created.
4	4	MCU	None	Daisy bites Orlok. Then realises something's wrong and pushes him away.	None	Daisy, Orlok	Handheld shot. Daisy's vampire teeth req'd
4	5	MCU	None	Orlok raises his head, reveals his teeth, and bites Daisy.	None	Daisy, Orlok	Handheld shot. Orlok's vampire teeth req'd
4	6	MLS	None	On Orlok from push away to end of scene	All dialogue for scene	Daisy, Orlok	Handheld shot
4	7	MCU	None	On Orlok fr.	All dialogue for scene	Orlok	Handheld shot
4	8	MLS	None	On Daisy from push away to her walk out.	None	Daisy, Orlok	Handheld shot
4	9	MCU	None	On Daisy from push away to her walk out.	All dialogue until walkout	Daisy	Handheld shot
4	10	MLS	None	Daisy stops when called by Orlok. To end of scene.	Dialogue after walkout	Daisy	On as long a lens as possible for very shallow depth of field to suggest the distance.
4	11	MS	None	Daisy stops when called by Orlok. To end of scene.	Dialogue after walkout	Daisy	As 4.11
5	1	MCU-LS	Slow pull out	Daisy and Orlok happy in the pub. Pull out to reveal their victims.	Ad libbed for guide track	Daisy, Orlok and extras	This shot can run under the credits, or the pullout can be speeded up so the gag can be done quickly at the end of the credits.

Figure 17 Case Study Shotlist – Film Order

not quite as noticeable. How you then order the setups is down to practicality and more of a scheduling problem.

SCRIPT BREAKDOWN

You need to know what exactly you're going to have to find for your film, and this requires a script breakdown: going through every scene of the script to make a list of everything the script calls for, including stuff not mentioned but implied (in this case, I've given the characters drinks even though they're not mentioned).

GENERAL PRODUCTION PROBLEMS

- **How long will the shoot take?** We have a relatively small number of setups (seven), but we do have to complete a unit move at some point. Still, this should be doable in a day. The material in the pub (the first page of the script) will go much slower than the material outside, partly because it needs to be lit more carefully, and partly because there are production design requirements which will take time to make ready. While the material to be shot at the second location involves a lot of dialogue, the filming is intended to be handheld and largely without lighting, so it'll go much, much faster.
- **Where can I do this?** Pubs often have back rooms that look perfect, but which might cost money. If the place has windows you may need blackout material (or just lots of bin bags) to make it look like night. The

	TRENDY PUB	TOILET	ALLEYWAY
Location	Trendy Pub	Toilet	Alleyway
D/N	N	N	N (Day for Night?)
I/E	I	I	E
Scenes	1, 2, 5	3	4
Characters	Black-Haired Woman (Daisy), Black-Haired Man (Orlok)	Another Woman, Black-Haired Woman (Daisy)	Black-Haired Woman (Daisy), Black-Haired Man (Orlok)
Extras	Trendy pub people x10, barman	Women in toilet	None
Props	Wine glass, wine bottle, wine, Daisy's phone, Orlok's phone, drinks for all	Another Woman's make-up	Drinks, Alice's mobile
Costume	Red dress for Daisy, Black and red for Orlok, no red on anyone else	Red dress for Daisy, no red on anyone else	Red dress for Daisy, Black and red for Orlok
B/g Music	None	None	None
Special Lighting	None	None	Maybe a 2K or HMI/MSR for Day for Night
Set Dressing	Red drapes, mirrors covered with patterned wallpaper, gothic furniture	Posters for bands	None
Make-up	Vampish on Daisy, a bit pale on Orlok	Vampish on Daisy, Teeth for Daisy, normal evening make-up on Another Woman	Vampish on Daisy, a bit pale on Orlok, Teeth for both
Special/ Visual FX	None	Possibly show Daisy's teeth extending as a CGI shot	None

Figure 18 Case Study Script Breakdown

electrical system should generally be able to cope with your lights – but check to see where the sockets are, and check their quality if it's an old pub. If the pub is part of a chain or owned by a brewery, you may need their permission as well. As for the Alleyway, you might get lucky and find that it's nearby – or you may have to travel elsewhere. We found a nicely grotty place, complete with a set of stairs coming up from a basement which looked like they could double for the pub entrance, round the side of a disused church, where we only had to get permission from the local council.

– **When can I do this?** The pub managers/landlords might be willing to let you use the back room in the morning when there's no chance of hiring it out. Best of all would be Sunday morning, as this tends to be the quietest time of all – so long as you don't mind the sound of the cleaners doing their job, and luckily we didn't have much dialogue to worry about. The biggest problem might be blacking out all the windows to hide the fact that it's daytime. The Alleyway location can be shot at night, if enough lighting is available; or you can do what we actually did and shoot day for night, taking advantage of high walls nearby to obscure the sky. And doing this on a Sunday helps make sure the place is quiet.

– **How many people do I need?** Cast and crew are discussed below. Your biggest problem is extras. Some of the shots in the pub seem to need dozens of customers – but getting people to hang around a pub all day, repeating the same things over and over and being bored rigid while the scene is lit isn't easy. You'll need to canvas friends and family and maybe contact the local paper to get them to do a story. However you do it, make sure each one of them signs a release form, and ask for twice as many as you need because you'll get half as many as you ask for.

– **What do I need to find?** Beyond kit (discussed below), much of what's needed might already be in the location. Use your script breakdown as a check-list. Glasses will be there but you'll need some non-alcoholic substitutes to fill them – blackcurrant juice for red wine, apple juice for white wine, cold tea for whisky, ginger beer for champagne, and so on. The biggest prop requirement is vampire teeth, but basic ones that can be fitted on top of normal teeth can be bought for less than £15 ($30) a set (we ordered them from a large fancy-dress supplier on the Internet). Beyond that, it's a matter of how you decide to dress the set, and you can do as little or as much as you like. We went for a somewhat over-the-top red and purple colour scheme, based around a very nice chaise longue which happened to already be in the location.

Schedule

Before The Shoot

- **Preproduction** begins 6 weeks before shoot. First priority: find location, crew & cast.
- **Auditions** 4 weeks before shoot (Level 2 & 3 only).
- **Record Music** Sometime before the shoot.
- **Location Recce** 2 weeks before shoot.
- **Prepare info pack** for everyone involved (maps, schedules, scripts, shotlists, storyboards as necessary): 1 week before the shoot.
- **Article in local paper begging for extras** 1 to 2 weeks before shoot.
- **Kit Pickups** The last weekday before the shoot (Friday).

– **Kit Check** The evening after the pickup (Friday).
– **Rehearsal** The evening before the shoot.

Shoot Day: Sunday

08:00	RDV:	Pub Location 10 Any Street Any Town AN8 7GH CREW & CAST CALL
09:00	SHOOT:	<u>INT. TOILET</u> Scene 2
09:30	EXTRA CALL	
10:00	SHOOT:	<u>INT. TRENDY PUB</u> Scene 1, 2, 5
13:00	LUNCH	
14:00	SHOOT:	<u>INT. TRENDY PUB</u> Continue shooting
15:00	UNIT MOVE TO:	Alleyway Location 10 Any Alley Any Town AN8 6JH
16:00	SHOOT:	<u>EXT. ALLEYWAY</u> Scene 4
19:00	WRAP	

After the Shoot

– **Kit drop-offs** The first weekday after the shoot.
– **Logging** ½ day.
– **Picture Edit** 1 week (level 1 & 2), 2 days (level 3).
– **Final Mix** ½ day.
– **Grading/Online Edit/Mastering** ½ day.

Notes

The timings for this schedule assume that filming is taking place between April and October in the UK, when sunrise and sunset times allow for filming this late. This would be impossible if the sun sets not long after 4pm – a winter shoot would require very different timings. We assume here that you can get into the pub at 8 o'clock. The crew will take at least half an hour to get themselves and the kit in, after which they'll be heading straight to the toilet to set up. Make-up on the characters for the first scene to be shot will take at least an hour, so the Make-Up artist and the actors need to be getting on with this straight away. Meanwhile, the Art Department are getting on with dressing the pub set, something that could easily take a couple of hours.

If the first scene actually starts shooting at 9am, it'll take a good hour or more – it may not be a long scene, but the first scene of the day always takes longer. Extras for subsequent scenes start turning up at 9:30, ready just in case the crew get through the first scene fast. Then it's downstairs to cover the angle towards the door, which needs the least setup and can therefore be done first; after which the camera is turned around to cover the main body of the pub.

Despite the fact that all this only takes a single page in the script, the material for the pub is scheduled to last until 3pm (and that's precisely how long it did take in real life). After this there's a unit move to the alleyway location. The director and actors should travel first so that they can rehearse and block the scene while everyone else is tidying up and packing at the last location. Shooting should recommence at 4pm and continue for another three hours or so. Overall this is a relatively short day at 11 hours (including lunch) – schedules on professional shoots are more likely to be 12 hours.

LIGHTING PLAN

The first major issue is one to resolve during a recce and possibly a visit while the location is open: what lighting is already there and is it useful? The pub may already have some nicely moody lighting intended to look good at night, but that probably means that it won't be bright enough to be useful. The toilet may well have the same issue. At Level 1, the cameras used will probably be able to cope with this level of lighting, but at levels 2 & 3, the cameras involved will likely need a little more.

Lighting in the pub should generally be from overhead, and it might be nice to use 650W fresnels with barn doors closed down and a fair amount of diffuser to create nice soft pools of light, which flatters most people quite nicely. It may be necessary to get something else in like a large kinoflo to add a wash which will raise the overall illumination levels to something the camera can cope with, as well as adding some very soft fill light.

Outside, the lighting will depend on whether you shoot at night or not. If shooting at night, a 2kW Blonde or a 1.2 kW MSR will work as a good key light that throws a lot of dramatic shadows; if shooting day for night, daylight should be enough but a key light placed in a position that helps it act as a backlight may help sell the sense of it being night once the day for night effect is added.

SOUND ISSUES & WILDTRACK LIST

When on recce, take a moment to listen to what the place sounds like when it's (apparently) silent. In the pub, there may well be air conditioning and fridges making small background noise. Ask the owners if these can be switched off for the shoot, but be prepared to live with it if they say no. In the toilet, you may have to be careful to make sure that no one uses the flush, even in the toilets next door, as the plumbing noises can then go on for some time.

Wildtrack	How & Where to record
Dialogue in scenes 1 & 2	While the characters are talking, no dialogue is specified for these scenes as music and background noise are intended to dominate the mix; the actors will ad lib lines, but record them anyway as a guide track just in case it turns out to be useful.
Background pub hubbub	If the pub can be made silent, record with the extras, cast and crew on location.
Mobile ringtone	Record a ringtone from one of the phones. DO NOT use a copyrighted tune, just a range of ordinary ringtones.
Door opening	Get a clean sound of the pub door opening in case it's required to motivate Daisy looking towards the door.
Background toilet hubbub	Record with female cast, crew & extras in the toilet to get the right sound.
Footsteps in scene 4	Should get separate tracks of footsteps (especially Daisy's as she walks away).
Atmos (really, you shouldn't need to list this. It should be automatic)	Just get everyone to shut up. If air conditioning or fridges cannot be switched off, make sure the atmos includes them.

Figure 19 Case Study Wildtrack List

Wildtracks often get left to the last minute, but I recommend planning them out as much as possible because it's all too easy to do a half-arsed job and then find yourself hiring more kit in postproduction to go out and get the sounds anyway. Some issues:

– **Background Music** Unless you're shooting at Level 1 with no chance of distribution, you need original music. A quick, cheap way to get music to sound like it's being played in a pub is to record the sound of it being played in a pub, so it would be a good idea to have the music ready during the shoot (or at least an early version with the same tempo).
– **Hubbub** You'll also need to record general background hubbub without the music; the ability to change the relative levels of every component of the soundtrack is vital, so get your extras to act like they're having fun for a couple of minutes and record the noise.

KIT LIST

Level 1

– **Format**: Consumer – Mini-DV or low-end HDV

'Handycam' size Mini-DV or HDV camera.
Basic tripod (e.g. Velbon D700).
Shure SM58 Dynamic Mic (with a broom handle for boompole if necessary).
Home-made reflector.
Wheelchair for dolly.

Much of this equipment should be your own, easily borrowed, or hired for very small cost. This is the absolute minimum required to accomplish the film – you need a tripod for shots that must be steady, a wheelchair if you want to try a dolly move for scene 5, and most importantly, an external microphone. If your camera can't cope with an external mic input, get another camera.

Level 2

– **Format**: Semiprofessional – High-end Mini-DV, DVCAM, DVCPro, HDV, low end DVCProHD, XDCAM EX

Sony PD170 DVCAM camera or Sony Z1 HDV Camera or Panasonic HVX200 DVCProHD camera.
Wide Angle Adapter.
Sony PVM 9020 Field Monitor or Sony LMD-9030 (which can take a component HD signal if necessary)
Manfrotto Tripod.
Sennheiser 416 Rifle Mic with basic boompole.
Lavalier (tie-clip) mic.
Basic minijack headphones (e.g. Audio Technica).
3× 800W 'Redhead' lights.
2× 2kW 'Blonde' lights (for use if shooting at night)
Lastolite reflector.
Wheelchair for dolly (or build one).

Most of the kit should be sourced from a media centre with some kind of subsidy or discount. These are the best semi-pro cameras you can get. They're still of the smaller size so handheld work will still be shaky. You should be able to get hold of the Sennheiser 416 rifle mic, a top-end piece of kit, but be careful – you've got to keep it pointed directly at the source of the sound. You'll have to plug it directly into the camera, so whoever's doing sound needs to stick close to the camera to keep an eye on levels. The tie-clip mic is there strictly for the wild-tracks of the inside of Sean's pocket – it's the only mic small enough. You can still use a wheelchair dolly, but people with practical skills might try and build one. The lights are pretty basic, but better than nothing.

Level 3

– **Format**: Professional – Betacam SP, DVCAM, DVCPro, DVCPro50, Digital Betacam, DVCProHD, HDCAM

Sony DSR570 16:9 DVCAM Camera (or an equivalent from the other formats), including wide angle lens if possible and if not, a wide angle adapter. Also possible is a lower end DVCProHD camera like the HVX200, but with a lens adapter system like the SG Pro or RedRock, which will allow you to mount cine lenses. If you do this, bear in mind that they will need a lot more light than a standard video lens.

Matte Box & Filter Set.

Professional Vinten or Sachtler tripod (e.g. Vinten Vision 100).

Sennheiser 416 Rifle Mic with Panamic boompole.

Lavalier (tie-clip) mic.

SQN stereo mixer with Bayer DT–100 ¼–inch jack headphones.
Sony PVM 9L2 16:9 Field Monitor or Sony LMD-9050 (which can take HD-SDI).
3× 650W Fresnel lights.
1× 1.2 kW HMI or MSR daylight balanced light.
Lastolite reflector.
Polyboard.
Box of Lighting Grip accessories inc. extra stands.
Basic dolly (e.g. Hague Tracker or 'Wally Dolly,' but bring the wheelchair anyway).

At full price, this kit will be too expensive, but by now you should be able to get onto a production scheme, call in some favours or otherwise manage to get the kit for less. We've moved to full scale professional cameras with almost no automatic functions. The choice of formats is wide – an HD format would be ideal but you may have to settle for what you can afford. The widescreen cameras should all be true 16:9 so proper widescreen is finally possible. The SQN mixer makes more work for the sound recordist but the benefits are more than worth it. The lighting kit is still basic by professional standards but the 1.2kW daylight balanced light is worth its weight in gold; the downside is that you might have to hire it from a professional hire company. You probably can't afford a full-scale professional dolly but you ought to be able to get hold of a semi-pro version from Hague's range, or possibly a Wally Dolly. Track length will be limited, though, so hang on to the wheelchair.

CAST & CREW LIST
Level 1

Director/Producer/Editor/Lighting Camera.
Sound Recordist/Runner.
Runner/Grip.
3× Actors (friends with talent).
Extras: as many as you can get.

This is you and two friends as the crew, the best two actors you know to play Daisy and Orlok, someone who can at least manage the line to play the woman in the toilet, and then all your other friends to play the people in the pub.

Level 2

Director/Producer/Editor.
Assistant Director.
Lighting Camera.
Camera Assistant/Grip.
Sound Recordist.
Runner.
Make-up Artist.
Continuity.
3× Actors (local talent).
Extras: At least 10.

Some of you may have experience working as runners on more professional shoots, so you should be able to act like a real crew with definite roles; the Director and Lighting Camera person should definitely be different people. The Make-up Artist might be professional but probably starting out on his or her career. Actors have been found through local theatre groups, student societies, or by running an audition after an article in the local paper.

Level 3

Director/Producer.
Assistant Director (possibly professional).
Editor (possibly professional).
Lighting Camera (possibly professional).
Camera Assistant/Grip (×2).
Sound Recordist (possibly professional).
Boom Operator.
Runner (×2).
Make-up Artist.
Continuity.
Stills Photographer.
3× Actors: (professional talent).
Extras: 20–30 (if there's enough room in the location).

The main difference, apart from your own growing experience, is that you should be starting to work with professionals in the early stages of their own career, although it's always fun working with grizzled elders if you can – the endless stories of nightmare shoots in the distant past are worth it. You might also be working with an editor for the first time, which is something of a learning curve – your impatience will be the main problem, even though they're probably faster on the keyboard than you are. The actors should be professionals by now.

POSTPRODUCTION ROUTE

Level 1

- **Editing**: iMovie or equivalent free editing software on home computer.
- **Mixing**: Very basic on this kit – you might only have one track to play with.
- **Music**: Raid your music collection.
- **Mastering**: Mastering to file and playing the film out onto Mini-DV.
- **Distribution**: Forget it (well, maybe local film clubs).

Use something you can get for free to see what editing is like, and to realise why more expensive software is better. You'll be capturing via Firewire and going back out the same way as long as your camera is capable – if it isn't, you might need another one, or a small Mini-DV deck.

Level 2

- **Editing**: Premiere/Avid Xpress DV/Final Cut Express on home computer.
- **Mixing**: Multi-track but limited by PC/Mac speakers.

- **Music**: Ask local musicians/composers for something they've already done.
- **Mastering**: Mastering to file, playing out to Mini-DV or close to a professional master onto DVCAM.
- **Distribution**: Local film clubs, some smaller festivals, maybe Internet.

It's amazing what you can do on your home computer – the only limitations are the picture quality you get through Firewire, the speed of the computer, the quality of the speakers and the size of the hard drive.

Level 3

- **Editing**: Avid Media Composer or Final Cut Pro edit suite.
- **Mixing**: Should be pretty good with a decent pair of speakers. Possibly taken out to a professional dubbing suite if you can find a way.
- **Music**: Recorded for you, possibly after the shoot but in this case preferably before.
- **Mastering**: Mastering to file but also a broadcast master on Digibeta or an HD format.
- **Distribution**: Any eligible festivals, Internet, possibly TV.

By now we're working with either professional or near professional equipment. Try and spend some time using the colour correction (grading) facilities, as well as being finicky and perfectionist with the sound (or if you get to work with a dubbing mixer, sit back and watch as they do it all in two hours and make it sound fantastic). If you've shot on a tapeless format, it may even be possible to achieve this level of quality on your own system at home, as you won't need professional tape decks to get hold of the footage – you can just transfer the files.

BUDGET

These figures are rough estimates but it's immediately obvious that Level 1 is more expensive than you might expect. There are lots of little costs in filmmaking which

PREPRODUCTION	Level 1	Level 2	Level 3
Camera Hire for Audition	-	£25 ($50)	£25 ($50)
Room Hire for Audition	-	£50 ($100)	£50 ($100)
Tape for Audition	-	£5 ($10)	£5 ($10)
Phones & Fax	-	-	-
Photocopying & Printing	£20 ($40)	£20 ($40)	£20 ($40)
Postage		£5 ($10)	£10 ($20)
PRODUCTION	**Level 1**	**Level 2**	**Level 3**
Catering	£30 ($60)	£40 ($80)	£50 ($100)
Cast/Crew transport	£10 ($20)	£30 ($60)	£100 ($200)
Van/Car Hire	-	-	£100 ($200)
Accommodation	-	-	£100 ($200)
Location Fee	-	-	£50 ($100)
Props & Set Dressing	£20 ($40)	£40 ($80)	£100 ($200)
Tea, Coffee, Munchies	£10 ($20)	£20 ($40)	£30 ($60)
General Supplies	£10 ($20)	£25 ($50)	£25 ($50)
Tape Stock (2 hrs)	£10 ($20)	£25 ($50)	£40 ($80)
Rough Kit Cost	£30 ($60)	£150 ($300)	£400 ($800)
Professional Actor Fee (x2)	-	-	£100 ($200)
POSTPRODUCTION	**Level 1**	**Level 2**	**Level 3**
Online Suite Hire	-	-	£200 ($400)
Transfers	-	-	£20 ($40)
Tape Stock for Mastering	-	£10 ($20)	£10 ($20)
Making Distribution Copies	£20 ($40)	£50 ($100)	£50 ($100)
TOTALS	**£160 ($320)**	**£495 ($990)**	**£1,485 ($2,970)**

Figure 20 Case Study Budget

add up – catering, photocopying, general supplies etc. Level 2 falls happily into the microbudget bracket but a good producer really ought to be able to get this for less. Level 3 is very much not in the microbudget league but only because I've thrown in rough prices for almost everything. Many of these costs can be reduced or eliminated – you should still be able to get the location and actors for free, van hire might not be necessary if there are cars available, kit might be found for a lot less, you might be able to get a free online suite – the list is endless. Just be ready for the unexpected extra costs which can easily push the budget over the edge...

AFTERWORD: THE TWELVE MOST COMMON MICROBUDGET MISTAKES

I've been positive and helpful and even diplomatic up until now, but just like a politician, I'm about to go negative. So if you're likely to be discouraged by a brief rant, maybe you shouldn't read this section just yet. In my experience, no amount of advice will prevent a filmmaker from making these errors. So go away and make a few films and then come back...

1: Bad Script

Bad scripts alone could fill this section. Some of the worst mistakes:

– **Not Enough Drafts** If you really think you've spent enough time writing your script, then you really ought to be doing another couple of drafts. Changing a few lines of dialogue here and there does not, repeat, NOT constitute a new draft.

- **Not Visual** Why do so many films consist of people speaking to each other without anything visual happening? Or indeed, anything happening at all? Dialogue is often an excuse to avoid telling a story – there ought to be a law forcing all filmmakers to make a film without it to teach them what film actually is. If you can turn the pictures off and still understand what's going on, it's not film – it's radio. There's nothing wrong with radio, but why did you waste all that effort making a film?

- **No Beginning, No End** Also annoying: a film that's halfway through before anything really happens, and/or ends halfway before you actually get to the credits. If the audience have to sit through ages of nonsense after a good ending, they'll forget there was a good ending. And they might not get that far if they have to sit through endless minutes of people introducing themselves and setting up the story.

- **Exposition** One of the hardest things to get right. Try too hard and the audience will feel patronised. Don't try hard enough and they'll be confused. Put yourself in their heads and think: what do they know? What might they have worked out by now? And don't think that putting something on the screen means the audience have actually noticed it. They're watching the actors, not the tiny detail on the wall behind them that makes sense of the film.

- **Symbolism** Avoid. Anyone who spots obvious

symbolism in a movie has stopped watching the movie so they can start watching out for symbolism.

- **Plagiarism** The most depressing thing: a whole film blatantly copied from someone's favourite bit of their favourite film because it's, like, cool. If you must make a copy of someone else's film for the sake of practice, please don't ask anyone else to watch it.

2: Bad Planning

Advice for planning: Be paranoid. Be very paranoid.

- **Mobility** Make sure there's someone on the shoot with a car who can run off and get things if necessary – NOT someone you need to keep shooting.
- **Tell the police** what you're doing if it's likely to look illegal or dangerous to even the most demented halfwit. Stopping the shoot while the Armed Response Unit search your house from top to bottom is a good way to wreck your shoot and your crew's confidence in you.
- **Catering** Feed your cast and crew properly or get ready for mutiny. Make sure food and drink is available and as varied as possible from day to day.
- **Check your kit** before you use it. Even professional hire companies screw up and forget to include things – such as the tripod plate that means the tripod is useless and you can't do any of your planned shots.
- **Weather Cover** Think of something you can do when it rains or else you'll be sitting around losing any chance of finishing your film.

- **Legal Cover** If there's even the remotest possibility that the film will be distributed, make sure that everyone recognisable on screen has signed a release form, that professional actors have signed a contract, and that you have written permission to use the music in your film. If you don't, you'll end up either falling out with people you thought you had a verbal agreement with, or pursued by agents and lawyers looking to make money out of you because you haven't covered yourself.
- **Over-optimism** The biggest problem is over-optimistic scheduling. Allow more time than you think you'll need – if there isn't enough time, then plan to shoot less. Less footage is better than crap footage you can't use.

3: Bad Camerawork

- **Auto Hell** Autofocus, autoaperture, gain and digital zoom all look amateurish. Play with them to see why they degrade the image or do odd things in the middle of takes, and then say goodbye forever.
- **Handheld Camerawork** Handycam–sized cameras can look horribly shaky compared to a weighty professional or semipro camera, but a lot of microbudget filmmakers handhold as the default rather than as a carefully considered option. The default should always be the tripod – get hold of one and learn to use it. If you have to handhold, hold it close to your body for maximum stability and rehearse the movement thoroughly.

- **Composition** shouldn't just be the first random thing you choose – take care to plan your images, vary the shot sizes, and please, please, please, learn about headroom.
- **Clean the Lens Regularly** or you'll find that the most striking feature of your film is the massive thumbprint halfway across the screen that you couldn't even see when you were shooting.
- **Whoops! There's the Crew!** Any reflective surface can reveal you and your friends if you're not careful. And of course there's the boom – make sure your sound recordist is asking for framelines. And if there's a tally light on your camera, switch it off or it'll be in your film, reflected from any surface covered in gloss paint.
- **The Technology Trap** Just because the camera or the format is new and they've managed to shrink the thing into a tiny space, doesn't mean it's better. DV and HDV cameras are cheap and reliable but they do not give the same results as better formats, no matter how new they are and how many bells and whistles they have. It may be wiser to use an older but more professional format – even an old Beta SP analogue camera – as the professional controls will force you to pay more attention to what you're doing and learn more about the basic concepts of camerawork.

4: Bad Lighting

The main problem is that beginners generally don't light anything, relying on the magic of technology to do it for them. They end up with flat, underexposed, grotty images that make the audience think they're watching a holiday video, or hideously overexposed images with no detail left in them. Get used to using ND and a reflector to deal with the enormous contrast range in sunlit exteriors. What really shows up an amateur is lighting discontinuity – a cut to a different shot size of the same subject ought to look at least roughly the same. This can be difficult in exteriors because the sun has a nasty habit of moving – so take a compass with you on recce and plan your setups around the movements of the sun.

5: Bad Sound

There's nothing quite as disastrous as bad sound, especially on a film that's otherwise accomplished. Sometimes this is because the filmmaker thought the onboard mic could do the job of an experienced sound recordist with thousands of pounds of professional equipment, and sometimes because they thought that mixing was as simple as putting one sound on top of another. And don't use copyrighted music you can't afford. There's just no point.

6: Bad Continuity

Even the professionals screw up from time to time. But that's no excuse for you to do so, particularly when some continuity errors are so common:

- **Reverse Angle** You need to be very careful about placement of objects between characters in reverse angles. It may not be immediately obvious when you're shooting but it'll jump out of the screen when you edit – where was that candle meant to be? Whoops…
- **Glasses** Actors don't always remember to put them back on when they come back from a break, and you absolutely cannot have glasses disappearing and reappearing on someone's face in the middle of a scene.
- **Background** If you have any kind of complex background (or foreground) clutter, take a snap of it so you can reconstruct it if any of it falls over, gets knocked about or otherwise tries to make itself teleport around from shot to shot.
- **Make-up** Especially special effects make-up – where exactly was that bloodstain meant to be? Take a photo!
- **Cigarettes & Drinks** Getting this right can be almost impossible sometimes. Make sure someone knows what level the glass has to be refilled to between takes, and have lots of cigarettes available so you can use fresh ones and keep continuity roughly correct.
- **Clocks** Yep, you're going to have to reset them at the beginning of each take. Or find one without a second hand which can just sit there and not move – better than having it jump around all over the place.

7: Cheapo Special Effects

The audience is used to Hollywood and anything less looks at best distracting and at worst pathetic. The very worst offender is over-ambitious CGI. If it's bad, it's awful; and if it's good, it'll show up the other flaws in your work because it takes so long to do that you'll almost certainly have skimped on something else that was far more important.

There's one exception: comedy. Cheap special effects can be hilarious if your film is meant to be funny (especially in horror films). But sadly, lots of serious films end up becoming funny without meaning to.

8: Not Enough Coverage

I've sat through too many films where the camera stayed locked on one angle, not because it was artistically right but because there was no other take the editor could use. A master angle of a scene isn't enough – unless it's utterly exceptional, the audience will be bored to death within a minute or two. Long takes covering an entire scene can sometimes be amazing, but you must shoot basic coverage as a back-up and learn how to schedule it with enough time to get all the shots you need. Some people spend all their time trying to get a perfect master with perfect performances and then find they haven't enough time left to do singles and cutaways. The master is usually only on screen for a tiny portion of the overall scene, and if you can cut away, you don't need a continuous master –

just use bits and pieces from what you have.

9: Title & Credit Limbo

It's possible to doom your film before it starts. Welcome to the endless limbo of the title sequence that runs on forever so the amateur filmmaker can put in all those bits and pieces they've seen on the front of Hollywood films; this does nothing but inform the audience they're in the presence of an idiot. You're making a short film, so keep it short! Get the title up on the screen, leave it there long enough for the audience to settle down, then get on with the story. And please bear in mind the horrible truth about credits: nobody cares except the people who already knew their name was going to be in there. Keep it down to thirty seconds or less.

10: Out-Takes & Behind the Scenes

Filmmaking is a great laugh. But really, you had to be there. Most short films aren't in production long enough to generate the truly exceptional moments of unintended comedy that are worthy of a decent gag reel, so don't inflict what little you have on the audience. The same goes for the dreaded behind-the-scenes video: if you absolutely have to do one, do it for distribution to cast and crew only. As every extra in the history of cinema has discovered, watching a film being made is the most tedious pastime imaginable.

11: It's Not Quite Finished Yet...

Development Hell is bad enough, but Postproduction Limbo is worse. If you don't plan out everything about your edit, sound mix, effects, music and mastering, you'll find yourself six months, nine months, even a year down the line and still with an unfinished film. Thankfully, most films that get stuck like this won't be inflicted on an audience until the hallowed day in the distant future when they're finally finished (probably both badly and expensively), but be warned: if you leave postproduction until after the shoot, you'll get what you deserve.

12: Arrogance

Out of all these sins, the worst – and in fact, the cause of many of them – is arrogance. Self-belief is vital to getting your film made, but self-belief without experience to back it up often steps over the line into arrogance. And arrogance renders impossible the main reason for making short films: to learn. It commonly comes in two flavours...

– **I'm Going to Hollywood!** Parroting the language and mannerisms you've observed in behind-the-scenes videos and DVD commentaries won't help. Nor is it a good idea to defend to the death a dumb idea because Kubrick or Spielberg or Tarantino did something similar. You can't compare your work to them because a) they don't show the films (and the mistakes) they made at your level which taught them how to make correct choices, and b) if their first film was apparently one of genius, they had long histories of working in the industry or accomplishment in another field or – since we're talking features – they were forced to rely on an experienced crew pointing out where they were going wrong. It's fine to aspire to the quality of your favourite director, but you must exercise judgement in doing so. What was right for them in one situation may well be dead wrong for you in another.

- **I'm an Artist!** Many filmmakers have a burning desire to express themselves but also, it seems, utter contempt for the audience. The shocking and unacceptable truth is that the audience is not guaranteed to be interested in your work just because you feel the need to express yourself. This doesn't mean you should be pandering to the audience and making only that which is absolutely commercial, but you must bear in mind that there is such a thing as an audience, even if it's a very small one. Please don't assume that you have the inalienable right to impose your 'vision' on them or you'll find them exercising their inalienable right to ignore you and your film.

Which only goes to show there's no one as zealous as a reformed offender. I've made all (well, most) of these mistakes and more than enough films suitable only for landfill. But even more sad and depressing than a badly made film is a film that was never made at all. If you never get round to it, if you're afraid of failure, if you constantly keep filmmaking in the back of your mind as something you'd like to do if only you had the time, then you won't even get to make the mistakes which might teach you how to be a good filmmaker. And you'll miss out on an awful lot of fun. So get on with it!

References

These lists of information can never be entirely complete, but were as accurate as I could get them at the time of writing.

MEDIA CENTRES/WORKSHOPS

Some of these are community initiatives, some are dedicated to high-end training, some are a bit like art galleries, some see film and video as only a tiny part of what they do – the only common thread is they've got some kit they might be willing to hire and/or teach you to use. Alternatively, many local colleges have equipment and training programmes (but there are way too many to list here).

BELFAST: Northern Visions, 4 Lower Donegall Street Place, Belfast BT1 2FN tel: 028 9024 5495 fax: 028 9032 6608 web: www.northernvisions.org

BIRMINGHAM: Vivid, 140 Heath Mill Lane, Birmingham B9 4AR tel: 0121 766 7876 fax: 0871 251 0747 web: www.vivid.org.uk

BRIDGWATER: Somerset Film & Video, The Engine Room, 52 High Street, Bridgwater, Somerset TA6 3BL tel: 01278 433187 fax: 01278 433172 web: www.somersetfilm.com

BRIGHTON: Lighthouse, 1, Zone B, 28 Kensington Street, Brighton BN1 4AJ tel: 01273 647197 web: www.lighthouse.co.uk

BRISTOL: Picture This Moving Image, 40 Sydney Row, Bristol BS1 6UU tel: 0117 925 7010 fax: 0117 925 7040 web: www.picture-this.co.uk

COLCHESTER: Signals Media Arts, Victoria Chambers, St Runwald St, Colchester, CO1 1HF tel: 01206 560255 web: www.signals.org.uk

COVENTRY: Herbert Media, Herbert Art Gallery & Museum, Jordan Well, Coventry CV1 5QP tel: 024 7683 2310 web: www.theherbert.org/herbertmedia

DERRY: Nerve Centre, 7–8 Magazine St, Derry BT48 6HJ tel: 028 7126 0562 fax: 028 7137 1738 web: www.nerve-centre.org.uk

EDINBURGH: Pilton Video, 30 Ferry Road Avenue, Edinburgh EH4 4BA tel: 0131 343 1151 Fax: 0131 343 2820 web: www.piltonvideo.org

EXETER: Exeter Phoenix New Media Centre, Bradninch Place, Gandy Street, Exeter EX4 3LS tel: 01392 667080 web: www.phoenixmedia.org.uk

GLASGOW: Glasgow Media Access Centre (GMAC), 3rd Floor, 34 Albion Street, Merchant City, Glasgow G1 1LH tel: 0141 553 2620 fax: 0141 553 2660 web: www.g-mac.co.uk

HEREFORD: Rural Media Company, Sullivan House, 72–80 Widemarsh Street, Hereford HR4 9HG tel: 01432 344039 fax: 01432 270539 web: www.ruralmedia.co.uk

KIRKCALDY: Mimac-Rushes, Suite 20-22, The Round House, Priory Campus, Karkcaldy KY1 2QT

LEICESTER: Line Out, Fosse Neighbourhood Centre, Mantle Road, Leicester LE3 5HG tel: 0116 262 1265 web: www.lineout.org

LIVERPOOL: Mersey Film and Video, 13–15 Hope Street, Liverpool L1 9BQ tel: 0151 708 5259 fax: 0151 707 8595 web: www.mersey-film-video.co.uk

LONDON: Connections Communications Centre, Palingswick House, 241 King Street, London W6 9LP tel: 020 8741 1766 fax: 020 8563 9134 web: www. cccmedia.co.uk

Four Corners, 121 Roman Road, Bethnal Green, London E2 OQN tel: 020 8981 6111 web: www.fourcornersfilm.co.uk

VET (Video Engineering & Training), Lux Building 2–4 Hoxton Square, London N1 6US tel: 020 7505 4700 fax: 020 7505 4800 web: www.vet.co.uk

London Film Academy, The Old Church, 52a Walham Grove, London SW6 1QR tel: 020 7386 7711 fax: 020 7381 6116 web: www.londonfilmacademy.com

MANCHESTER: WFA Media And Cultural Centre, 9 Lucy Street, Manchester M15 4BX tel: 0161 848 9782/5 fax: 0161 848 9783 web: www.wfamedia.co.uk

NOTTINGHAM: Intermedia Film and Video, 19 Heathcoat Street, Nottingham NG1 3AF tel: 0115 955 6909 fax: 0115 955 9956 web: www.intermedianotts.co.uk

Broadway, 14–18 Broad Street, Hockley, Nottingham NG1 3AL tel: 0115 952 6611 web: www.broadway.org.uk

OXFORD: Oxford Film & Video Makers, 54 Catherine Street, Oxford OX4 3AH tel: 01865 792732 web: www.ofvm.org

SHEFFIELD: Sheffield Independent Film, 5 Brown Street, Sheffield S1 2BS tel: 0114 272 0304 fax: 0114 249 2293 web: www.sifmedia.org.uk

SWINDON: Create Studios, The Wyvern Theatre, Theatre Square, Swindon, Wiltshire SN1 1QN tel: 01793 465399 fax: 01793 480278 web: www.createstudios.org.uk

SOUTHAMPTON: City Eye, Swaythling Neighbourhood Centre, Broadlands Road, Southampton SO17 3AT tel: 023 8067 7167 web: www.city-eye.co.uk

WOLVERHAMPTON: Light House, The Chubb Buildings, Fryer St, Wolverhampton WV1 1HT tel: 01902 716055 fax: 01902 717143 web: www.light-house.co.uk

REGIONAL/NATIONAL SCREEN AGENCIES

As well as a vital source of information, these organisations administer Film Council and local production schemes. There are also a number of local film offices for smaller regions and individual towns and cities.

EAST OF ENGLAND (Bedfordshire, Cambridgeshire, Essex, Hertfordshire, Norfolk, Suffolk): **Screen East**, 2 Millennium Plain, Norwich, Norfolk NR2 1TF tel: 01603 776920 fax: 01603 767191 web: www.screeneast.co.uk

EAST MIDLANDS (Derbyshire, Leicestershire, Lincolnshire, Northamptonshire, Nottinghamshire, Rutland): **EM Media**, 35–37 St. Mary's Gate, Nottingham NG1 1PU tel: 0115 934 9090 fax: 0115 950 0988 web: www.em-media.org.uk

ISLE OF MAN: Isle of Man Film, First Floor, Hamilton House, Peel Road, Douglas, Isle of Man IM1 5EP tel: 01624 687173 fax: 01624 687171 web: www.gov.im/dti/iomfilm/

LONDON: Film London, Suite 6.10, The Tea Building, 56 Shoreditch High Street, London E1 6JJ tel: 020 7613 7676 fax: 020 7613 7677 web: www.filmlondon.org.uk

NORTHERN IRELAND: Northern Ireland Screen, Alfred House, 21 Alfred Street, Belfast BT2 8ED tel: 028 9023 2444 fax: 028 9023 9918 web: www.northernirelandscreen.co.uk

NORTH OF ENGLAND (Tyne & Wear, Northumberland, County Durham, Tees Valley): **Northern Film & Media**, Central Square, Forth Street, Newcastle-upon-Tyne NE1 3PJ tel: 0191 269 9200 fax: 0191 269 9213 web: www.northernmedia.org

NORTH WEST OF ENGLAND (Lancashire, Greater Manchester, Merseyside, Cheshire, Cumbria): **North West Vision**, BBC, Oxford Road, Manchester M60 1SJ tel: 0870 609 4481 web: www.northwestvision.co.uk

SCOTLAND: Scottish Screen, 249 West George Street, Glasgow G2 4QE tel: 0845 300 7300 web: www.scottishscreen.com

SOUTH OF ENGLAND (Kent, Buckinghamshire, Oxfordshire, Hampshire, Surrey, Berkshire, East/West Sussex, Isle of Wight, Channel Islands): **Screen South**, The Wedge, 75–81 Tontine Street, Folkestone, Kent CT20 1JR tel: 01303 259777 fax: 01303 259786 web: www.screensouth.co.uk

SOUTH WEST OF ENGLAND (Gloucestershire, Wiltshire, Bristol, Somerset, Dorset, Devon, Cornwall): **South West Screen**, St. Bartholomews Court, Lewins Mead, Bristol BS1 5BT tel: 0117 952 9977 fax: 0117 952 9988 web: www.swscreen.co.uk

WALES: Film Agency for Wales, Suite 7, 33–35 West Bute Street, Cardiff CF10 5LH tel: 029 2046 7480 fax: 029 2046 7481 web: www.filmagencywales.com

WEST MIDLANDS (Herefordshire, Staffordshire, Shropshire, Birmingham & West Midlands, Warwickshire, Worcestershire, Telford & The Wrekin): **Screen West Midlands**, 9 Regent Place, Birmingham B1 3NJ tel: 0121 265 7120 fax: 0121 265 7180 web: www.screenwm.co.uk

YORKSHIRE (Humberside, North/South/West Yorkshire): **Screen Yorkshire**, Studio 22, 46 The Calls, Leeds LS2 7EY tel: 0113 294 4410 fax: 0113 294 web: www.screenyorkshire.co.uk

OTHER ORGANISATIONS

Dazzle, Unit P102, Penn Street Studio, 23–28 Penn Street, Hoxton, London N1 5DL tel: 020 7739 7716 web: www.dazzlefilms.co.uk – Short film distributors

Institute of Amateur Cinematographers (IAC), 24c West Street, Epsom, Surrey KT18 7RJ tel: 01372 739672 fax: 01372 741057 web: www.theiac.org.uk – Established way back in the 1930s but still going strong.

Mechanical Copyright Protection Society (MCPS) Media Licensing, Copyright House, 29/33 Berners St, London W1T 3AB tel: 020 7306 4500 fax: 020 7306 4380 web: www.mcps-prs-alliance.co.uk – The MCPS now prefer enquiries about music use to be made via the Internet rather than the phone.

New Producers' Alliance (NPA), Unit 7.03 The TEA Building, 56 Shoreditch High Street, London W1RP 7PJ tel: 020 7613 0440 web: www.npa.org.uk – Independent producers' organisation.

Onedotzero, Unit 212c Curtain House, 134–146 Curtain Road, London EC2A 3AR web: www.onedotzero.com – Onedotzero distribute short films, among many other things.

Raindance, 81 Berwick Street, London W1F 8TW tel: 020 7287 3833 fax: 020 7439 2243 web: www.raindance.co.uk – A film festival plus shedloads of courses and useful info.

The Script Factory, The Square, 61 Frith Street, London W1D 3JL tel: 020 7851 4890 fax: 020 7851 4858 www.scriptfactory.co.uk – Training, support, competitions and more for screenwriters.

Shorts International Ltd, 25 Beak Street, London W1F 9RT tel: 020 7734 2277 fax: 020 7734 2242 web: www.britshorts.com – Short film distributors ready to take submissions.

UK Film Council, 10 Little Portland Street, London W1W 7JG tel: 020 7861 7861 fax: 020 7861 7862 web: www.ukfilmcouncil.org.uk

Women In Film & Television, 4th Floor, Unit 2 Wedgwood Mews, 12–13 Greek Street, London W1D 4BB tel: 020 7287 1400 fax: 020 7287 1500 web: www.wftv.org.uk

WEBSITES

BBC Training – www.bbctraining.com – Contains a

number of online training resources you can use for free.

BBC Film Network – wwwbbc.co.uk/network – Short films to watch, filmmaking guides, articles and all kinds of other useful stuff.

BFI – www.bfi.org.uk – The BFI handbook (a directory of media organisations and useful contacts) is now available online at the BFI website.

Britfilms – www.britfilms.com – A site run by the British Council which has listings of many British shorts, a search engine for the UK film industry and a directory of international film festivals.

Current TV – www.current.com – A TV channel with online presence that looks for content from us lot; more about documentary than drama, though.

Icewhole – www.icewhole.com – Filmmaker social networking site with prizes for the best films.

Mandy – www.mandy.com – Online advertising for cast, crew, used equipment and all sorts of stuff.

Netribition Film Network – www.netribution. co.uk – News and stuff for filmmakers.

PCR – www.pcrnewsletter.com – Casting newsletter now available online. Placing casting ads is free.

The Screenwriter's Store – www.thescreenwritersstore.com – lots of good books, and useful info on screenwriting.

Shooting People – www.shootingpeople.org – Email newsletters for filmmakers, plus huge amounts of online resources. Annual subscription required but well worth it.

Short Film Depot – www.shortfilmdepot.com – An online film festival entry service that specialises in short films.

Spotlight – www.spotlight.com – UK actor's directory. Here you can find details of any actor's agent, but it costs to find out any more.

Talent Circle – www.talentcircle.co.uk – Another place to put ads for cast and crew.

TwelvePoint – www.twelvepoint.com – ScriptWriter magazine, long a source of excellent articles on the subject of screenwriting, has recently abandoned the world of print and goes online as TwelvePoint.com, making it cheaper and adding forums for screenwriters.

Withoutabox – www.withoutabox.com – Online application service for many film festivals. Saves having to fill in what seems like the same form over and over again.

PERIODICALS

Broadcast, Emap Communications, Greater London House, Hampstead Road, London NW1 7EJ web: www.broadcastnow.co.uk – Weekly journal of the UK television industry.

Micro Mart, Dennis Publishing Ltd, 30 Cleveland Street, London W1T 4JD tel 020 7907 6000 fax: 020 7901 6020 web: www.micromart.co.uk – Best place to find ads for cheap computers so you can put together an affordable edit suite.

Screen International, Emap Communications, Greater London House, Hampstead Road, London NW1 7EJ web: www.screendaily.com – Weekly journal of the international film industry.

BOOKS

Adventures in the Screen Trade by William Goldman, Abacus, 1996, 432 pages, ISBN 034910705X – Goldman tells the tale of his life in films and the lowly status that writers have to live with. A great read, though not a technical screenwriting book.

The DV Rebel's Guide by Stu Maschwitz, Peachpit Press, 2007, 320 pages, ISBN 0321413644 – Another great guide to filmmaking, especially for those of you who want to make action films.

Media 08 by Janine Gibson, Guardian Newspapers Ltd, 2008, 544 pages, ISBN 0852650914 – The Guardian's yearly contacts book for everything to do with the media and journalism. Also contains the official contact info for everything in the UK (and much of what lies beyond).

The Guerrilla Film Makers' Handbook (3rd Edition) by Chris Jones & Genevieve Jolliffe, Continuum Publishing Group, 2006, 756 pages, ISBN 082647988X web: www.livingspirit.com – Pretty much everything you need to know about making a feature film, although most of it is applicable to shorts as well.

How to Make Money Scriptwriting (2nd Edition), by Julian Friedmann, Intellect Books, 2000, 224 pages, ISBN 184150002X – About the only book on the British screenwriting market, with some interesting observations on the craft of writing.

Rebel Without a Crew by Robert Rodriguez, Faber and Faber, 1996, 296 pages, ISBN 057117891X – Rodriguez' diaries from the production of *El Mariachi* (made with $7,000 and shot in a little town in Mexico) and what followed. Includes a Ten-minute Film School.

Screenplay by Syd Field, Delta, 2005, 336 pages, ISBN 0385339038 – An excellent examination of the screenwriter's craft, though a little dogmatic about the three-act structure and Hollywood style.

Story by Robert McKee, Methuen Publishing Company, 1999, 480 pages, ISBN 0413715604 – About the most comprehensive and yet the most flexible explanation of how stories work that I know of.

GLOSSARY

1080 – 1920×1080 **HD**. The larger of the two HD screen sizes. Sometimes written as 1080p or 1080i, depending on whether it is **Interlaced** or **Progressive**. See **720**.

14:9 – A compromise **Widescreen** format used because broadcasters fear that viewers might find **16:9** annoying when **Letterboxed**. Created by chopping the sides off a 16:9 image.

16:9 – The **Widescreen** ratio adopted for video. See **4:3**, **Aspect Ratio**, **CCD**, **Fullscreen**, **Letterboxing**, **Anamorphic**.

180° Rule – A fundamental rule of camerawork and editing. You must not cut to a point on the other side of an imaginary line between two characters. AKA **Crossing the Line**.

24p – Short for 24 **FPS**, **Progressive** scan video (used to mimic film, especially in **HD** formats). 25p and 30p are also possible.

2K – (1) A screen size used for projecting Digital Cinema. Slightly larger than the more standard **1080 HD** screen size. Actual number of pixels varies according to **Aspect Ratio**. (2) A 2 kW light, AKA **Blonde**.

2-Machine Suite – A **Linear Editing** suite with two VCRs: a player and recorder. It cannot perform **Transitions** like **Fades** and **Wipes**.

2-Shot – A shot with two people in the **Frame**.

360° – A lighting setup which allows filming in every direction. Very difficult and time-consuming.

3CCD – See **CCD**.

3-Machine Suite – A **Linear Editing** suite with three VCRs: two players and a recorder. It can perform **Transitions** like **Fades** and **Wipes**.

4:2:2, 4:2:0, 4:1:1, 4:4:4:4 – See **Sample Rate**.

4:3 – The standard frame ratio of normal TVs, sometimes called **Fullscreen** and equivalent to the Academy frame of film. See **16:9**, **Aspect Ratio**, **CCD**, **Widescreen**, **Letterboxing**, **Anamorphic**, **Academy**.

4K – a very large screen size, much larger than standard **HD** screen sizes. Considered to be roughly equivalent in quality to 35mm film. Actual number of pixels varies according to **Aspect Ratio**.

720 – 1280×720 **HD**. The smaller of the two standard HD screen sizes. Sometimes written as 720p or 720i, depending on whether it is **Interlaced** or **Progressive**. See **1080**.

8mm – A defunct **SD** semiprofessional **Analogue** tape format which was indeed 8mm wide. Replaced by **Hi8** and then **Digital 8**.

Academy – The standard **Aspect Ratio** of 4:3, as defined by the Academy of Motion Picture Arts And Sciences (yes, *that* one). This was later used for TV, and described as **4:3** or **Fullscreen**.

AD – See **Assistant Director**.

ADC – Analogue to Digital Converter. A device which turns an **Analogue** signal into a **Digital** one. See **DAC**.

ADR – Automated Dialogue Replacement. A system of re-recording dialogue in **Postproduction** if the original dialogue is faulty.

AIFF-C – Audio Interchange File Format-Condensed. An audio file format without **Compression** which uses the file extension .aif. Sometimes used to encode and interleave audio within a video file. See **MP3** and **WAV**.

Alpha Channel – An extra layer of video which provides information on how transparent the video signal should be. Often saved within an **AVI** or **Quicktime** file, and sometimes used as part of a **High Definition** signal.

Analogue – Any recording system which records video or audio as waveforms. Subject to **Generation Loss**. Only a few **SD** analogue formats are still in use. See also **Digital**.

Anamorphic – An anamorphic process, electronic or optical, squeezes a **Widescreen** image into a **Fullscreen** shape, and unsqueezes it later. When squeezed, people and objects seem very tall and thin.

Angle – A Camera Angle. See **Setup**.

Animatic – An animated **Storyboard** using the images from the original storyboard and limited sound. Mostly used for complicated action sequences and **CGI**. Compare to **Video Storyboard**.

Aperture – AKA **Iris**. The opening between the **Lens** and the receptors (**CCD**s), which is used to control how much light is coming into the camera (the **Exposure**). Also affects **Depth of Field**. See **F-Stop**.

Artifact – a glitch in **Digital** video created by **Compression**. See **Codec, Cascading Codec**. Compare to **Dropout**.

Aspect Ratio – The ratio of the horizontal edge of the screen to the vertical edge – e.g. a standard **Fullscreen** TV is **4:3**, and a **Widescreen** TV is **16:9**. See **CCD, Anamorphic**.

Assemble Editing – A form of **Linear Editing** which does not use a **Control Track**. Shots can only be laid down one after another.

Assistant Director – AKA **AD**; Member of the crew responsible for running the set. On more professional productions, the job is divided into three: the **First** AD is in overall charge, the **Second** AD is off-set making arrangements for the next day of filming, and the **Third** AD is the First's second in command.

Atmos – Background noise recorded to assist continuity when mixing the soundtrack. AKA **Room Tone, Buzz Track**. Compare to **Wildtrack**.

Audio Scrub – A feature on **Non-Linear Editing** systems which allows audio to be monitored as a pointer is dragged across the **Timeline**.

Auteur Theory – A major source of arrogance and stupidity among filmmakers. Originally created by enterprising critics so they could get jobs as directors.

Authoring – The process of creating a **DVD**. Not to be confused with **Mastering**.

Autofocus – A feature on a camera which automatically adjusts the focus. Can be very unpredictable and problematic to use for drama, and doesn't work at all in some lighting conditions.

Available Light – Light sources already available in a location, e.g. the sun or street lamps.

AVCHD – Advanced Video Codec High Definition, a consumer/semipro **HD** video format comparable to **HDV** in terms of quality, but with better compression and lower data rates. Originally designed for optical disc recording (compare to **XDCAM**), but now also record-able on hard drives and memory cards. Discs can be played back on **Blu-Ray** players.

AVC Intra – A version of **DVCProHD** which records **1080p** at a 1:1 **Pixel Aspect Ratio** onto **P2** cards, and therefore is of better quality than **HDCAM**, which it is intended to compete against.

AVI – A video file format which can also contain audio, using the file extension .avi. Can be either compressed or uncompressed depending upon the choice of **Codec**. See also **Quicktime**, **MPEG**.

Back Light – AKA **Hair Light**. A light shining from behind the subject. An element of **Three-Point Lighting**.

Background Action – (1) The actions of extras. (2) A **Cue** given to extras to begin their performance before the cast.

Background Music – Music in a scene that can be heard by characters. See **Featured Music, Diegetic Sound**.

Balanced Leads – Balanced audio leads (**XLR**s, AKA **Cannons**) are protected against unwanted radio interference. **Unbalanced** audio leads (**Phonos**, **Jacks**, **Minijacks**) are vulnerable over distances of a few metres or more.

Ballast – A power transformer that comes with a **Daylight Balanced Light** such as an **HMI** or **MSR**.

Bantam – A higher quality version of a **Jack** (incompatible with standard jacks) sometimes used in audio **Patch Bays**.

Barn Doors – The flaps on the front of a light which can be used to cut down or control light, and also to hang **Gels** or **Diffusers** from.

Barney – A light camera covering which protects from rain and minimises camera noise.

Bars & Tone – **Colour Bars** and 1kHz **Tone**, recorded at the beginning of camera tapes so that an edit suite can be properly calibrated to correctly interpret your footage, and as something to fill up the less reliable beginning of a tape.

Also used in **Mastering** so another edit suite or broadcast equipment can be calibrated to match your film.

Batch Digitising – AKA Batch Capture. A process on **Non-Linear Editing** systems in which the computer automatically digitises footage based upon logging information.

Bazooka – A column often found on a **Dolly** which is topped by a **Bowl** into which a **Head** can be mounted. A source of great hilarity when passing through customs.

BCU – Big Close-Up. A shot size that shows the middle portion of the face.

Best Boy – On professional productions, the **Gaffer**'s second in command.

Beta – Short for **Betacam SP**.

Betacam – An obsolete **SD** professional **Analogue** tape format which used the same basic tape size as the unfortunate Betamax consumer format.

Betacam SP – The standard **SD** professional **Analogue** tape format, still in use though gradually being replaced. An improvement over the original **Betacam**; 'SP' stands for Superior Performance. Digital replacements: **Betacam SX** and **Digital Betacam**.

Betacam SX – A professional **Digital SD** tape format which uses **MPEG**–2 compression to give a very low data rate but relatively high quality; nevertheless, overall quality is lower than **Digibeta**, which was already on the market when SX was launched.

Bin – A folder in a **Non-Linear Editing** program which contains **Clips** and **Subclips**.

Birdie – A small 12V quartz lamp with a bulb of low wattage e.g. 50W, 75W, 100W. Used mainly for small highlights.

BITC – Burnt-In TimeCode. A **Timecode** display on video which is part of the picture and cannot be removed. See **VITC**, **LTC**.

Bit Depth – (1) The number of bits used to describe colour in a video signal – the more bits there are, the bigger the numbers that can be used, and the more detail available. Usually either 8 bits for most **SD** formats, or 10 bits for **Digital Betacam** and many **HD** formats. (2) The number of bits used in a digital audio signal, usually either 8 or 16.

Bleaching – Overexposing an image or part of an image to the point where no detail remains. See **Blown Out**.

Blimp – A casing for the camera which blocks camera noise.

Blocking – A rehearsal process to plan out the movements of actors (and camera, and anything else that needs planning).

Blonde – A 2000 watt (2kW) **Tungsten** light without a **Fresnel** lens. See **Redhead**.

Blown Out – Part of an image overexposed (suffering from **Bleaching**) to the point where no detail is visible can be said to be blown out. Windows can easily be blown out due to the difference in intensity between the sun and ordinary interior lights.

Bluescreen – A blue sheet or background intended to be replaced with other imagery in postproduction. See **Chromakey**, **Keying**, **Compositing**, **Greenscreen**.

Blu-Ray – An optical disc format that can be used for **HD** video, using a shorter wavelength laser to pack 25GB (or 50GB for the dual layer version) onto a single disc. Intended as the replacement for **DVD**.

BNC – A coaxial video cable (not the same as a TV aerial cable!) commonly used on professional equipment. Can carry all kinds of different signals and generally used because it locks onto the socket and cannot easily be yanked off. On the other hand, BNCs are usually the first cable to go wrong. See also **Phono**, **S-Video**, **MUSA**, **XLR**, **Minijack**, **Jack**.

Board – Short for **Clapperboard**.

Boom – Can mean **Boompole**, **Boom Mic**, or both at once. Confusing, isn't it?

Boom Mic – Any **Mic** which fits on a **Boompole**. Usually a **Rifle Mic**.

Boom Operator – Crewmember responsible for setting mics and holding the **Boom**.

Boompole – A pole upon which a **Mic** (usually a **Rifle Mic**) is mounted so it can be held closer to a performer without the sound recordist getting in the way of the shot.

Bottletop – A cover for a **Reflector** (especially the **Lastolite** type) which changes it to a different type, e.g. adding a gold or silver surface.

Bowl – On a professional **Tripod** or camera mount (such as a **Dolly**, **Jib** or **Bazooka**), the receptacle for the **Head** which the camera will actually sit on. See also **Legs, Sticks, Plate, Pan Bar, Spreader**.

Broadcast Quality – Video which meets the standards for television broadcast. However, these standards keep changing as technology moves on. In **SD**, **Betacam SP**, **Betacam SX**, **Digibeta**, **DVCAM**, **DVCPro**, **Digital S**, **MPEG IMX** and the various **D1**, **D2** etc. formats usually qualify, but standards vary depending upon the type of programme. **Mini-DV** is often frowned upon. **HD** is usually fine, although there's still confusion between **720** and **1080** screen sizes and **HDV** can sometimes be dubious.

Bubble – Professional slang for the (very expensive) bulbs used in film lights.

Business – Physical actions performed by actors, often added during rehearsal and **Blocking**.

Buzz Track – See **Atmos**.

Cable Bashing – The task of keeping cables running from a moving camera or microphone out of harm's way.

Call Sheet – A daily information sheet including the day's schedule, special arrangements, weather, contact information etc.

Camcorder – A camera which has a built in recording unit. Almost all non-studio cameras are camcorders these days; 'camcorder' tells you nothing about the size, quality or format you might expect.

Camera Tape − White tape (similar to electrician's tape) which can be written on and used for labelling.

Cannon − AKA **XLR**. A **Balanced** audio lead.

Capture − See **Digitisation**.

Car Rig − A system of suction cups that allows you to mount a camera onto a car.

Cascading Codec − When encoding video to a new file format, the **Codec** used to do so may become an obstacle, compressing the information and throwing data away. If the video is recaptured and then encoded and compressed again (as may happen when moving footage between different computer applications), the loss in picture quality can build up in a form of digital **Generation Loss**. See **Compression, Artifact**.

CCD − Charge Couple Device. A light receptor in a camera. **3CCD** means that three receptors are used, one for each of the primary colours. Most cameras have CCDs in the **4:3** shape, meaning that **16:9** modes require further processing and are of lower quality. True 16:9 needs CCDs in the 16:9 shape. See **Aspect Ratio**, **Component**, **CMOS.**

CGI − Computer Generated Images. Any footage or element within the image which was created by a computer. Ranges from subtle cleaning up of the image, to **Compositing**, to creating the film from scratch.

Cheating − The common practice of achieving a shot with a compromise camera position/angle, or shuffling people, **Props** or **Set Dressing** around if the technically correct position is too difficult. Saves time and effort, and works as long as the cheat is not identifiable in the edit.

Chromakey − The process of replacing an even coloured background with other footage, often referred to as **Bluescreen** or **Greenscreen**. Originally accomplished through **Analogue** equipment but now usually available in **Non-Linear Editing** Systems. **Digital** formats with lower **Sample Rates** for colour (**4:1:1** or **4:2:0**) will not be as useful for chromakey as formats with high sample rates (**4:2:2**) See **Keying**, **Compositing**.

Chrominance – The 'colour' part of a video signal.

CineAlta – A brand used by Sony to refer to their **HD** products intended for high end drama/feature film production and capable of **24p** recording.

Clapperboard – AKA **Slate**, **Board**. The board placed in front of a film camera before a shot, used to identify it and provide a cue for syncing up sound. Sometimes used in longer video productions (e.g. if a whole TV series is being shot at once) to make it easier to identify footage.

Clip – (1) A piece of footage. (2) A video or audio file on a **Non-Linear Editing** system. See **Subclip**.

Clip Distortion – Distortion resulting from excessive audio **Levels**. Caused by the signal exceeding the capacity of the system to record it.

Clipping – Short for **Clip Distortion**.

Clock – A countdown in the form of a clockface placed before the film during **Mastering** which allows the film to be properly cued up for playback. See **Leader**, **Pip**.

Clone – A copy of video or audio which has been transferred by a purely **Digital** process with no conversion and therefore no **Generation Loss**. See **Dubbing**, **Cascading Codec**.

CMOS – A newer and better form of light receptor for cameras, now starting to supersede the older **CCD** type. Not all the bugs are quite worked out yet, though.

Codec – A particular system for encoding and decoding **Digital** video information. Each digital video format has it's own Codec. Other Codecs are also used to compress video into particular file formats and vary enormously in quality, effectiveness and compatibility. See **Cascading Codec**, **Compression**, **Artifact**.

Colour Bars – A sequence of standardised vertical coloured bars used by cameras to calibrate **Monitors** and also important in **Mastering**.

Colour Correction – Changing colour levels in video

footage to amend errors, improve continuity or achieve an aesthetic effect. See **Grading**.

Colour Temperature – The absolute temperature of a light source, which affects the colour of light it emits. Measured in **Kelvins**. See **Daylight, Tungsten, Fluorescent, White Balance, Gels**.

Component – An **Analogue SD** or **HD** video signal split into one **Luminance** and two **Chrominance** cables. Provides the highest quality analogue connection. See **Composite, S–Video, Firewire, SDI, HDMI, HD-SDI**. AKA **YUV**.

Composite – An **Analogue SD** video signal in which **Luminance** and **Chrominance** are carried upon a single lead, and therefore the lowest quality connection. See **S–Video, Component, Firewire, SDI, HDMI, HD-SDI**.

Compositing – That part of computerised visual effects work which involves the combination of different images from different sources into a single, final image. Can include **Keying** and **Bluescreen/Greenscreen** processes.

Composition – The choice and balance of the elements that make up the **Frame**. See also **Framing, Headroom**.

Compression – (1) The process of reducing **Digital** information in volume by throwing away unneeded data. **Lossless Compression** doesn't reduce quality but can only reduce file size by a limited amount; **Lossy Compression** gives smaller files but can result in loss of quality, including **Artifact**ing. See **Codec, Cascading Codec**. (2) The audio effect created by a **Compressor**.

Compressor – An effects box in a **Dubbing Studio** or a feature in computer software which controls incoming audio levels by setting limits upon a signal. Can help to make voices sound nearby and intimate. Compare to **Normalisation**.

Condenser Microphone – A microphone that uses an electrical process to pick up sound. Requires **Phantom Power** either from batteries, a **Sound Mixer** or sound desk, and is more fragile than a **Dynamic Microphone**. Generates a signal at **Mic Level** which must then be amplified. See also **Line Level**.

Consolidation – The process whereby a **Non-Linear Editing** system copies portions of **Media** files actually used in a **Project**, allowing unused footage to be deleted and thus recover hard disc space.

Control Track – A continuous video signal upon a tape (e.g. a blank screen or a television programme) used by **Linear Editing** systems to enable **Insert Editing**.

Corpsing – Fits of uncontrollable laughter that sometimes afflict actors when they really ought to be acting.

Coverage – A system of covering action within a scene with a standard selection of shots, such as a **Master**, **Singles**, and **Cutaways**.

Crabbing – Moving the camera sideways.

Crash Zoom – A very fast zoom only possible on cameras with a manual zoom control (rather than the rocker switch common on most cameras). See **Zoom Lens**.

Crossfade – See **Dissolve**.

Crossing the Line – See **180° Rule**.

CU – Close-Up. A shot size showing most of the face.

Cue – (1) (Performers) An action or piece of dialogue which an actor will use as a signal for some part of their own performance. (2) (Music) Short for **Music Cue**. (3) (Video) The shuffling of a videotape to a predetermined location ('cueing up').

Cue Card – a large piece of card with dialogue written on it for the benefit of forgetful actors. See **Idiot Board**.

Cutaway – A shot used in editing to cut away momentarily from the main action – perhaps the reaction of another character, or a simple physical action. See **Coverage**.

D1, D2, D3, D5, D6 – A variety of high quality **Digital** tape formats which are used primarily for **Mastering** rather than filming. There is no 'D4' because the number 4 looks like the word for 'death' in Japanese.

DAC – Digital to Analogue Converter. A device which turns a **Digital** signal into an **Analogue** signal. Even if a camera or VCR is **Digital**, all outputs will be **Analogue** unless specifically labelled as **Digital**, for instance a **Firewire** or **SDI** connection. See **ADC**.

Day for Night – A technique for shooting night scenes during the day using a blue **Filter**, or via **Grading** in **Postproduction**. Works as long as the sky isn't visible in shot.

Daylight – Daylight has a **Colour Temperature** of approximately 5600 **Kelvins**, and appears blue if the camera is not correctly **White Balanced**. See also **Gels, Tungsten, Fluorescent**.

Daylight Balanced Lights – A type of professional film light, either of the **HMI** or **MSR** type, which has the same **Colour Temperature** as **Daylight**. See also **Kinoflo**.

Depth of Field – The depth of area which is in focus at any one time. Deeper on **Wide-Angle Lenses** than **Telephoto Lenses**. Made greater by closing down the **Aperture/Iris** (raising the **F-Stop** number).

Desaturated – Colours that look faded and dull. See **Saturation**.

Development – The stage of a film or video project in which the idea and script are developed into something ready to shoot. See **Preproduction**, **Production**, **Postproduction** and **Distribution**.

Diegetic Sound – Any sound which appears to come from a source somewhere within the scene (as opposed to **Non-Diegetic Sound**, e.g. **Featured Music**).

Diffuser – Anything which softens light, such as **Trace**, smoke machines, some **Filters**, some **Reflectors** etc. See **Soft Light** and **Hard Light**.

Digibeta – Short for **Digital Betacam**.

Digital – Any device which records or uses video or audio information as a series of noughts and ones, as opposed to **Analogue**. If video or audio is copied digitally (**Cloned**), it suffers no **Generation Loss** so long as it's not also undergoing **Compression**. Most **SD** formats in current use are now Digital, as are all **HD** formats. See also **ADC**, **DAC**, **Codec**, **Cascading Codec**.

Digital 8 – An **SD** semipro **Digital** tape format which uses the same tapes as the old **Hi8** format.

Digital Betacam – An **SD** professional **Digital** tape format developed from **Betacam SP**. One of the best **SD** formats and good for **Mastering**. See **Betacam SX**, **XDCAM**.

Digital Meter – A **Levels Meter** found on **Digital** audio equipment (including **Non-Linear Editing** systems) which reads the audio **Levels** from the digital information and uses a scale with 0dB at the top (and maybe another for comparison). See also **VU**, **PPM**.

Digital S – An **SD** professional **Digital** tape format.

Digital VHS – AKA D-VHS. Died quickly because of **DVD**.

Digitisation – AKA **Capture.** The process of encoding video or audio information into computer files on **Non-Linear Editing** systems. Similar to sampling in music. See **Batch Digitisation**.

Directional Microphone – A microphone designed to pick up sound from one direction only. See **Rifle Mike**.

Director of Photography (DoP or DP) – Member of the crew responsible for lighting and camerawork.

Dissolve – A **Transition** from one shot to another in which the two pictures mix together. AKA **Cross-Fade**.

Distribution – The final stage of a film or video project in which it is sold or screened or otherwise shown to audiences. See **Development**, **Preproduction**, **Production** and **Postproduction.**

DivX – A **Codec** (not a format!) for computer video files based upon the **MPEG**-4 codec which allows near-**DVD** quality video with relatively small file size. Mainly used for web distribution (as with **MP3** for audio).

Dogme – A set of restrictive filmmaking rules intended to allow experienced directors to focus on story and character rather than the technology of filmmaking.

Dolly – A wheeled camera mounting which runs on tracks or rubber wheels. Often comes with a **Bazooka** and usually operated by a **Grip**.

Dongle – A hardware device used to enable copyrighted software (such as the more expensive types of **Non-Linear Editing** systems).

Downconvert – The process of converting video to a lower quality format, especially going from **HD** to **SD**. See **Upconvert**.

Dress – The placement of **Set Dressing**, e.g. 'Can you dress in a bit more clutter, please?'

Dressing – Short for **Set Dressing**.

Dropout – A line of a video signal that has 'dropped out' i.e. gone blank. Usually only found in **Analogue** formats like **Betacam SP**. Compare to **Artifact**.

Dry Hire – Hiring equipment by itself without people to operate it. Compare to **Wet Hire**.

Dub – The **Final Mix**.

Dubbing – (1) Copying video or audio from one tape to another. If analogue, can result in **Generation Loss**. Compare to **Cloning**. (2) Replacing original dialogue with new (usually foreign language) dialogue. Compare to **ADR**. See **M&E**.

Dubbing Studio – A facility for the mixing of audio for film and television productions.

Dutch Angle – A camera angle off kilter from horizontal. Can look cool and add a sense of weirdness or alienation but can also be a cliché.

DV – Digital Video. (1) Any **SD** video transferred via **Firewire**. (2) An **SD** consumer **Digital** tape format, the more common smaller version of which is known as **Mini-DV** (3) Sometimes used confusingly to refer to any or all of the digital video formats.

DVCAM – An **SD** semipro **Digital** tape format, probably the most popular of these.

DVCPro – AKA DVCPro25. An **SD** semipro **Digital** tape format. See **P2**.

DVCPro50 – An **SD** professional **Digital** tape format with twice the data rate of **DVCPro**. See **P2**.

DVCProHD – AKA DVCPro100. A **HD** format that uses double the data rate of **DVCPro50**. Sometimes known as **Varicam**. See **P2**.

DVD – Digital Versatile Disc, a higher quality but still compressed **SD** video disc using the **MPEG**-2 file format. DVD **Authoring** programs will allow you to 'author' these on your computer. DVDs now come in a variety of mutually incompatible formats: the one-use-only DVD-R and DVD+R, and the rewritable DVD-RW, DVD+RW and DVD-RAM. See also **Video CD, Blu-Ray**.

DVI – Digital Video Interface, a common computer video connection which is also used for some consumer video equipment. Largely being supplanted in this field by **HDMI**.

Dynamic Microphone – A microphone which uses a mechanical process to pick up sound, and is less fragile than a **Condenser Microphone**. Generates a signal at **Mic Level** which must then be amplified. See **Sound Mixer**.

Dynamic Range – In audio, the range between the highest and lowest **Level** of a signal. Needs to be carefully controlled (e.g. with a **Compressor**) or things get messy. See **Headroom, Noise Floor**.

ECU – Extreme Close-Up. Used to refer to any extremely close shot, but in terms of the face, usually means a shot showing just the eyes.

Edit Controller – A device used in **Linear Editing** to issue commands to the VCRs.

EDL – Edit Decision List. A text file created by a **Non-Linear Editing** system which contains basic information about an edit.

EFP – Electronic Film Production.

ELS – Extreme Long Shot. Any shot in which the subject is very small in **Frame**.

ENG – Electronic News Gathering.

EPK – Electronic Press Kit. The video material used to sell films, e.g. behind the scenes, 'featurettes' etc.

EQ – Equalisation. An audio control which adjusts the **Levels** of individual frequencies of sound.

Establishing Shot – A shot (usually an exterior **WS**) which introduces the audience to a scene by showing them where it's taking place.

Exposure – The quantity of light reaching the **CCD**s of a camera, affected by **Aperture** and **Shutter** speed.

EXT. – Short for Exterior. Used mainly in the **Sluglines** of screenplays.

Featured Music – AKA **Incidental Music**. Music not heard by the characters in a scene. See **Background Music, Non-Diegetic Sound**.

Feedback – An audio signal which is being picked up from itself via a loudspeaker or input channel and trapped in a loop. If you have a sound desk in an edit suite, it's all too easy to cause this hideous screech by mistake when **Digitising**. Video feedback is also possible but just looks weird.

Field – Half of a video **Frame**. Two of these are interlaced to make each frame, effectively doubling the frame rate of video. See **Film Look, Field Dominance, Interlaced Scan, Progressive Scan**.

Field Dominance – The order in which the two interlaced fields of a video frame are displayed, either Odd/Upper (lines 1, 3, 5 etc) or Even/Lower (lines 2, 4, 6 etc). Mini–DV is always Lower, **HDV** is always Upper, but other formats and machines can vary. See **Interlaced Scan** and **Progressive Scan**.

Field Monitor – A small TV which is used to watch footage directly from the camera during production. See also **Monitor**.

Fill Light – A light (usually **Soft Light**) used to fill in shadows. An element of **Three-Point Lighting**.

Film Look – The process of making video look like film.

Can involve doubling or blending the **Fields** to mimic the frame rate of film, **Grading**, styles of lighting used during the shoot etc.

Filter – A glass or plastic plate, usually placed in front of the lens in a **Matte Box** but sometimes available as an internal device inside a camera, which can cut the levels of light entering the lens (e.g. **ND**), act as a **Diffuser** (e.g. a Promist), as a **Polariser**, change the **Colour Temperature** of incoming light (used mostly for film cameras), enable **Day for Night**, or add a cosmetic effect such as a **Grad**.

Final Mix – The stage of **Postproduction** in which the final soundtrack for the film is mixed from elements such as dialogue, **Atmos**, sound fx and music.

Firestore – A small portable hard drive that can record video material and replace tapes. Usually used as a backup as they are occasionally unreliable.

Firewire – (1) A compressed **digital** audio/video signal with no **DAC** or **ADC** between the two machines. The signal **Compression** (5:1) sets a limit on picture quality for **SD** signals. Can also be used for **HDV** signals. AKA **IEEE 1394** or **I.Link**. See also **Composite**, **S-Video**, **Component**, **SDI**, **HDMI**, **HD-SDI**. (2) The actual cable carrying a Firewire signal. The 4-pin version plugs into cameras while the 6-pin version also carries power and plugs into computers and peripherals – you may need both 4-pin to 6-pin and 6-pin to 6-pin cables to cover all applications. See also **BNC**, **MUSA**, **Minijack**, **Jack**, **Phono**, **XLR**.

First – See **Assistant Director**.

First Assembly – The first complete edit of the film. Almost certainly too long by about a third.

Fishpole – A **Boompole** which telescopes out for greater length.

Flag – A large, flat object used to mask out unwanted light. Often the best solution to **Lens Flare**.

Flare – See **Lens Flare**.

Flight Case – Hard metal case commonly used to store and transport film and video equipment.

Flood – Using the **Spot**/Flood control on a light to widen the beam of light, make it a little softer and a little less intense.

Fluid Head – A particularly high-quality **Head** for a **Tripod** with very smooth movement.

Fluorescent – A form of lighting which uses an electrically charged gas to emit light. Tends to cast a green tinge onto the subject. Problematic when mixed with **Daylight** or **Tungsten** light sources. Can be dealt with by **White Balance** or **Gels**. See **Colour Temperature**.

Focus Assist – One of several different systems, which make it possible to get focus on **HD** cameras without access to an HD **Monitor**.

Focus Pulling – (1) Changing focus during a shot. Compare to **Pulling Stop**. (2) The work done by a Focus Puller on a more professional shoot.

Foley – Sound effects recorded in a studio during postproduction. Named after Jack Foley, who pioneered the technique. AKA **Footsteps** and **Spot Effects**.

Footsteps – See **Foley**.

Flash – an animation system intended largely for web use, but which can also include video.

FPS – Frames Per Second. The normal frame rate for **PAL** video is 25 fps. Film is normally shot at 24 fps.

Frame – (1) A single picture of video or film (see **FPS**, **Field**) (2) The TV or film screen (see **Framing**, **Composition**).

Frameline – The edge of the frame in real space. **Boom Operators** in particular must be aware of this.

Framing – The choice of shot size, usually in relation to a human subject. See **Frame**, **Composition**.

Fresnel Lens – A lens used on professional lights to make them more directional and controllable.

F-Stop – A measurement of the degree to which an **Aperture** is opened or closed, affecting the **Exposure**

and the **Depth of Field**. The higher the number, the more closed it is. See also **Stop**, **Pulling Stop**.

Fullscreen – The **aspect ratio** of a normal **4:3** TV screen, known in cinema as **Academy** format. See **Widescreen**, **16:9**, **Anamorphic**.

Gaffer – On professional shoots, the member of crew in charge of the lighting team of **Sparks** and responsible to the **Director of Photography**. See also **Best Boy**.

Gaffer Tape – 2˝ wide cloth adhesive tape (similar to duct tape) used extensively to hold productions together, keep cables out of harm's way, make **Gobos**, prevent the director from screaming too loud etc.

Gain – (1) (Audio) The input **Level** control. (2) (Video) A function on a video camera which electronically amplifies light levels. Gain brightens the picture but adds grain and therefore reduces picture quality.

Gels – Sheets of translucent plastic which affect the quality of light passing through them. Can be used to correct **Colour Temperature** or **Fluorescent** lights, control light levels (see **ND**) or add a cosmetic effect.

Generation Loss – The inevitable result of copying **Analogue** video or audio. Since the copy is not exact, interference is added with every new generation, eventually leading to complete loss of signal. Compare to **Cascading Codec**.

Genny – Professional slang for a generator.

Gobo – An object used in lighting to cast a specific shadow and break up light, e.g. a tree branch or strips of **Gaffer Tape** to simulate a barred window.

Grad – A 'Graduated' **Filter** has a filter effect gradually increasing across its width. Useful for darkening a specific area of the frame (such as the sky) while leaving the rest unaffected.

Grading – The process of adjusting colour levels in footage to correct mistakes, improve continuity or add effects (such as a sepia tone). 'Grading' is a term used more for film than video. Americans add to our confusion by calling it 'Colour Timing.' See **Colour Correction**.

Greenscreen – A green sheet or background intended to be replaced with other imagery in postproduction. See **Chromakey**, **Keying**, **Compositing**, **Bluescreen**.

Green Room – An ante-room near to the set or studio where performers can relax.

Grip – A member of crew responsible for camera mountings like **Dollies**, **Jibs** etc.

Guide Track – Sound recorded during a shoot with some imperfection (background noise, copyrighted music etc.) meaning it cannot be used for the **Final Mix** but only as a guide for creating the final sound.

H.264 – A video **Codec** designed by Apple, which is particularly good for retaining quality while keeping file size down. Often used in web video, and incorporated into several **HD** formats.

Hair Light – See **Back Light**.

Handycam – A name used by Sony to describe many of their small consumer cameras and sometimes applied to any camera of about that size.

Hard Cut – A cut in which both sound and picture cut at the same time. Can be very obtrusive. See **Soft Cut**.

Hard Light – Directional light (e.g. from the sun or a naked light bulb) which throws harsh, well–defined shadows. See **Soft Light**, **Diffuser**.

Head – On a professional **Tripod**, the part that fits into the **Bowl** and which holds the **Plate** upon which the camera is mounted. Also holds the mechanisms for **Tilting** and **Panning**. See also **Legs**, **Pan Bar**, **Sticks**, **Spreader**, **Fluid Head**.

Headroom – (1) (Camera) The space left between the top of the **Frame** and the head of a subject. A fundamental concept of **Composition**. (2) (Sound) The space left between the **Peak** and the top of the scale of a **Levels Meter**. If **Levels** are incorrectly set with not enough headroom, **Clip Distortion** is a real risk. See **Noise Floor**.

HD – Abbreviation of **High Definition** video.

HDCAM – Sony's original **HD** format, which uses the same tape chassis as the various **Betacam** formats, and records **1080** screen size. Due to limitations in bandwidth, the actual recorded frame is 1440x1080, with a **Pixel Aspect Ratio** of 1.33:1 to make up the difference. See **HDCAM SR, CineAlta.**

HDCAM SR – A development of **HDCAM** which allows the recording of full **1080** frames with lower compression rates. Now commonly as an **HD** mastering format and for high end filming.

HDMI – High Definition Multimedia Interface, a consumer AV cable which is commonly used to carry **HD** signals. Has been designed to carry most AV signals without changes to the physical cable. See **Composite, S-Video, Component, Firewire, SDI, HD-SDI.**

HD Ready – A label on consumer TVs which are (supposedly) appropriate for **HD** use. 'HD Ready 1080p' indicates that the TV can handle the highest quality of consumer HD.

HD-SDI – An HD version of **SDI** which can also carry a high quality signal on a single **BNC** cable. See **Composite, S-Video, Component, Firewire, SDI, HDMI.**

HDV – A consumer and semiprofessional **HD** format which is very heavily compressed and usually recorded onto standard **Mini-DV** or **DV** tapes, although **XDCAM** optical discs and **XDCAM EX** cards can record it as well. Sony cameras usually record a **1080i** signal, while JVC cameras use **720p** in their **ProHD** variant. Compare to **AVCHD**.

Hertz – A measurement of frequency per second which can apply to many different things – the vibrations that we hear as the pitch of sound, the number of samples in a **Digital** signal etc. Abbreviated as **Hz**. One **Kilohertz** is 1000**Hz**.

Hi8 – An obsolete **SD** semipro Analogue tape format, developed from the original **8mm** format and later replaced by **Digital 8**.

High Definition (HD, Hi–Def) – A range of **Digital** video formats with larger screen sizes e.g. 1920x1080. Can approach the quality of film and are usually **16:9** by default. **Sample Rate** and **Bit Depth** are often higher than **SD**. See **1080, 720, 2K, 4K, HDCAM, HDCAM SR, CineAlta, DVCProHD, Varicam, HDV, ProHD, AVCHD, Blu-Ray, HDMI, HD-SDI**.

High Key – A style of lighting in which subjects and backgrounds are well-lit with primarily **Soft Light** (but which has no relation to the term **Key Light**). See also **Low Key**.

HMI – The older form of **Daylight Balanced Light**, cheaper but heavier. Can suffer from flickering.

Hz – Short for **Hertz**.

I.Link – Sony's name for **Firewire** AKA **IEEE 1394**.

Idiot Board – A less polite term for **Cue Card**.

IEEE 1394 – The standard for the DV cable also known as **Firewire** or **I.Link**.

i – **Interlaced Scan**. The lower case letter is often used in combination with screen size and/or frame rate when referring to one of the many types of **HD**, eg 1080i, 50i. See **p**.

Image Stabiliser – A device in small, lightweight video cameras which counters camera shake by either digital or optical means. Optical is the better of the two.

Ingesting – the action of transferring footage from a non-tape based system into an edit program.

In Point – Programmable point at which an editing system will begin recording, digitising, playing etc. See **Out Point**.

Inbetweening – The creation of intermediate frames to fill gaps, either in animation or when creating slow motion for video.

In-Camera – Visual FX shots done entirely on-set with no **Postproduction** element are said to have been filmed 'in-camera,'

In-Camera Editing – Filming in shoot order with only

one take for each shot, so that the shoot tape is actually the final edit of the film. Not recommended unless you're absolutely desperate.

Incidental Music – See **Featured Music**.

Insert Editing – A form of **Linear Editing** which allows for shots to be dropped in at any point of a tape which has **Control Track** recorded on it.

INT. – Short for Interior. Used mainly in the **Sluglines** of screenplays.

Interlaced Scan – The two **Fields** of standard video are said to be interlaced, i.e. alternate lines are displayed as though they were two separate images, but the eye sees only one image. See **Field Dominance**, **Progressive Scan**.

Iris – See **Aperture**.

Jack – A ¼" wide **Unbalanced** audio lead, which can carry either stereo or mono sound. Often used for headphones and in audio **Patch Bays**. Compare to **Bantam**. See also **BNC**, **Phono**, **S-Video**, **MUSA**, **XLR**, **Minijack**, **Firewire**.

Jackfield – A synonym for **Patch Bay** sometimes used in the music industry.

Jib – AKA Jib Arm. A small counterweighted mini-crane, sometimes only a metre or two long, upon which the camera can be mounted for smooth motion in many directions. Usually has a **Bowl** for the purpose of holding a **Head**. Can sometimes be mounted on a **Dolly** for even greater freedom of movement, and is usually operated by a **Grip**.

Jump Cut – A picture cut which maintains the same shot size. Can be disconcerting if used in isolation.

K – Abbreviation for **Kelvin**.

Kelvin – A measure of temperature in which the degrees are equivalent to those of Celsius/Centigrade, but which starts counting from absolute zero (−273.15°C). Usually written without the degree (°) symbol, e.g. 3600 Kelvins or 3600K. Used to measure **Colour Temperature**.

Key Light – The main illumination on a subject, usually **Hard Light**. An element of **Three-Point Lighting**.

Keyframe – In **Non-Linear Editing** systems, effects work and animation: a single frame selected as a point at which any of a number of possible values might change, e.g. audio **Levels**, stereo **Pan**, effects parameters etc.

Keying – the process of replacing part of one piece of footage with another using as a guide a particular colour (**Chromakey**), brightness level (**Lumakey**) or pre-defined mask (a **Matte**). Originally accomplished with **Analogue** equipment but now commonly available in **Non-Linear Editing** Systems. See also **Bluescreen**, **Greenscreen**, **Compositing**, **Alpha Channel**.

kHz – Short for **Kilohertz**.

Kilohertz – See **Hertz**.

Kinoflo – A bank of fluorescent tubes, adjusted to either **Daylight** or **Tungsten**, to be used as a very flattering **Soft Light**.

Lastolite – A company whose name has become synonymous with **Reflectors** consisting of reflective fabric stretched within a collapsible ring.

Lavalier – A tie-clip mic which might be plugged directly into a **Sound Mixer** or camera, or used as a radio mic.

Leader – A countdown in the form of decreasing numbers placed before the film during **Mastering** which allows the film to be properly cued up for playback. Leaders are more often used in film than video. See **Clock**, **Pip**.

Legs – On a professional **Tripod**, the actual legs, which have a **Bowl** on top into which fits the tripod **Head**. See also **Sticks**, **Plate**, **Pan Bar**, **Spreader**.

Lens Flare – A stray reflection of direct light hitting the lens at such an angle that a bright patch appears on the screen. See **Flag**.

Letterbox – A way of recording a **Widescreen** picture onto a **Fullscreen** picture which leaves black bars at the top and bottom of the screen but preserves the original **Aspect Ratio**. Compare to **Pan and Scan**.

Levels – (1) The 'volume' at which incoming audio is recorded (the actual volume control affects the overall sound mix going out to speakers rather than sound coming in). Set with **Gain** control. Can also apply to individual tracks of sound already recorded onto a system. See also **EQ**, **Compressor**, **Clip Distortion**, **Noise Floor**. (2) The loudness of an actor's performance (or any other sound) which must be established so audio can be adequately recorded, e.g. 'Can you give me a level, please?'

Levels Meter – A device on a **Sound Mixer**, camera, VCR or **Non-Linear Editing** system which measures the **Levels** of an audio signal. See **VU**, **PPM**, **Digital Meter**, **Headroom**.

Lighting Cameraman – The same as a **Director of Photography**, but the Lighting Cameraman **Operates** the camera as well.

Lighting Grip – Equipment which supports lights.

Line Level – Audio signals sent at a higher level, usually from a mixer, deck, or camera. Can sound very distorted if your mixer or camera is expecting **Mic Level**.

Linear Editing – Any editing system which works by recording video from one VCR to another. An inherent problem is that new material cannot be inserted earlier on the tape – it can only be copied over material already present. See **Scratch Editing**, **Assemble Editing**, **Insert Editing**, **2-Machine Suite**, **3-Machine Suite**, **Non-Linear Editing**.

Lines Off – AKA **Reading In.** Lines delivered off camera.

Lock – Short for **Picture Lock**.

Logging – The process of compiling a list of what footage is on a tape. Often used to make a list of **Clips** for **Batch Digitising**.

Long Lens – See **Telephoto Lens**.

Looping – See **ADR**.

Lossy Compression, Lossless Compression – See **Compression**.

Low Key – A style of lighting which allows for a lot of

shadows in frame and often uses **Hard Light** to throw some more (but which has no relation to the term **Key Light**). See also **High Key**.

LS – Long Shot. A shot size in which a human figure is shown from head to foot.

LTC – Longitudinal Time Code. A form of **Timecode** recorded invisibly on a separate track running alongside the video on a tape. This is usually compatible with **SMPTE** Timecode. See **BITC**, **VITC**.

Lumakey – See **Keying.**

Luminance – The 'brightness' part of a video signal.

M&E – Music & Effects. A final soundtrack without dialogue, used by foreign distributors to create a foreign language (dubbed) version of a film. Short films are usually subtitled for foreign markets so this generally isn't required.

Magic Hour – The thirty minutes or so each day when the sun is below the horizon but the sky is still light enough to enable shooting. A scheduling nightmare that nevertheless looks gorgeous on screen.

Mark – A marking on the floor (often done with **Gaffer Tape** or **Camera Tape**) which shows where an actor is supposed to be at a specific point during their performance.

Master – (1) A shot which encompasses the whole of the action within a scene. See **Coverage**. (2) The tape with the final version of the film from which you can then make viewing copies.

Mastering – The process of preparing and laying down the final version of the film onto tape. See **Bars & Tone**, **Clock**, **Leader**, **Pip**.

Match Action – A cut which goes from one action to the same action seen from a different angle. Creates an illusion of smooth motion.

Matte – A mask used to obscure part of a video or film image, usually so that another image can be laid on top without the two images mixing together. See **Keying**.

Matte Box – An apparatus on the front of a professional camera which both shields the lens from **Flare** and provides space to slot in **Filters**.

MCU – Medium Close-Up. A shot size encompassing the head and shoulders of a subject.

Media – Video or audio **Digitised** or **Captured** onto a **Non-Linear Editing** system.

Memory Effect – The tendency of older Nickel-Cadmium (NiCad) batteries to 'remember' the point at which they stopped charging, and to only charge to that point in future. Newer NiCad and Lithium-Ion (Li-Ion) batteries should not suffer from this.

Mic – A common written abbreviation for 'microphone,' pronounced 'mike'.

Mic Level – Audio signals sent at a lower level, usually generated by a microphone. Can sound very quiet if your equipment is set to expect **Line Level** – make sure the inputs on your **Sound Mixer** or camera are correctly set.

Mid-Shot – See **MS**.

Mini-DV – The standard consumer **Digital** tape format, a miniature version of **DV**.

Minijack – Usually an audio connector, this is a miniature version of the **Jack**, also **Unbalanced** and capable of both stereo and mono. Commonly used for headphones. Some **Mini-DV** cameras have a version which carries video as well as both channels of audio. See also **BNC**, **Phono**, **S-Video**, **MUSA**, **XLR**, **Jack**, **Firewire**.

Mise-en-Scéne – (literally 'putting on stage') (1) Posh word favoured by critics to describe **Composition** and the choices of lighting, production design etc, that go into the shot. (2) A wide shot that shows everything in the scene can be said to be showing the 'mise-en-scéne.'

Mixing – The adjustment of audio **Levels** for individual tracks which is necessary to produce an acceptable (or even audible) soundtrack.

Mizar – Originally a compact light with a **Fresnel** lens which had interchangeable bulbs of 300W, 500W and

650W. Now used as a generic term to describe any similar fresnel light of about those wattages.

MLS – Medium Long Shot. A shot size in which the subject is shown from the head to the knees.

Modelling – The effect created by lighting in which light and shade combine to bring out the depth of a subject. Usually created by a combination of **Hard Light**, **Soft Light**, and **Back Light** as in **Three-Point Lighting**.

Monitor – (1) (Video) AKA **Production Monitor**. Any high-quality TV used in the production process. See also **Field Monitor**. (2) (Audio) The high-quality pair of monitor speakers used in edit suites and **Dubbing Studios**.

Montage – (1) French for 'editing.' (2) A 'montage sequence' is a series of thematically related shots which are usually used to show time passing. (3) A theory originating in 1920s Russia which (put very simply) states that the cutting together of two shots can create a third meaning (e.g. 1st shot: an axe falls, 2nd shot: a man stumbles bleeding from a room, 3rd meaning: the man was hit with the axe – although the action was never seen).

Morticians' Wax – A putty-like substance which can be moulded to look like human skin. Used in conjunction with make-up to create realistic wounds, scars etc.

MP3 – Short for **MPEG** level 3, an audio file format that uses **Compression** to drastically reduce file size. If using this, compress the signal as little as possible or else audio quality may be affected. Uses the file extension .mp3. See also **AIFF-C** and **WAV**.

MPEG – Short for Motion Picture Experts Group, who came up with this range of **Codecs** for compressed video file formats with various file extensions (as well as **MP3**). MPEG-1 is used in CD-ROM, **Video CD** and Web applications, and the larger but higher quality MPEG-2 is used for **DVD**. MPEG-4 is the next level up, used in **DivX** and several **HD** codecs including **XDCAM EX**. See also **AVI**, **Quicktime**.

MPEG IMX – an **SD** video format by Sony which uses **MPEG** compression like **Betacam SX** but at a higher data rate. Can be recorded on its own tape format, or on **XDCAM** discs.

MS – Medium Shot, or Mid-Shot. A shot size showing a subject from head to abdomen.

MSR – The newer form of **Daylight Balanced Light**, more expensive but smaller and lighter.

Murphy's Law – See **Production Reality**.

MUSA – A kind of video lead used almost exclusively in video **Patch Bays**. Each cable carries one signal which might be a whole **Composite** signal, half an **S-Video** signal, one third of a **Component** signal, or a whole **SDI** signal. See also **BNC**, **Phono**, **S-Video**, **XLR**, **Minijack**, **Jack**, **Firewire**.

Music Cue – A specific piece of music used in a film.

Mute – Video or film footage recorded without sound. See **Sync Sound**.

MXF – Material eXchange Format. A file format that can contain many different types of video. Designed for use in **Non-Linear Editing** systems. **P2** cards will record in this format.

Natural Framing – The use of a natural frame (such as a window or tree branches) to create a frame within the video frame.

ND – Neutral Density. A **Filter** or **Gel** which cuts down light without colouring it.

Negative Bounce – Using a dark surface to absorb light instead of reflect it.

Nervous – Slang for a final check of a location for anything that might have been left behind.

Neutral Density – See **ND**.

Noise – (1) (Audio) The hiss inherent when recording **Analogue** audio onto magnetic tape, caused by some of the grains of iron oxide used to store information refusing to have their magnetic polarities fiddled with. (2) (Video) The 'snow' seen in analogue video which isn't actually receiving a signal.

Noise Floor – The level of the hiss on **Analogue** tape (**Digital** audio is free from this problem). Requires that input **Levels** be set high enough to rise above it. See **Headroom**.

Noise Gate – An effects box in a **Dubbing Studio** which can be set to only allow sound through above a certain volume, e.g. it can be used to cut out background noise inbetween the words spoken by a performer.

Non-Diegetic Sound – See **Diegetic Sound**.

Non-Linear Editing (NLE) – Any form of editing system with the capability to insert ('splice in') footage at any point in the edit, pushing aside that which was there before without deleting it. Applies to film editing as well as computer-based systems. See **Digitisation**, **Capturing**, **Batch Digitising**, **Timeline**, **Bin**, **Clip**, **Subclip**, **Project**, **Media**.

Non-Square Pixel – See **Pixel Aspect Ratio**.

Normalisation – A process which smoothes out high and low **Levels** in an audio signal. Not as useful as **Compression** for controlling levels.

NTSC – National Television System Committee, the body that set the US **SD** television standard which is incompatible with **PAL** and **SECAM**. The frame size is 720×480 and the frame rate is 29.97 or 30 fps (I know, it's bizarre). The worst of the three SD formats, but if you need to send stuff to the US, you'll have to deal with it.

Offline – The rough edit of a video. On **Linear Editing** systems, the offline is the rough stage before the **Online** stage, which can be on almost any video format, usually the cheapest. On **Non-Linear Editing** systems, an edit made with lower-quality (more compressed) footage prior to the **Online**.

Online – The final edit of a video. On **Linear Editing** systems, this is done on the highest quality video format available, and **Grading**, titles and other video effects are added. In **Non-Linear Editing** systems, these may already have been done, leaving only the redigitisation of footage at higher quality, possibly on the same system.

Operate – Professional slang for using (operating) a camera, e.g. 'I'm going to be operating on this shoot.'

OS – Short for Off Screen. Used in scripts to indicate that a piece of dialogue is being spoken by someone not actually on the screen at that point. Compare to **VO**.

Out Point – Programmable point at which an editing system will stop recording, digitising, playing etc. See **In Point**.

Outline – (1) A rough working out of the plot of a story, sometimes done on index cards. (2) A short description of the film with a general outline of the story. Compare to **Treatment**.

p – **Progressive Scan**. The lower case letter is often used in combination with screen size and/or frame rate when referring to one of the many types of **HD**, e.g. 1080p, 25p. See **i**.

P2 – Professional Plug-in. Panasonic's memory card system onto which video footage can be recorded, replacing tapes. Records files in **MXF** format, but the video content can be **DV, DVCPro, DVCPro50,** or **DVCProHD**.

PAL – **SD** TV standard adopted in the UK, incompatible with **NTSC** and **SECAM**. Has a frame size of 720×576 pixels and is 25fps (or 50i to be more accurate).

Pan – (1) (Camera) Turning the camera left or right, usually on a **Tripod**. See also **Tilt**. (2) (Audio) Moving the perceived position of sound between two stereo speakers.

Pan and Scan – The system used to transfer most **Widescreen** films to video. The sides of the frame are cut off, but the TV screen 'pans' across the frame if it needs to. Compare to **Letterbox**.

Pan Bar – The adjustable arm on the **Head** of a **Tripod** which is used to **Pan** and **Tilt** a camera. See also **Plate**, **Legs**, **Spreader**, **Bowl**.

Panamic – A company who make very good **Boompoles** and are sometimes synonymous with the same.

Paper Edit – A rough edit of the film done on paper.

PAR Can – PAR stands for Parabolic Aluminised Reflector. A PAR Can is a light normally used for theatrical and stage work which looks a bit like a tube (or a can). Has no **Spot/Flood** control and therefore not the best light for film work.

PAT Test – Portable Appliance Test, a safety test for electrical devices. Large organisations and local authorities might want all your kit to be PAT tested if you film on their premises, and this can be expensive.

Parenthetical – AKA **Personal Direction**. The notes that appear in brackets one line beneath a character name in screenplay format. These should only be used when there is absolutely no other way to indicate what's happening.

Patch Bay – AKA **Jackfield**. A system of sending video or audio signals between a number of pieces of equipment. Outputs and inputs for each bit of kit are all plugged into a line of sockets which can then be connected with patch leads. See **Jack, MUSA, Bantam**.

Peak –The highest **Level** of an audio signal, e.g. 'It's peaking at around −12dB.' See **Headroom, Levels Meter**.

Personal Direction – See **Parenthetical**.

Phantom Power – Power supplied to a **Condenser Microphone**. Can come from a sound desk or through batteries.

Phase Converter – A device which matches the frame rate of a TV or computer monitor to that of the camera.

Phono – AKA **RCA**. An **Unbalanced** lead that can carry one channel of audio or video. See also **BNC, S-Video, XLR, MUSA, Minijack, Jack, Firewire**.

Pickup – A shot to be filmed separately from the rest ('picked up'), often something that was overlooked in the original schedule or discovered during editing.

Picture Lock – AKA **Lock.** The point during **Postproduction** at which the picture edit is completed, and locked down before the film goes to a sound mix at a **Dubbing Studio**.

Picture Safe – See **Safe Area**.

Pip – A one frame long 1kHz beep used to mark an individual frame. Can usually be found when a **Clock** or **Leader** gets to 3 seconds before the start of programme.

Pixel Aspect Ratio – In video, pixels are not always exactly square. They're **Non-Square** with an aspect ratio of 1:1.066 (for **4:3 PAL**) or 1:1.422 (for **16:9 PAL**) or 1:1.33 (for **HDCAM**), although these are not the only possibilities. Changing the shape of the pixels allows the encoding of widescreen into a smaller screen shape. Make sure your **Non-Linear Editing** system is set correctly if it has an option for pixel aspect ratio.

Plate – A small mount which can be screwed into the bottom of the camera, which is then held in place on the **Head** of a **Tripod**. One of the easiest things to lose on a shoot. See also **Legs**, **Bowl**, **Sticks**, **Spreader**.

Playback – Audio playing facilities on set, usually used to play music so performers have something to dance to. Can also refer to video playback if that's required.

Polariser – A type of **Filter** which can exclude light passing through at an angle – can be used to cut down diffusion, improve colour **Saturation** and definition in heavily saturated areas such as the sky, and (most remarkably) reduce or eliminate reflections from surfaces such as windows.

Polecat – A type of lighting stand which has rubber feet at both ends and is extendible to allow it to be wedged between any two surfaces. Requires a clamp to actually fix a light to the pole.

Polyboard – A sheet of polystyrene used as a **Reflector**, or, when painted black, for **Negative Bounce**.

Pop Shield – A fabric shield placed between a performer and a microphone to prevent 'pops' caused by 'plosive' consonant sounds (e.g. P, B).

Post – Short for **Postproduction**.

Postproduction – The stage of a project after shooting, when the film is edited, music is composed and recorded and sound is mixed. See **Development**, **Preproduction**, **Production** and **Distribution**.

Postproduction Route – The methods by which you choose to **Post** your film (including choice of editing system, effects work, music composition, **Final Mix** and **Mastering**), which requires very careful planning. Ignoring this can result in postproduction dragging on forever.

POV – Short for Point Of View. A shot from the point of view of a particular character (or anything else that might have visual powers).

PPM – Peak Programme Meter. A **Levels Meter** for **Analogue** audio which is more accurate than a **VU** and is designed to fall away gradually from a **Peak**. Just to be confusing, there are several different PPM scales; in the UK, though, you should be using the BBC type, running from 1 to 7. The peak should be between 4 and 5. Tends to be used in professional edit suites and **Dubbing Studios**. See also **Digital Meter**.

Practical – Used to describe any **Prop** or item on screen which actually works. Also used to describe a light in vision which is used as part of the lighting setup (as opposed to most ordinary lights which are too dull for film and television).

Preproduction – Stage of a project in which the shoot is planned and prepared. See **Development**, **Production**, **Postproduction** and **Distribution**.

Preroll – The amount of time a VCR will run backwards before the **In-Point** and then start playing. Used to make sure the VCR is running at a stable speed before it plays or records; the minimum is usually 3 seconds.

Presence – See **Atmos**.

Preview – A function of **Linear Editing** systems which allows a cut to be checked before it is made.

Production – The shoot of the film or video. See **Development**, **Preproduction**, **Postproduction** and **Distribution**.

Production Mixer – See **Sound Mixer**.

Production Monitor – See **Monitor**.

Production Reality – See **Murphy's Law**.

Progressive Scan – Video which does not use an **Interlaced** system of **Fields** to make up **Frames**. Instead, the lines are displayed in their proper 'progressive' order, making the footage look more like film. See **24p**.

ProHD – JVC's variant form of **HDV**, that records a **720** frame. A quite heavily compressed semiprofessional **HD** format that can record onto standard **Mini-DV** and **DV** tapes.

Project – Term used to refer to a complete set of **Bins**, **Clips**, **Timelines** etc., on a **Non-Linear Editing** system.

Prop – Short for 'property.' Any item that might actually be handled by the actors. Some props are **Practical** and some aren't. Compare to **Set Dressing**.

Prosumer – A general level of equipment quality somewhere between professional and consumer (so basically the same as semiprofessional). A hideous word that must be destroyed.

PSC – Personal Single Camera.

Pulling Stop – Adjusting the **F-Stop** (i.e. the **Aperture** or **Iris**) during a take. Not to be done lightly. See also **Focus Pulling**.

Quicktime – A video file format which can also contain audio (and all kinds of other things), using the file extension .mov. Can be either compressed or uncompressed depending upon the choice of **Codec**. See also **AVI**, **MPEG**.

RAID – Redundant Array of Independent Discs. A system of combining several hard drives together to provide a faster, more fault tolerant data recording system. A handy choice for a more advanced **Non-Linear Editing** system, especially if the material was not recorded on tape and cannot be recaptured if lost.

RCA – See **Phono**.

Reading In – AKA **Lines Off**. Lines delivered off camera.

Recce – A trip to potential location(s) undertaken during **Preproduction** to ascertain if it's worth filming there, and to gather necessary information if it is.

RED – A company making highly advanced **HD** cameras, shooting 'Redcode' format onto cards or hard drives at screen sizes a bit larger than **4K**, but downconvertable to more standard sizes. Designed to replace 35mm film in a way that **HDCAM** hasn't quite managed, while still being affordable to people shooting low budgets. A semipro camera, 'Scarlet', is in the works.

Redhead – A 800 watt **Tungsten** light without a **Fresnel** lens. Some redheads are actually painted red, but some aren't and might look very different. See **Blonde**.

Reflector – Any surface used to bounce light, such as walls, **Polyboards**, **Lastolites** etc. A silvery surface reflects **Hard Light** while a light-coloured matt surface reflects **Soft Light**. A gold foil surface might be used to reflect a warmer light onto a face. See **Bottletop**.

Rendering – The often time-consuming calculations made by a **Non-Linear Editing** system or computer effects program to prepare or add effects to digitised footage.

Repeat – (1) (Audio) A repeated or reflected sound, such as an echo. (2) (Props & Costumes) A replacement item identical to another which must be destroyed or soiled during a take.

Reverb – (1) The continuous reflections of sound that come from hard surfaces in an enclosed area, which seem to make a sound linger. (2) The effects box which recreates this in a **Dubbing Studio**.

Reverse – i.e. Reverse Angle. A shot or angle which is roughly 180° round from the previous shot or angle.

RGB – The three primary colours (red, green, blue), occasionally used as the three channels of a **Component** video signal (especially in computer files), though the **YUV** system is more normal.

Rifle Mic – AKA **Shotgun Mic**. A particularly

Directional Microphone often mounted on a **Boompole**.

Room Tone – See **Atmos**.

Rostrum – i.e. Rostrum Camera, a camera mounted above a still image so the still can be filmed with greater control.

Rule of Thirds – A guideline for **Composition** which states that important elements of the picture should be placed roughly one third of the distance up or down the **Frame**, either horizontally or vertically.

Safe Area – The area of the **Frame** which should be visible on the screen of even the worst domestic TV set. Can be displayed on most **Non-Linear Editing** systems and comes in two varieties: **Picture Safe** and the slightly smaller **Title Safe**. See **Underscan**.

Safety – An extra take made just in case all the previous takes were faulty in some way.

Sample Rate – In digital video and audio, the rate at which the original **Analogue** signal is measured for encoding as **Digital** information. Audio sampling is measured in samples per second, e.g. 44100 (44.1 **kHz**) for CD quality. Video sampling is measured in terms of the relative quantity of samples between the three channels of a **YUV** (**Component**) signal (or sometimes four if you add an **Alpha** channel), and written as a ratio e.g. **4:2:2**, **4:1:1** etc. See **Chromakey**.

Saturation – The purity of any given colour in a video signal. It's better to have a saturated image than a desaturated one, since it looks more appealing to the human eye and having to raise the saturation in **Postproduction** isn't ideal – although you might of course want a **Desaturated** look for aesthetic reasons. See **Polariser**.

SCART – 21 pin European AV connector, often used on **SD** consumer equipment.

Scratch Editing – The process of **Linear Editing** with a system which can be put together from ordinary consumer equipment.

Scrim – Perforated sheet clipped to **Barn Doors** (like **Gels**

or **Trace**) in order to cut down light.

Script Supervisor – Member of crew responsible for continuity.

SD – Abbreviation of **Standard Definition**.

SDI – Serial Digital Interface. An uncompressed **digital** connection with no **DAC** or **ADC** involved, carrying either video or video interleaved with audio. SDI is the best available video connection for **SD**. See **Composite**, **S-Video**, **Component**, **Firewire**, **HDMI**, **HD-SDI**.

SECAM – Séquential Couleur à Memoire. **SD** TV standard used in France and the former Soviet Union (among others). Incompatible with **PAL** and **NTSC**.

Second – See **Assistant Director**.

Set Dressing – AKA **Dressing**. Anything in shot on a set which is there for design purposes rather than to be used as a **Prop** (although it's nice if it can be used – if it is **Practical** – just in case).

Setup – AKA **Angle**. Every major change in the lighting or camera position creates a new 'Setup' and 10 major ones per day is common for most crews, especially when lighting is involved.

Shoot Ratio – The ratio between the length of the film and the length of footage actually shot.

Shooting Script – A script which has been made ready for production by adding scene numbers to the **Sluglines** (vital for planning) and incorporating anything else the director thought useful. Compare to **Spec Script**.

Shotgun Mic – See **Rifle Mic**.

Shotlist – A comprehensive list of what shots you plan to shoot.

Showreel – A short promotional video containing previous work of an individual or organisation.

Shutter – The device within a camera which opens to allow light through one time for each individual **Exposure** (which might be either a **Field** or a **Frame**). The longer it is open, the more blurred movement will be within the frame, and the greater will be the exposure.

Single – A shot on one character within a scene. See **Coverage**.

Slate – Common term for a **Clapperboard**.

SLR – Single Lens Reflex, the standard stills camera which uses interchangeable lenses, as opposed to a 'compact' camera which is stuck with the one lens.

Slugline – The location description line in a script e.g. INT. CABINET ROOM – DAY.

Smash Cut – A sudden, heavily contrasting cut. Mostly used by screenwriters trying to get the editor to do their bidding (and therefore completely pointless).

SMPTE – (pronounced 'simpty') Society of Motion Picture and Television Engineers, who have given their name to, among other things, a form of **Timecode** which is encoded on video as **LTC** but is also used in many other applications.

Softbox – A type of light which encloses the bulb in a large diffusing box to create a very flattering **Soft Light**.

Soft Cut – A cut which staggers the cutting of picture and sound. Assists continuity and masks the unnaturalness of the cut. AKA L-Cut, delay edit, split edit. See **Hard Cut**.

Soft Light – Non–directional light which radiates in a kind of glow. It casts a less distinct shadow than **Hard Light** and is created by using a **Diffuser**.

Solo – A control on **Sound Mixers**, sound desks and sometimes within **Non-Linear Editing** systems which allows the user to listen to a single audio track without having to actually turn off all the other tracks.

Sound Mixer – A device used on location to mix incoming sound and set levels before sending it to a recording device (usually either the camera or a **DAT**). See **SQN**, **Mic Level**, **Line Level**.

Spark – An electrician responsible for lights and generators (also known as **Gennies**). See also **Gaffer**, **Best Boy**.

Spec Script – A script written 'speculatively,' i.e. it hasn't been commissioned for production and the writer is just hoping it'll be taken on by someone or win a competition. The main difference between this and a **Shooting Script** is that it doesn't have scene numbers.

Special FX – Environmental effects such as snow, wind, rain, smoke etc.

Splicing – (1) The action of physically cutting film and putting it back together. (2) An equivalent operation performed by a **Non-Linear Editing** system.

Spot – Using the Spot/**Flood** control on a light to narrow the beam of light, make it a little harder and a little more intense.

Spot Effects – See **Foley**.

Spreader – A restrictive device which keeps the **Legs** of a **Tripod** from spreading too far and thus collapsing. See also **Bowl, Head, Plate, Sticks, Pan Bar**.

SQN – A very nice company from the Isle of Man who make very good **Sound Mixers**, and whose name is sometimes used as a synonym for same.

Standard Definition – The basic video and TV screen size standard since the 60s and 70s. Varies according to what part of the world you're in; see **PAL**, **NTSC** and **SECAM**.

Steadicam – A camera mounting which rests upon a camera operator and keeps the camera steady while the operator is able to move around. Very expensive, requires special training to use, and not terribly good for the back.

Stepping Ring – A screw-on adapter which changes the lens diameter to allow **Filters** and adapter lenses of different diameters to be used.

Sticks – Professional slang for a **Tripod**.

Stock – Professional slang for videotapes (tape stock). Also used for film and stills stock.

Stop – A single **F-Stop** (which may or may not actually be a whole number in terms of the F-stop measurement). See also **Pulling Stop**.

Storyboard – A sequence of drawings used to plan what shots will be required for a film. See **Video Storyboard**, **Animatic**.

Striping – (1) Recording a **Control Track** on a tape for **Linear Editing**. (2) Recording continuous **Timecode** on a professional tape for the purpose of **Mastering**. (3) A way of combining hard drives to make a single, larger drive. See **RAID**.

Subclip – A **Clip** in a **Non-Linear Editing** system which refers to part of another clip rather than directly to a **Media** file. Subclipping is a way of **Logging** footage which has been **Captured** all in one go rather than shot by shot.

Subtext – Meaning which is implied but not directly revealed. The implication can be created by performance or through information previously given to the audience.

S-Video – Separated Video (not S-VHS Video, as some people think). (1) A type of **Analogue SD** video signal originally associated with the S-VHS format but now found on many cameras and VCRs. Consists of both a **Luminance** and **Chrominance** signal and is the middle of the analogue connections in terms of quality. AKA **YC**. See also **Composite, Component, Firewire, SDI, HDMI, HD-SDI**. (2) The special 4-pin cable which is used exclusively to carry S-Video signals (although S-Video is sometimes carried on two separate **BNC** or **MUSA** cables). See also **Minijack, Jack, XLR, Firewire**.

SxS – Memory cards used in the **XDCAM EX** format. This format has a lower data rate than **P2**, and can consequently store more video.

Sync Clap – Any sharp sound with a visible source (e.g. a pat of the **Mic** while it's in shot) used in the absence of a **Clapperboard** so that sound sync can be established in **Postproduction**.

Sync Sound – Sound recorded in sync with the picture. See also **Wildtrack, Clapperboard, Mute**.

Tally Light – A teensy red light on the front of some cameras which switches on when the camera is recording.

TC – Short for **Timecode**.

Telecine – AKA **TK**. The process of transferring film to video.

Telephoto Lens – Commonly known as a **Long Lens**. Includes less of the picture in the frame, making the subject seem nearer. Gives a flatter (and more flattering) picture and has a narrow **Depth of Field**. See also **Wide-Angle Lens** and **Zoom Lens**.

Temp Music – Music used during editing in place of music to be composed later.

Third – See **Assistant Director**.

Three-Point Lighting – A textbook system of lighting mainly used for interviews but containing the basic ideas that go towards lighting in general. The three points are three lights: **Key Light, Fill Light** and **Back Light**.

Tilt – Tilting the camera up and down on a **Tripod** or other camera mounting. See **Pan**.

Timecode – AKA **TC**. A frame-by-frame numbering system, encoded alongside video information or between frames. Appears in the format HH:MM:SS:FF. See also **BITC, VITC, LTC, SMPTE**.

Timecode Break – Any discontinuity in **Timecode** (usually caused by forgetting to set the camera correctly after reviewing footage), which can prevent VCRs and **Non-Linear Editing** systems from finding the footage they need. **Batch Digitising** in particular depends upon there being no breaks in timecode.

Timeline – The part of a **Non-Linear Editing** system which graphically shows the edit as a timeline composed of video and audio tracks.

Title Safe – See **Safe Area**.

TK – Short for **Telecine**.

Tone – A 1kHz audio signal generated by **Sound Mixers** to calibrate input **Levels** on cameras and by **Non-Linear Editing** systems for **Mastering** purposes.

Trace – A type of fireproof paper used as **Diffuser** by pegging it onto the **Barn Doors** of a light.

Tracking – A smooth form of camera movement using a

Dolly, which may or may not actually be on tracks.

Tramlines – Annotations on a script, usually vertical lines, which indicate how much of the script an individual shot will cover.

Transition – Any movement between two shots which is not a simple cut, such as a **Crossfade** or a **Wipe**.

Treatment – A telling of the story usually used as a selling document. Actual definitions of the content of a treatment vary enormously, but it's usually a detailed point-by-point description of the events of the film. Compare to **Outline**.

Tripod – The most common camera mount and a vital filmmaking tool. Consumer versions usually come in one piece, but semipro and professional tripods will consist of separate **Legs** and **Head**. See also **Bowl, Sticks, Plate, Spreader, Pan Bar**.

Tungsten – Tungsten lights have a **Colour Temperature** of approximately 3200 **Kelvins**, and appear orange if the camera is not correctly **White Balanced**. See also **Gels, Daylight, Fluorescent**.

Turn Over – (1) Starting up a film or video camera (literally turning over the motor) (2) Starting to film e.g. 'We didn't start turning over until midday.'

Tx – Short for transmission (i.e. broadcast).

U–Matic/U–Matic SP – An obsolete **SD** professional **Analogue** format. U-Matic SP was an improvement but is now also obsolete.

Unbalanced – See **Balanced**.

Underscan – An option on professional **Monitors** which shrinks the image in size to allow you to see the portions of the picture which would normally lie outside the frame. See **Safe Area**.

Unit – i.e. Film Unit. The group of people and equipment making a film. See **Unit Move**.

Unit Move – The often time-consuming process of moving a **Unit** from one location to another.

Upconvert – The process of converting a lower quality

format to a higher quality format, especially when going from **SD** to **HD**. Can cause problems as the inadequacies of the lower format become very obvious. See **Downconvert**.

Varicam – A brand name used by Panasonic to refer to some of their high end **DVCProHD** cameras which can record **HD** at a wide range of frame rates, mimicking the variable frame rates possible with film.

Vectorscope – A visual display showing the strength of a video signal (either the whole signal, the **Luminance**, or the **RGB** components). Used to spot if the signal has passed beyond the 'legal' limits for broadcast.

VHS – Video Home System, the venerable **SD** domestic tape format we all know and hate. Still in use as a basic viewing format to enter your film in festivals or seek distribution.

Video – sometimes used in retail to refer to **VHS** as opposed to **DVD**, despite the fact that DVD is also a kind of video.

Video CD – A lower quality, highly compressed **SD** video disc playable in most computers and **DVD** players, using the **MPEG**-1 file format.

Video Mixer – A device used in **Linear Editing** suites which can mix video signals and add video effects.

Video Storyboard – A method of working out how to shoot a scene by shooting a test version with a cheap camera and whoever may be at hand. See **Storyboard**, **Animatic**.

Vignetting – Used to refer to the edge of the lens coming into shot. Not good.

Visual FX – Almost any effects work including prosthetics, animatronics, **CGI** etc., but excluding environmental effects (see **Special FX**).

VITC – Vertically Integrated Time Code. A form of **Timecode** placed in spaces between **Frames** on videotape. See **BITC**, **LTC**.

VO – Short for Voice Over. Used in scripts to indicate

dialogue spoken as voiceover. Compare to **OS**.

VU – Volume Unit. A **Levels Meter** for Analogue audio which is cheaper and less accurate than a **PPM**. The scale usually places 0dB about two thirds of the way up. See also **Digital Meter**.

WAV – Waveform Audio File Format. An audio file format without **Compression** using the file extension .wav. See **AIFF-C**, **MP3**.

Wet Hire – Hiring equipment along with operators. Compare to **Dry Hire**.

Whip Pan – A sharp and sudden pan to a subject. You can have a whip **Tilt** as well, but it's not as common.

White Balance – A control on most cameras which adjusts to match the **Colour Temperature** of light. See also **Daylight, Tungsten, Fluorescent**.

Wide-Angle Adapter – An extra lens which screws onto the front of a camera lens to make it more of a **Wide-Angle Lens**. Focus can be difficult or impossible if you try to zoom in with such an adapter attached.

Wide-Angle Lens – Includes more of the picture in the frame, making the subject seem further away, but, in extreme cases, makes nearer objects bulge towards the screen. Gives a more three-dimensional look and has a large **Depth of Field**. See also **Telephoto Lens** and **Zoom Lens**.

Widescreen – Any film or video frame with an **Aspect Ratio** wider than **4:3** (**Fullscreen**). Widescreen TVs are **16:9**, but cinema films are usually either 1.85:1 or 2.35:1. See **Anamorphic**.

Wildtrack – Any sound recorded 'wild', i.e. not with picture. Generally used to refer to sound effects recorded on location. Compare to **Atmos**.

Windjammer – A fluffy covering for a microphone which cuts down wind noise. Some are designed to fit over **Windshields**.

Windshield – A rigid covering fitted around a microphone (usually a **Rifle Mic**) to cut down wind noise. Sometimes referred to as a 'Rycote' after the company that makes most of them.

Wipe – A form of **Transition** in which one picture replaces another by 'wiping' across it.

Wrap – (1) When work at a location is finished, the work of packing up equipment and getting out. (2) The very end of the shoot. (3) A performer can be said to be 'wrapped' when they have finished their work on a film, even if the shoot is still in progress.

WS – Wide Shot. A shot size incorporating the whole of the scene or lots of scenery, as opposed to most other shot size conventions which are based on the relative size of a person in frame.

XDCAM – An optical disc recording system manufactured by Sony which replaces tapes. Developed from **Digital Betacam**. Depending on the camera, can record **DVCAM**, **MPEG IMX** or **HDV**. Compare to **AVCHD**.

XDCAM EX – A development of **XDCAM** which records onto memory cards, specifically the **SxS** format. Records in an **MPEG-4** format. Compare to **P2**.

XLR – AKA **Cannon**. A type of connector which locks to the socket. Can carry **Balanced** audio if it's a 3-pin lead, or power if it's a 4-pin lead. See also **BNC**, **Phono**, **S-Video**, **MUSA**, **Minijack**, **Jack**, **Firewire**.

Y – An abbreviation for the **Luminance** part of a video signal.

YC – AKA **S-Video**. A video signal comprising **Luminance** (Y) and a single **Chrominance** channel.

YUV – AKA Y-Cr-Cb or **Component** (the version used in **PAL**, anyway). A video signal comprising one **Luminance** (Y) and two **Chrominance** channels (Cr and Cb). The two colour channels are actually red and blue with the luminance value subtracted, and from this the value for green is worked out. Apparently. Compare to **RGB**.

Zebras – Striped patterns used in viewfinders to indicate where the image is overexposed and **Blown Out**.

Depending on the camera, they may also appear on the **Monitor** but will not be recorded on the tape.

Zoom Lens – A lens (standard on most video cameras) which allows the user to 'zoom' in on a subject, making it seem apparently closer on the screen. Effectively, the zoom lens is both a **Wide-Angle Lens** and a **Telephoto Lens** (though not at the extremes of either); zooming in or out changes the properties of the lens from one to the other. See **Crash Zoom**.

Index